A Bibliography of Jazz

Da Capo Press Music Reprint Series

GENERAL EDITOR
FREDERICK FREEDMAN
VASSAR COLLEGE

A Bibliography of Jazz

By Alan P. Merriam

With the Assistance of Robert J. Benford

𝄞 DA CAPO PRESS • NEW YORK • 1970

A Da Capo Press Reprint Edition

This Da Capo Press edition of
A Bibliography of Jazz
is an unabridged republication of the
first edition published in Philadelphia
in 1954.

Library of Congress Catalog Card No. 75-127282

SBN 306-70036-0

Published by Da Capo Press
A Division of Plenum Publishing Corporation
227 West 17th Street, New York, N. Y. 10011

PUBLICATIONS

OF

THE AMERICAN FOLKLORE SOCIETY

BIBLIOGRAPHICAL SERIES

VOLUME IV

1954

A BIBLIOGRAPHY OF JAZZ

A Bibliography of Jazz

by ALAN P. MERRIAM

with the assistance of

ROBERT J. BENFORD

PHILADELPHIA

THE AMERICAN FOLKLORE SOCIETY

1954

PRINTED IN GERMANY AT J.J. AUGUSTIN, GLÜCKSTADT

CONTENTS

PREFACE

Jazz, as an identifiable musical system, originated in the last decade of the nineteenth century and has continued uninterrupted since that time. Richly expressive and honestly creative, it has taken its place in the culture of America and, indeed, the world, at first as a dance music exclusively and later as a serious artistic activity. It was in its role as dance music that jazz functioned almost entirely during the first thirty years of its recognizable existence, but in the 1920's it suddenly emerged from semi-obscurity and began to receive increasingly more attention in magazines, journals and newspapers as discussion broadened and controversy swelled. By the late 20's the first books and magazines devoted to jazz were appearing, and since that time spoken and written criticism of jazz has steadily increased.

To the present, however, there has been no published bibliography dealing extensively with the writing concerned with this specifically American music; even the connoiseurs of Europe, traditionally far ahead of America in the recognition of jazz, have attempted nothing of this sort. Thus there has been virtually no source to which the student, the layman, or the musician could turn to find what had been written about the music with which he was concerned. It is this gap in the bibliography of the arts of America that the present work attempts to fill.

The literature of jazz is as varied and exciting as the music itself, for not only has a group of competent critics grown up around the idiom but it has been, since the 20's, traditionally fair game for any writer with paper and an outlet for his self-expression. A critical look at this literature reveals much that is shoddy, poorly written and poorly conceived, and yet much that brings an understanding not only of the music but of the cultural milieu in which it has functioned for so many years. The cycles of change in public opinion alone are well worth a detailed interest, but it is the prevailing, vigorous atmosphere, the emergence of defined lines of development, the changes in attitude of musicians and writers alike that make jazz bibliography what it is. The range of content is enormous—from analysis and appreciation of the music to the problem of women in jazz, from history to personal controversies among jazz musicians, from discography to cartoons—and this very diversity brings the vitality and enthusiasm of the music itself to the published literature.

This bibliography is by no means selective, nor is it meant to be so. Rather, it has been compiled with the conviction that, for an initial attempt at least, selection on any basis would tend to distort rather than clarify the materials at hand. It is fully as important to include a recent article describing a writer's idea of "jazz in 1850," when neither the word nor the fact existed, as it is to document a sober analysis of the aesthetic values in jazz by a contemporary philosopher; or to include a savage attack on jazz from a racist viewpoint as it is a discussion of jazz as a magnificent contribution of the American Negro to world artistic culture. Each one in its own way presents a viewpoint and documents a reaction which is of importance not only to an understanding of the music but also to its struggle to assert itself against vigorous opposition. To select only those writings which are complimentary to jazz and to its performers would result in marked distortion of the field as a whole; to select on the basis of "good" writing would exclude most of what has been written; to leave out the foolish works by those who knew nothing of the subject to which they brought their doubtful talents would leave only a shell of the immensely vital story of jazz. Nor has there been any attempt to include or exclude any particular author or authors; if one appears in striking contrast to another it is the simple function of what was available to the present author.

The bibliography makes no claim to completeness. It is, rather, a beginning toward the orderly gathering of the tremendous literature which has grown up around jazz music. Indeed, an arbitrary line was drawn at the end of the year 1950 and no titles past that date were included in the present work.

The bibliography is divided into three parts beginning with the individual entries arranged alphabetically by author; this section includes periodical and newspaper articles, books, booklets, pamphlets and all other materials gathered. The various types are differentiated by standard bibliographic forms. In jazz bibliography, especially, many titles include names of individuals; these names have been alphabetized according to the last name, and thus an entry beginning with "Louis Armstrong," for example, is found under the letter A instead of the letter L as in the more common indexing system. Through this system it was possible to group references to individuals more closely, particularly under the anonymous entries.

Following each entry is a code system of letters enclosed by parentheses designed to give the reader immediate knowledge of the major stress of the entry; thus (J & D) is found after entry 1. This does not necessarily mean, however, that no other subject is discussed in the reference; in many cases more than one emphasis is indicated. Thirty-two of these code symbols are used, as follows:

A & A	Analysis and Appreciation	Chi	Chicago
Bibl	Bibliographies of Jazz	Crit	Criticism
Bl	Blues	Disc	Discography and Record
Bop	Bop		Information
BW	Boogie Woogie	Dix	Dixieland

Ed	Education	NO	New Orleans
Fict	Fiction	Ork	Jazz Orchestras
Gen	General	Pers	Individual Personalities
Geog	Geographic Subdivisions	Pic	Picture Stories
	and Surveys	Poet	Jazz Poetry
Hist	History	Poll	Jazz Polls
Infl	Influence of Jazz	Rad	Radio, Television, Movies
Inst	Jazz Instruments		and Jazz
J & C	Jazz and the Classics	Rag	Ragtime
J & D	Jazz and the Dance	Rev	Book Reviews
J & O	Jazz and Opera	Sw	Swing
KC	Kansas City	Tech	Technical Equipment
Lang	Language		Used in Jazz

Some explanation of those categories which are not necessarily self-explanatory must be made. "Analysis and Appreciation" includes entries in which an attempt is made by the author to analyze or evaluate jazz; this may mean violent criticism as well as commendation. In designating the various jazz styles, "Blues, Bop," etc., those terms which have received serious use have been accepted without consideration for controversy over what constitutes a particular style. Thus while one author may differentiate New Orleans from Dixieland, another may not; what is important is that enough authors have written about a particular style to make a bibliographic entry practical. "Criticism" here refers only to criticism of actual performance and to writing about the problems of critics and criticism, not to an evaluation of jazz as a musical form. "Education" refers to entries concerned with the teaching of jazz in various places and institutions. "Geographic Subdivisions and Surveys" indicates those entries which describe the jazz situation in certain specific locales delimited by the original writer; this may be restricted to a single city or apply to an entire continent. "Influence of Jazz" refers to entries in which the author has attempted to show how jazz has affected other institutions, the manners and morals of a nation, or "classical" music, for example. "Jazz Instruments" indicates discussions of specific musical instruments and their uses in jazz, while "Language" refers to studies of the special terminology of jazz. Finally, "Technical Equipment Used in Jazz" indicates studies concerning the use of recording equipment, reproduction equipment, or other technical instruments in reference to jazz. Many of the entries are also cross-referenced to allow the reader to follow through a series of articles or a controversy between two writers.

The second section of the bibliography consists of a listing of magazines which have been devoted wholly or in considerable part to jazz music. Most of these magazines are now defunct; many of them were published regularly over a very short period of time. The compilation of data for them is thus extremely difficult, but the importance of the listing cannot be minimized, for much original material has appeared in such periodicals. In entry form, the title of the magazine is given first, followed by the subtitle in parentheses. The name of the last editor, the name of the publisher and the place of publication, the frequency of appearance and the dates during which the periodical was extant are then given. The word "date" in the entries refers to the year 1950, the reference point for the present bibliography.

The third section consists of two indices. The first is a subject index based on the thirty-two categories previously explained; reference is to the entry numbers. Alphabetizing of the various categories is carried out under the abbreviations used throughout the bibliography; thus "Book Reviews," for example, comes under "Rev." Under "Ork" and "Pers" respectively, various jazz orchestras and individuals are listed alphabetically by name; in the case of the jazz performers reference is made not only to entries about them but also to articles or books which they have written, for these works often tell as much or more about the individual as those written about him by others. The second index lists the various periodicals cited, followed by their place of publication; thus the reader can find what has been published on jazz in any of the magazines from which materials have been drawn.

It is a pleasure to acknowledge the assistance given by individuals and institutions to the compilation of this bibliography. Several libraries lent their facilities and often gave special priveleges to the author; these include the Chicago Public Library; the John Crerar Library, Chicago; Deering Library, Northwestern University, Evanston, Illinois; the Harper Library, University of Chicago; the Library of Congress; Newberry Library, Chicago; and the New York Public Library. Special acknowledgment must be made the American Council of Learned Societies under whose auspices the author first began the present work. Early in 1949 and again in the summer of the same year, trips to Washington, D. C. and the Library of Congress were made possible by special grants from the ACLS in addition to an Advanced Graduate Fellowship under which the author was studying. Many individuals have also given their willing cooperation in collecting materials, and it is with special appreciation that the author expresses his thanks to Bob Anderson, Copenhagen; Alex Andrew, Glasgow; Albert Bettonville, Brussels; Hans Bluthner, Berlin; Clyde H. Clark, Toronto; Jehangir Dalal, Bombay; Paavo Einio, Helsinki; Jane Ganfield, Purdue University; Bill and Jane Grauer, New York; H. Meunier Harris, Brighton, England; Peter J. Kerin, Richmond, Australia; George Malcolm-Smith, Hartford, Conn.; Pat and Ed Minty, Washington, D. C.; Kurt Mohr, Basel; Nestor R. Ortiz Oderigo, Buenos Aires; Ralph J. Sturges, Hartford, Conn.; Emmanuel Ugge, Prague; E. J. Wansbone, Auckland, and Richard A. Waterman, Northwestern University. It is extremely difficult to express proper appreciation to Robert J. Benford who has contributed heavily to the successful realization of this work. Not only has he given time and effort to checking countless references, but he has also been an inexhaustible source of encouragement and enthusiasm throughout the long project. Without his constant support this bibliography might not have been realized in its present scope. To my wife, Barbara W. Merriam, goes special appreciation for the uncounted hours given to all manner of tasks. Finally, parts of the present work have previously appeared in the *Record Changer* (IX, July–Aug., 1950, 33–5) and *Notes* (X, Mar., 1953, 202–10), the editors of which have kindly given permission for reproduction.

It is the hope that despite whatever limitations it may have this bibliography will serve both those who wish to obtain an idea of the scope of the literature concerning jazz and those who have long hoped for the means by which they could implement their knowledge of more restricted problems within the same field. Jazz bibliography, however, must not stop here; the following pages represent but a beginning toward the orderly presentation of the writing, old and new, about jazz.

ALAN P. MERRIAM

Evanston, Illinois
15 September, 1953

ENTRIES

ENTRIES

1. Adams, Berle. "Dance Tempo 'The Basic Principle' of Band Biz," *Down Beat,* XXVII (May 19, 1950), 4. (J & D)
2. Adorno, T. W., with the assistance of Eunice Cooper. "Hobson, Wilder, *American Jazz Music*; Sargeant, Winthrop, *Jazz Hot and Hybrid.*" *Studies in Philosophy and Social Science,* IX (1941), 167–78. (Rev)
3. ——, with the assistance of George Simpson. "On Popular Music," *Studies in Philosophy and Social Science,* IX (1941), 17–48. (A & A)
4. Aldam, Jeff. "Mainly About Morton," *Jazz Music,* II (Feb.-Mar., 1944), 107–08. (Disc, Pers)
5. Aldrich, Richard. "Drawing a Line for Jazz," New York *Times,* Dec. 10, 1922, VIII, 4:1–3. (J & C)
6. Allen, Frederick Lewis. "When America Learned to Dance," *Scribner's,* CII (Sept., 1937), 11–17, 92. Condensed: *Readers' Digest,* XXXI (Oct., 1937), 104–07. (J & D)
7. Allen, Stuart S. *Stars of Swing.* London: British Yearbooks, 1946. 76 pp. (Pers, Sw)
8. ——. "A Weary Duke Errs by not Rehearsing with Ork," *Down Beat,* XV (July 28, 1948), 2. (Crit)
9. Alpert, Trigger. "Trigger Alpert on Bassists," *Metronome,* LIX (Oct., 1943), 31, 68. (Pers)
10. Altmann, Ludwig. "Untergang der Jazzmusik," *Die Musik,* XXV (July, 1933), 744–49. (A & A)
11. Anderson, Ernest (Ed). *Esquire's 1947 Jazz Book.* New York: Esquire, 1946. 90 pp.
12. Anderson, W. R. "Jazz and Real Music," (lr) *Musical Times,* LXXIII (Oct., 1932), 926–27. (A & A)
13. Andrico, Michel G. (Trans: Ian Munro Smyth). "Essay on the Harmonic Element in Hot Jazz," *Jazz Hot,* 11 (Sept.–Oct., 1936), 9–14. (A & A)
14. Angell, Roger. "African Drumbeat; New Recordings Capture the Rhythms of the Grandfather of American Jazz," *Holiday,* VIII (Dec., 1950), 6, 8, 9, 11, 12, 14. (Disc, Hist)
15. Anon. "'Accursed Jazz'—An English View," *Literary Digest,* XCI (Oct. 2, 1926), 28–9. (A & A)
    See: 17; 165; 406; 558; 559; 560; 2159; 2337; 3209.
16. ——. "Act of the Year: Art Tatum," *Metronome,* LX (Jan., 1944), 23. (Ork)
17. ——. "An Affront to Jazz," New York *Times,* Sept. 17, 1926, 22:4. (A & A)
    See: 15; 165; 406; 558; 559; 560; 2159; 2337; 3210.
18. ——. "The Air is Filled with Music," *Time,* LIII (Mar. 14, 1949), 44. (Pers)
    See: 28; 495; 1490; 1820; 2085.
19. ——. "All-Stars Wax Charity Jazz!" *Metronome,* LVIII (Feb., 1942), 7, 12. (Disc)
20. ——. "American Bandsmen in London," *Musical Opinion,* XLVI (May, 1923), 733–34. (Gen)

21. Anon. "American Dancer Jazzing the 'Marseillaise' Angers Friendly Audience in Paris Music Hall," New York *Times*, Jan. 31, 1926, 1:4. (J & C) *See*: 782.
22. —— —. "American Jazz Artists," *Common Ground*, VII (Autumn, 1946), 52–60. (Pic)
23. —— —. "America's Best Writers and Composers (Of Ragtime)," *Tuneful Yankee*, I (Jan., 1917), 37, 39, 41. (Pers, Pic, Rag)
24. —— —. "Apollo's Girl," *Time*, LV (Apr. 3, 1950), 70–1. (Pers)
25. —— —. "The Appeal of the Primitive Jazz," *Literary Digest*, LV (Aug. 25, 1917), 28–9. (A & A)
26. —— —. "Louis Armstrong," *in* Anna Rothe (Ed). *Current Biography 1944*. New York: H. W. Wilson, 1945. pp. 15–17. (Pers)
27. —— —. "Louis Armstrong Abroad," (lr) *Disques*, I (Feb., 1931), 535. (Pers)
28. —— —. "Louis Armstrong in Mardi Gras Role," *Variety*, CLXXIII (Jan. 12, 1949), 43. (Pers) *See*: 18; 495; 1490; 1820; 2085.
29. —— —. "Louis Armstrong in Scandinavia," *Melody Maker*, XXV (Oct. 15, 1949), 3. (Crit, Pers)
30. —— —. "Armstrong Sellout in Stockholm Bow," *Variety*, CLXXIII (Oct. 5, 1949), 36. (Crit, Pers)
31. —— —. "Armstrong to Make Another Europe Trip," *Down Beat*, XVII (Nov. 3, 1950), 3. (Pers)
32. —— —. "Armstrong's Nostalgia Envelopes Bop City," *Billboard*, LXI (Sept. 3, 1949), 14. (Crit, Pers)
33. —— —. "Arrangers of the Year: Eddie Sauter, George Handy," *Metronome*, LXIII (Jan., 1947), 22. (Pers)
34. —— —. "Arrivals of the Year: Warne Marsh, Terry Gibbs," *in* Barry Ulanov and George Simon (Eds). *Jazz 1950*. New York: Metronome, 1950. p. 12. (Pers)
35. —— —. "Arrivals of the Year: Bud Powell, Gerry Mulligan," *in* Barry Ulanov and George Simon (Eds). *Jazz 1950*. New York: Metronome, 1950. p. 13. (Pers)
36. —— —. "Arte Novissima," *Musica d'Oggi*, V (July, 1923), 220–21. (Gen)
37. —— —. "At Last! Action vs. Bootleggers," *Down Beat*, XVII (Aug. 25, 1950), 10. (Gen) *See*: 175.
38. —— —. "Leopold Auer, Violin Master, Becomes Citizen. Promptly Gives Views on Prohibition and Jazz," New York *Times*, Nov. 9, 1926, 26:4. (Gen)
39. —— —. "Les Avis de... sur le Be-bop," *Hot Club Magazine*, 17 (May, 1947), 8–9. (Bop)
40. —— —. "B.G. and Bebop," *Newsweek*, XXXII (Dec. 27, 1948), 66–7. (A & A, Bop, Ork)
41. —— —. "B.G. Swing King and Favorite," *Metronome*, LVI (Aug., 1940), 7, 15. (Pers)
42. —— —. "Bach: So Oder So," *Die Melodie*, III (1948/49), 7, 10–11. (A & A, J & C)
43. —— —. "Bachaus Discusses Jazz," *Musical Courier*, LXXXVII (Aug. 16, 1923), 24. (A & A)
44. —— —. "Back to Chicago,'' *Time*, XXXVIII (July 21, 1941), 40. (Chi, Ork)
45. —— —. "'Bad Music'," *Music Lover's Magazine*, I (June, 1922), 5–6. (A & A, Infl)
46. —— —. "Ban Against Jazz Sought in Ireland," New York *Times*, Jan. 7, 1934, IV, 3:4. (Infl) *See*: 328.
47. —— —. "Ban on Jazz Sacrilege," New York *Times*, Nov. 4, 1922, 4:4. (J & C)
48. —— —. "Band Business is on Way Up Again, Says Krupa," *Down Beat*, XVII (Aug. 25, 1950), 3. (Pers)

49. Anon. "Band of the Year: Dizzy Gillespie," *Metronome*, LXIV (Jan., 1949), 17–18. (Ork)
50. ——. "Band of the Year: Lionel Hampton," *Metronome*, LX (Jan., 1944), 21. (Ork)
51. ——. "Band of the Year: Stan Kenton," *Metronome*, LXIII (Jan., 1947), 17–19, 44–6. (Ork)
52. ——. "Bands That Stay on Top—And Why," *Metronome*, LI (Oct., 1935), 19, 57; (Nov., 1935), 19, 51. Pt. II entitled: "Analyzing the Stylists." (Ork)
53. ——. "William Count Basie," *in* Maxime Block (Ed). *Current Biography 1942*. New York: H. W. Wilson, 1943. pp. 55–7. (Pers)
54. ——. "Count Basie," *Look*, VIII (Mar. 21, 1944), 78. (Pers, Pic)
55. ——. "Basie Discography," *Down Beat*, XVII (Nov. 17, 1950), 14. (Disc)
56. ——. "Count Basie Picks the 12 Best Pianists," *Music and Rhythm*, II (Jan., 1942), 19, 45. (Pers)
57. ——. "Battle of Bands; Yen to See Tooters Brings a New Boom to Broadway," *Newsweek*, XXI (May 10, 1943), 64. (Gen)
58. ——. "Beale Street's Hero," *Time*, XXVII (May 25, 1936), 54, 56. (Pers)
59. ——. "'Beat' Begins 'Bouquets for Living' Series," *Down Beat*, XVII (Aug. 11, 1950), 10. (Gen)
60. ——. "'Beat Me, Ivan'," *Newsweek*, XXX (Aug. 4, 1947), 66. (Gen)
61. ——. "'Beat' Will Again Sponsor Ellington Chicago Concert," *Down Beat*, XVII (Feb. 10, 1950), 1. (Gen, Ork)
62. ——. "Bebop: New Jazz School is Led by Trumpeter Who is Hot, Cool and Gone," *Life*, XXV (Oct. 11, 1948), 138–42. (Bop, Pers, Pic)
63. ——. "Bebop Fashions; Weird Dizzy Gillespie Mannerisms Quickly Picked Up As Accepted Style For Bebop Devotees," *Ebony*, IV (Dec., 1948), 31–3. (Bop, Gen, Pers, Pic)
64. ——. "Before Long They Will Protest," New York *Times*, Oct. 8, 1924, 20:5. (Rad)
65. ——. "Benny, Tommy, Gene, Lionel, Carney Swamp Contest; Bing Tops Sinatra," *Metronome*, LX (Jan., 1944), 2, 26–7. (Pers, Poll)
66. ——. "Benny, Tommy Win Contest: Duke, Harry, Charlie Close," *Metronome*, LIX (Oct., 1943), 15, 58–9. (Pers, Poll)
67. ——. "Benny's Band Busts Up; Shaw Grabs," *Metronome*, LVI (Aug., 1940), 9. (Ork)
68. ——. "Billy Berg's; Hollywood Jazz Temple Draws Stars and Hoi Polloi," *Ebony*, III (Apr., 1948), 29–32. (Pers, Pic)
69. ——. "Bunny Berigan," *in* Maxime Block (Ed). *Current Biography 1942*. New York: H. W. Wilson, 1943. p. 74. (Pers)
70. ——. "Bunny Berigan Dies After Long Illness," *Down Beat*, IX (June 15, 1942), 1. (Pers)
71. ——. "Berlin Calls Jazz American Folk Music; Composer Predicts It Will Eventually Be Sung in Metropolitan Opera House," New York *Times*, Jan. 10, 1925, 2:7. (Infl)
72. ——. "Berlin Opera Mingles Auto Horn, Films, Jazz," New York *Times*, Mar. 3, 1927, 23:2. (J & O)
73. ——. "Berlin Says Jazz Is Dying," New York *Times*, Apr. 15, 1926, 14:2 (Gen)
74. ——. "Ben Bernie," *in* Maxime Block (Ed). *Current Biography 1943*. New York: H. W. Wilson, 1944. p. 39. (Pers)
75. ——. "Ben Bernie Indignant at British Exclusion," New York *Times*, July 24, 1926, 3:5. (Gen)
See: 702.
76. ——. "Bessie's Blues," *Time*, XXX (Nov. 22, 1937), 38, 40. (Bl, Pers)

77. Anon. "Best Solos of the Year 1941," *Music and Rhythm*, II (Mar., 1942), 31. (Disc)
78. —— —. "Big Apple," *Time*, XXXI (Sept. 13, 1937), 37, 38. Abr: *Digest*, I (Oct. 2, 1937), 22–3. (J & D, Pic)
79. —— —. "Barney Bigard Is Leaving Duke," *Down Beat*, IX (July 15, 1942), 2. (Pers)
80. —— —. "Bird, Backed By Strings, Disappoints at Birdland," *Down Beat*, XVII (Aug. 25, 1950), 4. (Crit, Ork)
81. —— —. "Bird Wrong; Bop Must Get A Beat: Diz," *Down Beat*, XVI (Oct. 7, 1949), 1, 12. (A & A, Bop)
82. —— —. "Biz Should Set Up Emergencies Fund," *Down Beat*, XVII (Mar. 10. 1950), 10. (Gen)
83. —— —. "The Blight of Jazz and the Spiritual," *Literary Digest*, CV (Apr. 12, 1930), 20. (A & A)
84. —— —. "Blow! Joshua! Blow! The American People Do Not Enjoy Having Their Beloved Melodies and Spirituals Carricatured," *Etude*, LIX (Apr., 1941), 221, 288. (J & C)
85. —— —. "Blues!" *Etude*, XLV (June, 1927), 434. (A & A, Bl)
86. —— —. "The Booking of Bands: Who Does It and What They're Like: And Why," *Metronome*, LXI (Oct., 1945), 18–22. (Gen)
87. —— —. "Bop," Chicago *Daily News*, May 13, 1949, 18. (Bop)
88. —— —. "Bopera on Broadway," *Time*, LII (Dec. 20, 1948), 63–4. (Bop)
89. —— —. "Both Jazz Music and Jazz Dancing Barred From All Louisville Episcopal Churches," New York *Times*, Sept. 19, 1921, 17 : 4–5. (Gen, J & D)
90. —— —. "Bouncy Blues Singer," *Time*, XLIX (Jan. 6, 1947), 63–4. (Pers)
91. —— —. "Brick's Boys Go Riding," *Time*, XLVI (July 30, 1945), 54. (Ork)
92. —— —. "British Bandman," *Time*, XXV (June 10, 1935), 58. (Pers)
93. —— —. "British Music Critic Excoriates Jazz," New York *Times*, Sept. 12, 1926, 1 : 6, 9 (A & A)
    See: 15; 17; 165; 168; 233; 558; 559; 560; 2337; 3209.
94. —— —. "Broadcasters Favor 'Swinging' of Bach," New York *Times*, Oct. 28, 1938, 28 : 6. (J & C, Rad)
    See: 621; 733; 742; 743.
95. —— —. "Broadway's Minstrel," *Top Notes*, I (May 10, 1930), 5, 8. (Pers)
96. —— —. "Brooklyn Academy Opens Its Door to Jazz; Paul Whiteman Concert Marks Debut There," New York *Times*, Jan. 8, 1934, 21 : 3. (Crit)
97. —— —. "The Bulwark Against Jazz Flood," *Pacific Coast Musician*, XI (Sept., 1922), 3. (Infl)
98. —— —. "Bunk Discography," *Down Beat*, XVI (Aug. 26, 1949), 6. (Disc)
99. —— —. "Bunny, Like Bix, Will Soon Be a Myth," *Metronome*, LVIII (July, 1942), 9, 20–1. (Pers)
100. —— —. "Burned Up By Hot Band, Hurls Instruments In Sea," New York *Times*, May 17, 1939, 17 : 2. (Infl)
101. —— —. "Bury Jelly Roll Morton On Coast," *Down Beat*, VIII (Aug. 1, 1941), 13. (Pers)
102. —— —. "'Buying American' In Music," *Literary Digest*, CXVIII (Dec. 29, 1934), 24. (A & A)
103. —— —. "Bye-Bye Boogie; Hazel Scott Leaves Night Clubs and Moves To Concert Stage," *Ebony*, I (Nov., 1945), 31–5. (Pers, Pic)
104. —— —. "Dr. Cadman Assails Jazz," New York *Times*, May 3, 1927, 19 : 5. (Gen)
105. —— —. "Cafe Society Concert," *Musician*, XLVI (May, 1941), 86. (Crit)
106. —— —. "Cabell (Cab) Calloway III," *in* Anna Rothe (Ed). *Current Biography 1945*. New York: H. W. Wilson, 1946. pp. 84–6. (Pers)

107. Anon. "Calls America Still Savage Musically," New York *Times*, Oct. 11, 1922, 15 : 2. (A & A, Gen)
108. ——. "Calls Jazz Musical Slang," New York *Times*, Aug. 1, 1926, 14 : 2. (Gen)
109. ——. "Car Crash Fatal To Hasselgard," *Down Beat*, XV (Dec. 15, 1948), 1. (Pers)
110. ——. "Hoagland Howard (Hoagy) Carmichael," *in* Maxime Block (Ed). *Current Biography 1941*. New York: H. W. Wilson, 1942. pp. 136–38. (Pers)
111. ——. "The Case Against Dave Matthews," *Metronome*, LX (Feb., 1944), 15. (Crit, Pers)
112. ——. "Case History of an Ex-White Man," *Ebony*, II (Dec., 1946), 11–16. (Pers, Pic)
113. ——. "Ce Que la Presse Pense au Sujet du Livre 'Duke Ellington', par Jean de Trazegnies," *Hot Club Magazine*, 10 (Oct., 1946), 7. (Rev)
114. ——. "Celestin's Tuxedo Jazz Band of 1946," *Record Changer*, VII (Dec., 1948), 6–7. (Ork, Pic)
115. ——. "Chamber Music Blues," *Time*, XXXVIII (Nov. 17, 1941), 63–4. (Rad)
116. ——. "Charinsky Defends Jazz," *Metronome*, XXXVIII (June, 1922), 36. (Gen)
117. ——. "Herman Chittison," *Jazz Hot*, 8 (May, 1936), 17. (Pers)
118. ——. "Charlie Christian Dies in New York," *Down Beat*, IX (Mar. 15, 1942), 1, 20. (Pers)
119. ——. "Chu's Golden Horn Is Stilled By Fatal Crash," *Down Beat*, VIII (Nov. 15, 1941), 2, 20. (Pers)
120. ——. "Church Jazz Wedding Utilizes Saxophone," New York *Times*, Nov. 14, 1926, IX, 22 : 3. (Gen)
121. ——. "El Circulo Jazz," *Newsweek*, XXIV (July 10, 1944), 92. (Gen)
122. ——. "Claim French Don't Yet Get With Bop," *Down Beat*, XVI (Oct. 7, 1949), 3. (Bop, Geog)
123. ——. "Classical vs. Jazzical Music," *Literary Digest*, LXV (June 12, 1920), 40–1. (J & C)
124. ——. "Classics in 'Jazz-Tempo'," *Sheet Music News*, II (Jan., 1924), 27. (J & C)
125. ——. "Rod Cless Passes Away," *Jazz Session*, 5 (Jan.-Feb., 1945), 5. (Pers)
126. ——. "Club of His Own," *Time*, XLVI (Dec. 31, 1945), 68. (Pers)
127. ——. "Nat, King Cole," *Look*, IX (Jan. 9, 1945), 40. (Pers, Pic)
128. ——. "Collectors Directory," *Recordiana*, I (June-July, 1944) 5–7. (Gen)
129. ——. "Collector's Items," *in* George S. Rosenthal (Ed). *Jazzways*. Cincinnati, 1946. pp. 93–4. (Disc)
130. ——. "Collegiate Band to Tour," New York *Times*, June 15, 1926, 42 : 6. (Ork)
131. ——. "Columbia Finally Gives In and Adds 45 RPM Discs," *Down Beat*, XVII (Sept. 22, 1950), 1. (Disc)
See: 132.
132. ——. "Columbia Lone Holdout Against 45 RPM Pops," *Down Beat*, XVII (Aug. 25, 1950), 1. (Disc)
See: 131.
133. ——. "Complete Contest Standings," *Metronome*, LV (July, 1939), 12. (Poll)
134. ——. "Complete Index of Articles Appearing in the *Record Changer* From First Issue, August 1942–Dec. 1947," *Record Changer*, VII (May, 1948), 22–3. (Bibl)
135. ——. "Composer Sees Jazz as Feverish Noise," New York *Times*, Sept. 3, 1929, 24 : 6. (Gen)
136. ——. "Composers Protest Jazzing the Classics," New York *Times*, Nov. 25, 1922, 16 : 2. (Disc, J & C)
137. ——. "Concerning Ragtime," *Musical Monitor*, VIII (Sept., 1919), 619. (Rag)
138. ——. "Concert and Opera," New York *Times*, July 24, 1938, IX, 5 : 8. (Gen, Sw)
See: 670; 727.

139. Anon. "Concertizing Kenton," *Newsweek*, XXXI (Mar. 1, 1948), 74. (Gen, Pers)
140. ——. "Concerto for Woody," *in* George S. Rosenthal (Ed). *Jazzways*. Cincinnati, 1946. p. 98. (Pers)
141. ——. "Condemns Age of Jazz," New York *Times*, Jan. 27, 1925, 22 : 8. (Infl)
142. ——. "Eddie Condon," *in* Anna Rothe (Ed). *Current Biography 1944*. New York: H. W. Wilson, 1945. pp. 106–08. (Pers)
143. ——. "Eddie Condon," *Look*, X (Sept. 17, 1946), 58–9. (Pers, Pic)
144. ——. "Condon Mob," *in* George S. Rosenthal (Ed). *Jazzways*. Cincinnati, 1946. pp. 29–35. (Ork, Pers)
145. ——. "Eddie Condon's Le Jazz Intellectuel: Inspired Ad-Libbing by Old Masters, *Newsweek*, XXIII (Jan. 24, 1944), 62. (Crit, Ork)
146. ——. "Conductors Biased, says Henry Hadley—Finds an Evil Lure in Jazz," New York *Times*, Nov. 1, 1932, 23 : 5. (Infl)
147. ——. "Constructive, Not Wanton Criticism," *Down Beat*, XVII (Feb. 10, 1950), 10. (Crit)
148. ——. "Cornetist to Queen Victoria Falls Dead On Hearing Our Coney Island Jazz Bands," New York *Times*, June 14, 1926, 1 : 6. (Infl)
149. ——. "Count One For ' Jazz'," *Pacific Coast Musician*, XI (May, 1922), 6. (Gen)
150. ——.-"Crash Kills 'Bus' Etri, Barnet Guitar," *Down Beat*, VIII (Sept. 1, 1941), 4. (Pers)
151. ——. "Credits Beethoven With Evolving Jazz," New York *Times*, Sept. 17, 1932, 9 : 1. (A & A)
152. ——. "'Crewcut' Contest's $1,000 Word," *Down Beat*, XVI (Nov. 4, 1949), 1. (Lang)
See: 556.
153. ——. "Crosby Band Breaks Up After Seven Years," *Metronome*, LIX (Jan., 1943), 9, 34. (Ork)
154. ——. "Damrosch Assails Jazz," New York *Times*, April 17, 1928, 26 : 2. (Infl)
155. ——. "Dance Bands Aren't Dead," *Metronome*, LXVI (Aug., 1950), 13, 20. (Ork)
156. ——. "Dance Business Keeps Picking Up," *Down Beat*, XVII (Nov. 3, 1950), 10. (J & D)
157. ——. "Dance Palace on Tour," *Newsweek*, XVIII (Nov. 10, 1941), 80. (Gen, Pers)
158. ——. "Dance Puzzle Stirs Teachers to Action," New York *Times*, Apr. 20, 1914, 9 : 3. (J & D)
159. ——. "Dancebandom Sure Misses Charlie Christian," *Metronome*, LVIII (Apr., 1942), 11. (Pers)
160. ——. "Dancing Boom Gains Speed," *Down Beat*, XVII (Mar. 24, 1950), 10. (J & D)
161. ——. "Dark Angel of the Violin," *Ebony*, III (Aug., 1948), 41–2. (Pers, Pic)
162. ——. "Beryl Davis," *Metronome*, LXIII (July, 1947), 17, 40–1. (Pers)
163. ——. "Meyer Davis Champions Jazz," *Melody*, VIII (Jan., 1924), 22–3, 25. (A & A)
164. ——. "Meyer Davis Thinks Jazz Symbolic of America," *Metronome*, XXXIX (Sept., 1923), 72, 171. (A & A)
165. ——. "Debunking Jazz," *Literary Digest*, XCII (Mar. 26, 1927), 26–7. (A & A)
See: 15; 17; 406; 558; 559; 560; 2159; 2337; 3209.
166. ——. "The Decline of Jazz," *Musician*, XXVII (May, 1922), 1. (Gen, Infl)
167. ——. "Decries 'Jazz Thinking'," New York *Times*, Feb. 15, 1925, 17 : 3. (A & A)
168. ——. "Defend Jazz Music; Hit British Critic," New York *Times*, Sept. 13, 1926, 21 : 7. (A & A)
See: 15; 17; 165; 406; 558; 559; 560; 2159; 2337; 3209.

169. Anon. "Defends 'Jazz Tempo'," *Sheet Music News*, II (Mar., 1924), 17. (J & C)
170. ——. "Delving Into the Geneology of Jazz," *Current Opinion*, LXVII (Aug., 1919), 97–9. (A & A)
171. ——. "The Descent of Jazz Upon Opera," *Literary Digest*, LXXXVIII (Mar. 13, 1926), 24–5. (J & O)
172. ——. "A Dialogue on Classical Music and Jazz," *Musical Canada*, XII (Nov., 1931), 2, 10. (J & C)
173. ——. "Differs With Kahn On Our Jazz Music," *New York Times*, Nov. 14, 1924, 17 : 1. (A & A)
174. ——. "Disapproved by Royalty," *New York Times*, Mar. 12, 1928, 20 : 6. (Gen)
       See: 422.
175. ——. "Disc Bootleggers are Waxing Fat on Stolen Goods," *Down Beat*, XVII (June 16, 1950), 10. (Disc)
       See: 37.
176. ——. "Disc Jockey of the Year: Jimmy Lyons," *in* Barry Ulanov and George Simon (Eds). *Jazz 1950*. New York: Metronome, 1950. p. 15. (Pers)
177. ——. "Discography: Leon Bismark (Bix) Beiderbecke," *Recordiana*, I (June-July, 1944), 3–4. (Disc)
178. ——. "Discography of Ragtime Recordings," *Jazz Forum*, 4 (Apr., 1947), 7–8. (Disc, Rag)
179. ——. "Discography of the Year," *in* Barry Ulanov and George Simon (Eds). *Jazz 1950*. New York: Metronome, 1950. pp. 84, 86, 88, 90, 92, 94, 96, 98, 100, 101, 102. (Disc)
180. ——. "Dissonance Turns Tragic," *Musician*, XLVII (Jan., 1942), 10. (Gen)
181. ——. "Dixieland Bandwagon," *Time*, LV (Apr. 24, 1950), 104. (Dix)
182. ——. "Dixieland Shrine," *Newsweek*, XXIV (Oct. 16, 1944), 105–06. (Gen)
183. ——. "Django Music," *Time*, XLVIII (Nov. 18, 1946), 53. (Pers)
184. ——. "DJs One Reason Men Are Jobless," *Down Beat*, XVII (June 2, 1950), 10. (Gen)
185. ——. "Do You Get It?" *Time*, LIII (May 23, 1949), 50–1. (Gen, Hist, Sw)
186. ——. "The Doctor Looks At Jazz," *Literary Digest*, XCIV (Sept. 3, 1927), 29. (Infl)
187. ——. "Johnny Dodds," *Jazz Information*, II (Aug. 23, 1940), 6–9, 24. (Pers)
188. ——. "Does Jazz Cause Crime?" *Musical Observer*, XXIII (Aug., 1924), 24. (Infl)
189. ——. "The Dollar: Sign of Our Times," *Down Beat*, XVII (Apr. 7, 1950), 10. (Gen)
190. ——. "Don't Stop Swinging the Classics—Scott," *Music and Rhythm*, II (Jan., 1942), 17, 45. (J & C)
191. ——. "Dope Menace Keeps Growing," *Down Beat*, XVII (Nov. 17, 1950), 10. (Gen)
192. ——. "Jimmy Dorsey's 'Even Groove' Philosophy Is Paying Off!" *Down Beat*, VIII (Mar. 1, 1941), 16. (Pers)
193. ——. "Jimmy and Tommy Dorsey," *in* Maxime Block (Ed). *Current Biography 1942*. New York: H. W Wilson, 1943. pp. 210–12. (Pers)
194. ——. "D'ou Vient S. M. le Jazz?" *Courrier Musical*, XXVIII (Mar. 1, 1926), 144. (Hist)
195. ——. "Drawing A Line For Jazz," *Metronome*, XXXIX (Jan., 1923), 29. (J & C)
       See: 5.
196. ——. "Driver Kills Chippie Hill," *Down Beat*, XVII (June 16, 1950), 12. (Pers)
197. ——. "Drummer In A Museum," *Time*, XXXVII (Apr. 28, 1941), 44. (Pers)

198. Anon. "Ducasse Uses Ragtime In New Tone Poem," *Musical America*, XXXVII (Mar. 10, 1923), 15. (J & C)
199. ——. "Eddy Duchin," *Look*, X (Apr. 30, 1946), 76. (Pers, Pic)
200. ——. "The Duke," *Time*, XLIX (May 19, 1947), 47. (Ork, Pers)
201. ——. "Duke and Duchess of Music World," *Ebony*, IV (Oct., 1949), 20–24. (Pers, Pic)
202. ——. "Duke, Benny, Artie Top 1941 Discs," *Metronome*, LVIII (Jan., 1942), 18, 27. (Disc)
203. ——. "Duke, James Lead Bands of 1942," *Metronome*, LIX (Jan., 1943), 10–11, 39. (Ork, Poll)
204. ——. "Duke Marks His Band's 20 Fabulous Years With Ellington Week and Carnegie Concert," *Newsweek*, XXI (Feb. 1, 1943), 50. (Ork, Pers)
205. ——. "The Duke of Jazz," *Time*, XLI (Feb. 1, 1943), 66. (Pers)
206. ——. "The Duke Steps Out," *Look*, VII (Jan. 26, 1943), 54–5. (Pers, Pic)
207. ——. "Duke Sweeps '48 Band Poll," *Down Beat*, XV (Dec. 29, 1948), 1, 12–13. (Ork, Pers, Poll)
208. ——. "Duke, T.D., B.G. Lead Year's Discs," *Metronome*, LIX (Jan., 1943), 16. (Disc)
209. ——. "Isadora Duncan Plans Greek Temple for Nice; She Is Reported to Have Bought the Theatre Promenade des Anglais to Fight Jazz," New York *Times*, May 1, 1925, 6 : 1. (Gen)
210. ——. "Billy Eckstine; A Lush Voice and Musical Imagination Have Made Him A Top Crooner," *Look*, XIII (Aug. 30, 1949), 92. (Pers, Pic)
211. ——. "Editorial," *Disques*, I (Oct., 1930), 291–92. (A & A)
212. ——. "Editorial Comment," *Musical Courier*, LXXXVII (Aug. 30, 1923), 20. (Pers)
213. ——. "Editorial Comment," *Musical Courier*, LXXXVIII (Mar. 27, 1924), 36. (Gen)
214. ——. "Editorial Comment," *Presto*, 1882 (Aug. 19, 1922), 5. (Gen)
215. ——. "The Editors Recommend an Important New Book, Jazz: A People's Music: Sidney Finkelstein," *Record Changer*, VIII (Jan., 1949), 8, 22. (Rev)
216. ——. "The Effort to Take Jazz Seriously," *Literary Digest*, LXXXI (Apr. 26, 1924), 29–30. (A & A)
217. ——. "1883 Metronome 1943," *Metronome*, LIX (Oct., 1943), 20–5. (Gen)
218. ——. "Duke Ellington," *in* Maxime Block (Ed). *Current Biography 1941*. New York: H. W. Wilson, 1942. pp. 260–62. (Pers)
219. ——. "Duke Ellington," *Look*, XI (July 22, 1947), 64, 66–7, 69. (Pers, Pic)
220. ——. "Ellington Cops Both Crowns," *Down Beat*, XIV (Jan. 1, 1947), 1, 20. (Pers, Poll)
221. ——. "Ellington Wins Swing Poll," *Down Beat*, X (Jan. 1, 1943), 1, 13–14. (Pers, Poll)
222. ——. "Enjoin 'Jazz' Palace to Protect New Born," New York *Times*, Feb. 4, 1926, 4 : 3. (Infl)
223. ——. "The Ethics of Ragtime," *Jacobs' Orchestra Monthly*, III (Aug., 1912), 27–9. (Rag)
224. ——. "Europe Violently Fer or Agin Stan's Music," *Down Beat*, XVI (Jan. 14, 1949), 1. (A & A, Geog)
225. ——. "Factory Tests Show Swing Causes Many Girl Employees to Spoil Their Work," New York *Times*, Sept. 8, 1938, 25 : 5. (Infl, Sw)
226. ——. "Fails To Stop Jazz, Is Arrested Later," New York *Times*, July 7, 1922, 11 : 1. (Gen)
227. ——. "FCC Dodges 'Swing' Issue But Urges Care In Its Use," New York *Times*, Nov. 3, 1938, 25 : 6. (Rad)
See: 484; 1323; 1461.

228. Anon. "Festival Is Opened of American Music," New York *Times*, May 5, 1937, 28 : 7. (Gen, Sw)

229. —— —. "Finds Jazz the Rage With Caucasian Folk," New York *Times*, June 29, 1932, 18 : 4. (Geog)

230. —— —. " 'First Nighters' of Songs," New York *Times*, Sept. 13, 1925, XIII, 23 : 4. (Gen)

231. —— —. "Ella Fitzgerald; Her Vocal Versatility Continues to Amaze Musicians," *Ebony*, IV (May, 1949), 45–6. (Pers)

232. —— —. "Flays Rag-Time As Not Reflecting Americanism," *Musical America*, XXVIII (July 20, 1918), 22. (Rag)
See: 2206.

233. —— —. "Folk Music of the Machine Age," *Literary Digest*, XCII (Mar. 26, 1927), 27. (A & A)
See: 15; 17; 165; 168; 406; 558; 559; 560; 2159; 2337; 3209.

234. —— —. "Folk Roots of Jazz," *in Music of the New World*, Handbook, Vol. IV, Course II, Pt. II "Folkways in Music." New York: Southern Music, 1944. pp. 41–2. (Hist)

235. —— —. "Folks Find New Word to Mangle," *Down Beat*, XVII (Dec. 15, 1950), 10. (Bop)

236. —— —. "Ford Wars on Jazz; Gives Party For Old Time Dances, Seeking to Revive Their Popularity," New York *Times*, July 12, 1925, II, 2 : 5. (J & D)

237. —— —. "Founds Jazz Academy," New York *Times*, June 28, 1931, III, 4 : 6. (Ed)

238. —— —. "Four New Faces in All-Stars," *Metronome*, LVIII (Jan., 1942), 7, 20, 22–3, 38. (Pers, Poll)

239. —— —. "4000 Listeners Tell What They Prefer On Radio," New York *Times*, Feb. 21, 1926, VIII, 17 : 1. (Rad)

240. —— —. "Fra Ragtime Til Be-Bop," *Berlingske Tidende*, Nov. 5, 1949, 9. (Gen)

241. —— —. "A Fragment of 1924," *Record Changer*, IX (June, 1950), 6–9; (Sept., 1950), 9–11; (Oct., 1950), 11–13; (Nov., 1950), 11. (Disc)

242. —— —. "France Orders Our Jazz Players Expelled," New York *Times*, May 31, 1924, 1 : 5. (Gen)

243. —— —. "Frazier Names His All-Time All-Stars," *Down Beat*, XVII (Feb. 10, 1950), 2. (Gen)

244. —— —. "French Find Our Jazz Too Soul-Disturbing," New York *Times*, Feb. 3, 1929, III, 6 : 8. (Geog)

245. —— —. "French Jazz Critic Tastes Hot Licks—American Style," *Parade*, April 10, 1949, 27. (Pers)

246. —— —. "A French Philosophy of the Musical and Literary Jazz," New York *Times*, Nov. 7, 1926, VIII, 8 : 7. (Gen)

247. —— —. "French Police Stop Jazz Band Burial; Dead Man Wanted It In Procession, But the Mourners Were Foxtrotting," New York *Times*, Oct. 18, 1923, 3 : 1. (Gen)

248. —— —. "Fresh Air on 52nd St.," *Time*, XLVIII (Oct. 28, 1946), 55. (Ork)

249. —— —. "From Jim Crow to Jazz," *British Musician*, X (Oct., 1934), 223–25; (Nov., 1934), 252–54. Pt. II entitled: "The 'Spiritual,' Its Public Debut." (Hist)

250. —— —. "Fur und Wider den Jazz," *Deutsche Musiker-Zeitung*, LX (Nov. 30, 1929), 1018; (Dec. 7, 1929), 1041. (A & A)

251. —— —. "Slim Gaillard et le Vout-O-Reeney," *Hot Club Magazine*, 19 (Aug. 15, 1947), 9. (Lang, Pers)

252. —— —. "Eva Gauthier Comments on Her Experiment in Jazz," *Musical Observer*, XXIII (July, 1924), 22. (Gen)

253. —— —. "German Coming to Seek Jazz Singers Here to Satisfy Craze Started by Phonograph," New York *Times*, Apr. 8, 1927, 4 : 3. (Gen)

254. Anon. "A German Interpreter of Jazz," *Literary Digest*, LXII (Aug. 23, 1919), 31. (A & A)
255. —— —. "Germans Would Oust American Jazz Bands," New York *Times* Dec. 11, 1924, 2 : 7. (Gen, Geog)
256. —— —. "Girls Ban Jazz, Petting, Cigarettes," New York *Times*, Feb. 18, 1922, 4 : 3. (Gen)
257. —— —. "Godowsky Utters Kind Word on Jazz," New York *Times*, Oct. 10, 1924, 22 : 3. (Gen)
258. —— —. "Good Music Gains Over Jazz Mania," New York *Times*, June 13, 1923, 31 : 5. (Gen)
259. —— —. "Benjamin David (Bennie) Goodman," *in* Maxime Block (Ed). *Current Biography 1942*. New York: H. W. Wilson, 1943. pp. 305–08. (Pers)
260. —— —. "Benny Goodman: Jazz Immortal," *Look*, IX (June 12, 1945), 34, 36, 38, 40–1. (Pers, Pic)
261. —— —. "Benny Goodman Makes A Comeback," *Life*, XIX (Aug. 20, 1945), 117. (Pers, Pic)
262. —— —. "Benny Goodman, Glenn Miller Voted Champs!" *Down Beat*, IX (Jan. 1, 1942), 1, 21–2. (Pers, Poll)
263. —— —. "Benny Goodman On Reedman," *Metronome*, LIX (Oct., 1943), 26. (Pers)
264. —— —. "Grainger Says Jazz Is Refining Our Taste," New York *Times*, Feb. 11, 1932, 19 : 3. (Infl)
265. —— —. "Grand Opera With Jazz," New York *Times*, Oct. 20, 1925, 29 : 2. (J & O)
266. —— —. "Gray Gives Shot In Arm to Coast Dance Business," *Down Beat*, XVII (Sept. 8, 1950), 3. (Ork)
    See: 1336.
267. —— —. "The Great American Composer—Will He Speak In the Accent of Broadway ?" *Current Opinion*, LXIII (Nov., 1917), 316–17. (J & C)
268. —— —. "The Great Songs," *Metronome*, LIX (Oct., 1943), 28–9, 53. (Gen)
269. —— —. "Green A Ventura Highspot," *Down Beat*, XVI (July 15, 1949), 2. (Pers)
270. —— —. "Group to Fight 'Jazzing' of the National Anthem," New York *Times*, Dec. 21, 1938, 21 : 3. (Gen)
271. —— —. "John Hammond… A Critic and A Crew Haircut," *Music and Rhythm*, II (Oct., 1941), 26. (Pers)
272. —— —. "Lionel Hampton," *Look*, VII (June 29, 1943), 66. (Pers, Pic)
273. —— —. "Lionel Hampton on Vibes et al," *Metronome*, LIX (Oct., 1943), 32, 68. (Pers)
274. —— —. "Lionel Hampton's Million-Dollar Band Business," *Ebony*, IV (Aug., 1949), 20–4. (Ork)
275. —— —. "William Christopher Handy," *in* Maxime Block (Ed). *Current Biography 1941*. New York: H. W. Wilson, 1942. pp. 361–62. (Pers)
276. —— —. "Harling's New Jazz Opera," *Christian Science Monitor*, Sept. 25, 1926, 8. (Crit, J & O)
277. —— —. "Harty Hits At Jazz," New York *Times*, Oct. 3, 1926, VIII, 7 : 4. (Gen)
278. —— —. "Has Jazz Hurt Concert-Giving ?… Managers Say 'No'," *Musical America*, XLIII (Nov. 14, 1925), 31. (Infl)
279. —— —. "Coleman Hawkins," *Look*, VII (Mar. 9, 1943), 62. (Pers, Pic)
280. —— —. "Erskine Hawkins," *in* Maxime Block (Ed). *Current Biography 1941*. New York: H. W. Wilson, 1942. pp. 269–71. (Pers)
281. —— —. "Herbie Haymer on Wax," *Down Beat*, XVI (June 3, 1949), 13. (Disc)
282. —— —. "He Calls It Progress," *Time*, LI (Mar. 1, 1948), 34, 37. (Ork, Pers)
283. —— —. "He Has No Scorn for Jazz ?" New York *Times*, Jan. 28, 1925, 16 : 5. (Gen)
    See: 1731.

284. Anon. "He Sees a Change For the Worse," New York *Times*, Oct. 13, 1924, 18 : 5. (Infl)
See: 655.
285. ——. "Here's Capsule Record of 1942 Music World," *Down Beat*, X (Jan. 1, 1943), 2–3. (Gen)
286. ——. "Woody Herman Tosses In Towel," *Down Beat*, XVI (Dec., 16, 1949), 1. (Pers)
287. ——. "He's Planning Quantity Production," New York *Times*, Jan. 12, 1925, 14 : 5. (Gen)
See: 493.
288. ——. "Higgy, Rey, New All-Stars," *Metronome*, LIX (Jan., 1943), 7, 14–15, 32–3. (Pers, Poll)
289. ——. "'High-Class' Jazz," *Musical Leader*, XLV (Apr. 26, 1923), 396. (Gen)
290. ——. "High Schools Plan Lectures On Jazz," New York *Times*, May 19, 1937, 25 : 6. (Ed)
See: 2786.
291. ——. "His Opinion Will Not Be Accepted," New York *Times*, Nov. 13, 1924, 22 : 6. (Gen)
See: 456.
292. ——. "La Historia de un Instrumento Musical," *La Razon*, Nov. 14, 1942, 2. (Inst)
293. ——. "'Hit the Road' Now A Big Headache: Tire, Gas Shortage Makes Location Stands Best Bet," *Down Beat*, IX (Mar. 15, 1942), 1, 19. (Gen)
294. ——. "Hitler Frowns On Jazz," *Literary Digest*, CXVII (Mar. 24, 1934), 24. (A & A)
295. ——. "Billie Holiday," *Look*, X (Sept. 3, 1946), 59. (Pers, Pic)
296. ——. "Billie Holiday Concert Makes Jazz History," *Down Beat*, XIII (Mar. 11, 1946), 1. (Crit, Pers)
297. ——. "Hollywood Debut for Pearl Bailey," *Ebony*, II (Apr., 1947), 38–9. (Pers)
298. ——. "The Home of Happy Feet," *Ebony*, I (Oct., 1946), 32–7. (Gen, Pic)
299. ——. "Home-Made Jazz for Italy," New York *Times*, July 16, 1926, 3 : 2. (Geog)
300. ——. "Honeysuckle Rose," *New Yorker*, XIX (Dec. 11, 1943), 26–7. (Ed, Pers)
301. ——. "Horn of Plenty," *Time*, LII (Aug. 23, 1948), 50–1. (Pers)
302. ——. "Lena Horne," *in* Anna Rothe (Ed). *Current Biography 1944*. New York: H. W. Wilson, 1945. pp. 310–12. (Pers)
303. ——. "Lena Horne Begins a New Movie," *Ebony*, I (Mar., 1946), 14–20. (Pers, Pic)
304. ——. "Lena Horne is Still on the Way Up," *PM*, Dec. 15, 1942, 19 : 2–3. (Pers)
305. ——. "Hot Drummers," *Look*, X (Mar. 5, 1946), 43–5. (Pers, Pic)
306. ——. "Hot Jazz Born When Dixieland Boys Wore Rompers," *Metronome*, LII (Sept., 1936), 24. (Hist, Ork)
307. ——. "Hot Jazz in Iceland," *Jazzfinder*, I (June, 1948), 5. (Geog)
308. ——. "Hot Music at Carnegie," New York *Times*, Jan. 18, 1938, 22 : 3. (Crit, Ork, Sw)
See: 1289.
309. ——. "Hot Royalty," *in* George S. Rosenthal (Ed). *Jazzways*. Cincinnati, 1946. pp. 56–7. (Pers)
310. ——. "Hot Society," *Time*, XXIX (May 17, 1937), 50. (Disc)
311. ——. "Hot Trumpeters," *Look*, X (Aug. 6, 1946), 32–5. (Pers, Pic)
312. ——. "How Deaf Can You Get?" *Time*, LI (May 17, 1948), 74. (Bop, Pers)
313. ——. "How To Do the Bop Hop; Benny Goodman Band Introduces New Dance Steps On Its Tour," *Ebony*, IV (July, 1949), 23–5. (J & D, Pic)

314. Anon. "Huge RCA Dance Band Buildup," *Down Beat*, XVII (Mar. 24, 1950), 2. (Disc, J & D)
315. —— ——. "Hungary Protects Home Jazz by Barring Foreign Bands," New York *Times*, Dec. 1, 1925, 2 : 7. (Geog)
316. —— ——. "An Idea From America," *Musical Opinion*, XLIII (May, 1920), 610. (Gen)
317. —— ——. "Immortals of Jazz," A Series of Biographical Sketches in *Down Beat*: (Pers)

> "Louis Armstrong," VI (Dec. 15, 1939), 10.
> "Mildred Bailey," VIII (July 15, 1941), 10.
> "Count Basie," VIII (June 15, 1941), 10.
> "Sidney Bechet," VII (July 15, 1940), 10.
> "Bix Beiderbecke," VII (Aug. 1, 1940), 10.
> "Benny Carter," VII (Sept. 15, 1940), 10.
> "Johnny Dodds," VII (Apr. 1, 1940), 10.
> "Jimmy Dorsey," VII (Sept. 1, 1940), 10.
> "Tommy Dorsey," VIII (May 15, 1941), 10.
> "Roy Eldridge," VIII (Apr. 15, 1941), 10.
> "Duke Ellington," VII (Jan. 15, 1940), 10.
> "Bud Freeman," VIII (June 1, 1941), 10.
> "Benny Goodman," VII (Feb. 1, 1940), 10.
> "Emmet Hardy," VII (Aug. 15, 1940), 6.
> "Coleman Hawkins," VII (Feb. 15, 1940), 18.
> "Fletcher Henderson," VI (Nov. 15, 1939), 23.
> "Jay C. Higginbotham," VIII (Mar. 15, 1941), 10.
> "Earl Hines," VII (July 1, 1940), 23.
> "Pete Johnson," VIII (July 1, 1941), 10.
> "Gene Krupa," VI (Nov. 1, 1939), 20.
> "Red McKenzie," VI (Oct. 15, 1939), 22.
> "Wingy Manone," VIII (Aug. 1, 1941), 10.
> "Salvatore Massano (Eddie Lang)," VII (Oct. 1, 1940), 11.
> "Miff Mole," VIII (Feb. 1, 1941), 10.
> "Jelly Roll Morton," VII (Apr. 15, 1940), 10.
> "Red Nichols," VI (Sept., 1939), 30.
> "Jimmy Noone," VIII (Feb. 15, 1941), 10.
> "Red Norvo," VII (June 15, 1940), 10.
> "King Oliver," VII (May, 15 1940), 13.
> "Ben Pollack," VIII (May 1, 1941), 10.
> "Leon Rappolo," VII (Oct. 15, 1940), 10.
> "Don Redman," VII (Nov. 15, 1940), 10.
> "Gil Rodin," VII (June 1, 1940), 22.
> "Muggsy Spanier," VII (May 1, 1940), 10.
> "Jess Stacy," VIII (Mar. 1, 1941), 10.
> "Jack Teagarden," VII (Dec. 1, 1940), 10.
> "Frank Teschmaker," VII (Mar. 15, 1940), 10.
> "Frank Trumbauer," VII (Nov. 1, 1940), 10.
> "Joe Venuti," VII (Mar. 1, 1940), 10.
> "Fats Waller," VIII (Jan. 15, 1941), 10.
> "Chick Webb," VIII (Jan. 1, 1941), 10.
> "Mary Lou Williams," VII (Dec. 15, 1940), 12.
> "Teddy Wilson," VIII (Apr. 1, 1941), 10.

318. —— ——. "In the Matter of Jazz," *Musical Courier*, XC (Feb. 19, 1925), 28. (Gen)
319. —— ——. "In the Name of Music," (lr) New York *Times*, July 30, 1939, IX, 6 : 6. (Gen)

320. Anon. "Index to Recent Records," *in* Orin Blackstone (Ed). *Jazzfinder '49.* New Orleans: Orin Blackstone, 1949. pp. 65–106. (Disc)
321. ——. "Indians Abandon Tom-tom For the White Man's Jazz," *Metronome,* XXXVIII (May, 1922), 61. (Gen)
322. ——. "The Influence of 'Jazz'," *Monthly Musical Record,* LVII (Aug. 1, 1927), 233. (Infl)
323. ——. "Influence of the Year: King Cole Trio," *Metronome,* LXIII (Jan., 1947), 23. (Ork)
324. ——. "Influence of the Year: Charlie Parker," *Metronome,* LXIV (Jan., 1948), 22. (Pers)
325. ——. "Die Internationale Republik des Jazz," *Die Melodie,* III (1948/49), 8–9; IV (June, 1949), 14–15. (Geog)
326. ——. "Introducing Duke Ellington," *Fortune,* VIII (Aug., 1933), 47–9, 90, 92, 94–5. (Pers)
327. ——. "The 'Inventors' of Tin Pan Alley," *Popular Mechanics,* LI (Jan., 1929), 74–7. (Gen, Pers)
328. ——. "Irish Denounce Jazz," New York *Times,* Jan. 2, 1934, 17 : 4. (Gen)
     See: 46.
329. ——. "Is Jazz 'The American Soul'?" *Musical America,* XXXIX (Nov. 24, 1923), 10. (A & A)
330. ——. "Is Jazz Going Hibrow? Hot Pianist Dorothy Donegan Is Newest Convert to the Classics," *Ebony,* I (July, 1946), 15–17. (Pers, Pic)
331. ——. "Is Jazz Music?" *Musical Courier,* XCVII (Aug. 16, 1928), 20. (A & A)
     See: 807; 843; 845; 2897.
332. ——. "Is Jazz Our National Anthem?" New York *Times,* Jan. 30, 1922, 11 : 3. (A & A)
333. ——. "Is Jazz the Pilot of Disaster?" *Etude,* XLIII (Jan., 1925), 5–6. (Infl)
334. ——. "Is a Music Boom on Way Back?" *Down Beat,* XVII (Oct. 20, 1950), 10. (Gen)
335. ——. "Is the Pendulum Swinging Back?" *Down Beat,* XVII (Sept. 8, 1950), 10. (Gen)
336. ——. "Is the Popularity of Jazz Music Waning?" *Radio Broadcast,* VIII (Dec., 1925), 177–78. (Infl)
337. ——. "Is Radio a Dead End For Negro Bands?" *Music and Rhythm,* II (Dec., 1941), 15. (Gen, Rad)
338. ——. "It's A Matter of Wanting to Live," *Down Beat,* XVII (Jan. 27, 1950), 10. (Gen)
339. ——. "Italians Sign Petitions Against Jazz, Says Milhaud," *Musical America,* XXXVIII (Sept. 29, 1923), 4. (Geog, Gen)
340. ——. "Jam!" *Esquire,* XXII (Dec., 1944), 107–14. (Pic)
341. ——. "Jam Session," *Life,* XV (Oct. 11, 1943), 117–24. (Pic)
342. ——. "Jam Session," *Look,* VII (Aug. 24, 1943), 64–6. (Pic)
343. ——. "Jam Session in Movieland," *Ebony,* I (Nov., 1945), 6–9. (Pic, Rad)
344. ——. "Harry James (Haag)," *in* Maxime Block (Ed). *Current Biography 1943.* New York: H. W. Wilson, 1944. pp. 340–43. (Pers)
345. ——. "Harry James," *Look,* VII (Feb. 9, 1943), 62. (Pers, Pic)
346. ——. "Jazz," *in* Henry Suzzalo (Ed). *The National Encyclopedia.* New York: P. F. Collier, 1932. pp. 578–79. (A & A)
347. ——. "Jazz," *Opportunity,* III (May, 1925), 132–33. (A & A)
348. ——. "Jazz," *Outlook,* CXXXVI (Mar. 5, 1924), 381–82. (Infl, Hist)
349. ——. "Jazz," *Scottish Musical Magazine,* XI (July, 1930), 156. (Infl)
350. ——. "Le Jazz," *Dissonances,* I (July-Sept., 1924), 150–51. (Gen)
351. ——. "Jazz A Form of Art," *Metronome,* XXXVIII (Sept., 1922), 65. (A & A)
     See: 1350.

352. Anon. "'Jazz A State of Mind'," New York *Times*, Apr. 2, 1925, 23 : 3. (A & A)
353. —— ——. "Jazz Abroad," New York *Times*, May 20, 1928, VIII, 7 : 7. (J & D)
354. —— ——. "Jazz Again," *Musical Courier*, LXXXVII (July 5, 1923), 21. (Ork)
355. —— ——. "Jazz All Over Europe," New York *Times*, Apr. 30, 1929, 14 :1 . (Gen, Geog)
356. —— ——. "Jazz am Konservatorium," *Der Auftakt*, VII (1927), 317–19. (Ed)
357. —— ——. "Jazz and the Disposition," New York *Times*, June 13, 1927, 18 : 5. (Gen, Infl)
     See: 402.
358. —— ——. "Jazz and Its Victims," New York *Times*, Oct. 7, 1928, V, 19. (Infl)
359. —— ——. "Jazz—and the Organist," *American Organist*, VI (Feb., 1923), 113–14. (Gen)
360. —— ——. "Jazz and Ragtime Are the Preludes to a Great American Music," *Current Opinion*, LXIX (Aug., 1920), 199–201. (A & A, Infl)
361. —— ——. "Jazz Artists Migrate," New York *Times*, Mar. 12, 1925, 9 : 1. (Gen)
     See: 451.
362. —— ——. "Jazz as Folk-Music," *Musical America*, XLIII (Dec. 19, 1925), 18. (A & A)
363. —— ——. "Jazz As a Form of Art," *Musical Leader*, XLIV (Aug. 10, 1922), 130. (A & A)
     See: 1350.
364. —— ——. "Jazz at the Fountainhead," New York *Times*, Apr. 12, 1929, 26 : 6. (Gen)
365. —— ——. "Jazz at the Philharmonic," *Scholastic*, L (Apr. 7, 1947), 36. (Pers, Ork)
366. —— ——. "Jazz at the Sorbonne," New York *Times*, June 20, 1926, VIII, 2 : 2. (Gen, Geog)
367. —— ——. "Jazz Back in Japan," *Metronome*, LXIII (Aug., 1947), 17. (Geog)
368. —— ——. "Jazz Bands Here and Abroad," New York *Times*, Dec. 12, 1924, 22 : 6. (Gen)
369. —— ——. "Jazz Bands Popular in Turkey," New York *Times*, Oct. 12, 1927, 27 : 2. (Geog)
370. —— ——. "Jazz Beyond the Alps," New York *Times*, Mar.11, 1926, 20 : 6. (A & A)
371. —— ——. "Jazz Bitterly Opposed in Germany," New York *Times*, Mar. 11, 1928, VIII, 8 : 4. (Ed, Geog, Infl)
372. —— ——. "Jazz, the Black Peril, and the Bigger Cheeses," *Musical Opinion*, L (4 May, 1927), 794–95. (Infl)
373. —— ——. "Jazz Boom in Europe," *Ebony*, III (July, 1948), 23–7. (Geog, Pic)
374. —— ——. "Jazz by· Django," *Newsweek*, XXVIII (Nov. 18, 1946), 100. (Pers)
375. —— ——. "The Jazz Cannibal," *Literary Digest*, LXXXIV (Jan. 10, 1925), 36. (Poet)
376. —— ——. "Jazz Club Concert," New York *Times*, Sept. 7, 1947, 63 : 4. (NO, Pers)
377. —— ——. "Jazz Comes to Stay," *Current Opinion*, LXXVII (Sept., 1924), 337–38. (A & A)
378. —— ——. "Jazz Coming On," *Musical Courier*, XCII (Jan. 7, 1926), 30. (Crit, J & O)
379. —— —— "Jazz Commission for Kahn," New York *Times*, May 19, 1927, 32 : 5. (Gen)
380. —— ——. "El Jazz, Con Sus Disonancias y Estridencias, Ha Conquistado Al Mundo," *La Razon*, Jan. 3, 1942, 2. (Infl)
381. —:—. "Jazz Concert Heard," New York *Times*, May 17, 1945, 15 : 1. (Crit)
382. —— ——. "Jazz Concert in Public Park on Sunday Stirs Up London," New York *Times*, June 10, 1925, 1 : 7. (Gen)
383. —— ——. "Jazz Concerts," *Ebony*, I (Sept., 1946), 29–34. (Gen, Pic)
384. —— ——. "A Jazz Conference," *Musical Leader*, XLIII (Apr. 13, 1922), 364. (Gen)

385. Anon. "Jazz Conservatory for Prague," New York *Times*, Nov. 22, 1931, III, 3 : 5. (Ed)
386. —— —. "Jazz 'Doomed and Dying'," New York *Times*, June 7, 1921, 10 : 3. (Gen)
387. —— —. "Jazz Dying, Says Sheldon," New York *Times*, Sept. 26, 1926, 26 : 8. (Gen)
388. —— —. "Jazz Enters the Laboratory For Psychological Study," *Science News Letter*, XXXVI (July 1, 1939), 12–13. (A & A)
389. —— —. "The Jazz Fiddler," *Etude*, XLI (June, 1923), 420–21. (A & A, Inst)
390. —— —. "Jazz Foundation Concert," New York *Times*, June 23, 1945, 10 : 3. (Crit)
391. —— —. "Jazz Frightens Bears," New York *Times*, Nov. 24, 1928, 16 : 5. (Infl)
392. —— —. "Jazz Gains in Popularity as Soviet Lifts Ban," New York *Times*, May 17, 1933, 15 : 2. (Geog)
393. —— —. "Jazz Grows Popular in China, Dance Record Sales Reveal," New York *Times*, Nov. 16, 1929, 5 : 2. (Geog)
    See: 398.
394. —— —. "The Jazz Hoot," *New Yorker*, XXVI (Apr. 1, 1950), 21–2. (Pers)
395. —— —. "Jazz Hymns Draw Fire," New York *Times*, Aug. 2, 1925, 27 : 2. (Rad)
    See: 438.
396. —— —. "Jazz in China," *Musical Courier*, LXXXVIII (June 26, 1924), 14. (Geog)
397. —— —. "Jazz in Italy," *Musical Leader*, LI (July 8, 1926), 10. (Geog)
398. —— —. "Jazz in the Orient," New York *Times*, Nov. 19, 1929, 28 : 5. (Geog)
    See: 393.
399. —— —. "El Jazz, Influencia y Expresion," *Ars Magazine*, II (Oct., 1941), 31. (Infl)
400. —— —. "Jazz Is Compared to Comic Cartoon," New York *Times*, Feb. 18, 1927, 24 : 4. (A & A)
401 —— —. "Jazz is Dead But Tang and Color Will Survive in America's Future Classicalism, Says Grofe, Founder of the 'New School'," *Musical Courier*, CIV (May 14, 1932), 9, 16. (Infl)
402. —— —. "Jazz is Not Music, Stresemann Asserts," New York *Times*, June 12, 1927, 19 : 4. (Gen)
    See: 357.
403. —— —. "Jazz Losing Caste, Mary Garden Finds," New York *Times*, Nov. 24, 1927, 28 : 2. (A & A)
404. —— —. "Jazz May Be Lowbrow, But..." *Musical Courier*, LXXXVIII (Jan. 10, 1924), 39. (A & A)
    See: 2719.
405. —— —. "Jazz Music and Digestion," New York *Times*, May 13, 1927, 22 : 5. (Infl)
406. —— —. "Jazz Music, and Its Particular Sting," *Musical Digest*, X (Sept. 21, 1926), 7. (A & A)
    See: 15; 17; 165; 168; 233; 558; 559; 560; 2159; 2337; 3210.
407. —— —. "Jazz Music Banned in France," *Musical Leader*, XLVII (June 19, 1924), 586. (A & A, Geog, Infl)
408. —— —. "Jazz Music Upheld by Otto H. Kahn," New York *Times*, Aug. 13, 1924, 17 : 6. (Gen)
409. —— —. "Jazz Not What It Once Was," *Musical Leader*, XLVIII (July 24, 1924), 84. (A & A)
410. —— —. "Jazz Now Syncopep," *Musical Leader*, XLVIII (Dec. 11, 1924), 568. (Gen)
411. —— —. "Jazz—Obsequies or Otherwise?" *Melody*, VI (July, 1922), 7–8. (Hist)

412. Anon. "Jazz on the River," *Newsweek*, XXX (July 7, 1947), 85. (Gen, Pic)
413. —— —. "Jazz on the Verge," *Time*, XXVIII (Dec. 7, 1936), 62–3. (Crit)
414. —— —. "Jazz Opera 'Deep River' to Open Here on Oct. 4," New York *Times*, Aug. 13, 1926, 12 : 2. (J & O)
415. —— —. "Jazz Opera in View for Metropolitan," New York *Times*, Nov. 18, 1924, 23 : 1. (J & O)
416. —— —. "Jazz Operas in Germany," *Living Age*, CCCXXXII (Apr. 15, 1927), 735. (J & O)
417. —— —. "Jazz Or—," *Musical Courier*, LXXXVIII (Feb. 7, 1924), 36. (Gen, Infl)
418. —— —. "Jazz or 'Modern Popular Music' To Be Heard and Discussed at Composers' League Lecture," *Musical Courier*, LXXXVIII (Feb. 7, 1924), 6. (Gen, J & C)
419. —— —. "Jazz or No Jazz ?" *Musical Standard*, XXII (Dec. 15, 1923), 187. (J & C)
420. —— —. "Jazz Origin Again Discovered," *Music Trade Review*, LXVIII (1919), 32–3. (Hist)
421. —— —. "Jazz Overadvertized," *Literary Digest*, LXXIX (Dec. 15, 1923), 28–9. (A & A)
422. —— —. "Jazz Pandemonium to Prince Joachim," New York *Times*, Mar. 11, 1928, 10 : 1. (A & A, Infl)
See: 174.
423. —— —. "Jazz Pianist Ammons Dies," Chicago *Daily News*, Dec. 3, 1949, 6 : 5. (Pers)
424. —— —. "Jazz Played Out," *Literary Digest*, LXXII (Jan. 14, 1922), 27. (A & A)
425. —— —. "Jazz Prize," *Musical Courier*, LXXXIX (July 17, 1924), 28. (Lang)
426. —— —. "Jazz Reduces Output of Tenors From Naples," New York *Times*, May 22, 1927, II, 8 : 2. (Infl)
427. —— —. "Jazz, Says Darius Milhaud, Is the Most Significant Thing in Music Today," *Musical Observer*, XXII (Mar., 1923), 23. (J & C)
428. —— —. "The Jazz Scene," *Ebony*, V (Nov., 1949), 24–7. (Disc)
429. —— —. "Jazz Stems From Whites Not Blacks, Says LaRocca," *Metronome*, LII (Oct., 1936), 20, 51, 53. (Hist, Ork)
430. —— —. "Jazz ? Swing ? It's Ragtime," *Time*, XLVI (Nov. 5, 1945), 62–3. (Ork, Pers)
431. —— —. "Jazz Symphony," *Time*, XXX (Dec. 20, 1937), 44–5. (J & C)
432. —— —. "Jazz Takes Root in Classics, Asserts Sigmund Spaeth," *Musical America*, XLI (Dec. 27, 1924), 23. (J & C)
433. —— —. Jazz Under Ban," *Music and Musicians*, VIII (Aug., 1922), 3. (Gen)
434. —— —. "Der 'Jazz' Vom Jazz," *Deutsche Musiker-Zeitung*, LXI (Apr. 26, 1930), 347. (A & A)
435. —— —. "'Jazz' Waits at This Church," *Music Trades*, LXIII (May 13, 1922), 44. (Gen)
436. —— —. "Jazzando," *Musical Courier*, LXXXV, (Aug. 24, 1922), 20. (Infl)
437. —— —. "A Jazzed Discussion," *Musical Courier*, LXXXVIII (Apr. 17, 1924), 37. (Infl)
438. —— —. "Jazzed Hymns Called Off," New York *Times*, Aug. 3, 1925, 18 : 3. (Rad)
See: 395.
439. —— —. "Jazzing the Classics," New York *Times*, Dec. 7, 1927, 28 : 6. (J & C)
440. —— —. "Jazzu," *Time*, LIV (Aug. 8, 1949), 40–1. (Geog)
441. —— —. "Jack Jenny Dies Suddenly," *Down Beat*, XIII (Jan. 1, 1946), 3. (Pers)
442. —— —. "'Jitterbug' Tunes Barred at Princeton Songfests," New York *Times*, May 1, 1939, 25 : 7. (Gen)
443. —— —. "Jitterbugs at Play," New York *Times*, May 31, 1938, 18 : 2. (Gen)

444. Anon. "Jive Bombers," *Scholastic*, XLVIII (Feb. 4, 1946), 32. (A & A, Ork)

445. — —. "Jive Papa," *Ebony*, I (Aug., 1946), 19–24. (Lang)

446. — —. "Bunk Johnson," *Ebony*, I (Mar., 1946), 33–7. (Pers, Pic)

447. — —. "Bunk Johnson Rides Again," *Time*, XLI (May 24, 1943), 63–4. (Pers)

448. — —. "Joint Rocked," *Time*, XXXI (Jan. 24, 1938), 58. (Crit)

449. — —. "Louis Jordan," *Ebony*, IV (Jan., 1949), 39–41. (Pers, Pic)

450. — —. "Louis Jordan," *Look*, IX (Oct. 2, 1945), 78. (Pers, Pic)

451. — —. "Journalism Gets Vindication," New York *Times*, Mar. 13, 1925, 18 : 6. (Gen)
     See: 361.

452. — —. "Judge Rails at Jazz and Dance Madness," New York *Times*, Apr. 14, 1926, 15 : 1. (J & D)

453. — —. "Jungle Band," *Life*, XIX (Nov. 5, 1945), 134, 137. (Ork, Pic)

454. — —. "Kahn on Jazz," *Musical Courier*, LXXXIX (Nov. 20, 1924), 26. (Gen)

455. — —. "Otto H. Kahn on Jazz Music," *Musical Courier*, XCI (July 16, 1925), 14. (Gen)

456. — —. "Otto H. Kahn Pays Tribute to Jazz," New York *Times*, Nov. 12, 1924, 14 : 1. (Gen)
     See: 291.

457. — —. "Kahn to Open Jazz School," New York *Times*, Sept. 2, 1925, 21 : 2. (Ed)

458. — —. "Kahn Wants a Jazz Opera to Produce on Metropolitan Stage," *Music News* XVI (Nov. 28, 1924), 3. (J & O)

459. — —. "Hal Kemp," *in* Maxime Block (Ed). *Current Biography 1941*. New York: H. W. Wilson, 1942. p. 465. (Pers)

460. — —. "Kenton Chances Blasting a Path to Prostration," *Down Beat*, XV (June 2, 1948), 10. (Gen)

461. — —. "Kenton Grabs Early Poll Lead," *Down Beat*, XVII (Dec. 1, 1950), 1, 19. (Poll)

462. — —. "Stan Kenton Ork Set for New York Debut at Door," *Down Beat*, VIII (Nov. 1, 1941), 1. (Pers)

463. — —. "Kenton Quits Music Business," *Down Beat*, XVI (Jan. 14, 1949), 1. (Pers)

464. — —. "Kenton Readies Ork for Concert Tour," *Down Beat*, XVI (Nov. 4, 1949), 2. (Ork)

465. — —. "Kenton, Shearing Poll Winners: All-Star Band Gets New Faces," *Down Beat*, XVII (Dec. 29, 1950), 1, 14–15. (Poll)

466. — —. "Jerome Kern Hits at Jazz Orchestra," New York *Times*, Apr. 12, 1924, 18 : 1. (Gen)

467. — —. "Killian Killed in L. A. By Psychopathic Murderer," *Down Beat*, XVII (Oct. 20, 1950), 9. (Pers)

468. — —. "King Jazz and the Jazz Kings," *Literary Digest*, LXXXVIII (Jan. 30, 1926), 37–8, 41–2. (Pers)

469. — —. "King Louis 1st," *Look*, VII (Mar. 23, 1943), 64–6. (Pers, Pic)

470. — —. "King of the Jook-Box," *Newsweek*, XV (Jan. 15, 1940), 30–1. (Pers)

471. — —. "King of the Ragtimers," *Time*, LVI (Oct. 30, 1950), 48. (Rev)

472. — —. "Kreisler Is Here For Concert Tour . . . Calls Jazz a Symptom . . ." New York *Times*, Oct. 9, 1936, 30 : 1. (Gen)

473. — —. "Fritz Kreisler Returns; Violinist Says Jazz Is a Clever Caricature and Transitory," New York *Times*, Jan. 11, 1925, 31 : 4. (A & A)

474. — —. "Eugene Bertram (Gene) Krupa," *in* Anna Rothe (Ed). *Current Biography 1947*. New York: H. W. Wilson, 1948. pp. 370–72. (Pers)

475. — —. "Gene Krupa; The Drummer Man Runs Wild," *Look*, VIII (Oct. 31, 1944), 40. (Pers, Pic)

476. Anon. "Krupa: Into This World Again," *Newsweek*, XXIV (July 31, 1944), 69. (Pers)
477. ——. "Gene Krupa Shows How to Play Drum in These Fantastic Sound Pictures," *Life*, X (June 9, 1941), 81. (Inst, Pic)
478. ——. "Lac Bug vs. Jitterbug," *Newsweek*, XIX (Apr. 27, 1942), 59–60. (Disc)
479. ——. "Lambeth Walk and the Yam," *Newsweek*, XII (Sept. 12, 1938), 20–1. (J & D)
480. ——. "Land of Oo-Bla-Dee," *Time*, LIV (Sept. 12, 1949), 77–9. (Pers)
481. ——. "Laud Jazz in High Places," New York *Times*, Aug. 16, 1921, 3 : 4. (Infl)
482. ——. "Leave 'Jazz' Alone," *Musical Courier*, LXXXV (Oct. 26, 1922), 21. (Gen, Infl)
See: 1151.
483. ——. "Franz Lehar on Jazz," *Living Age*, CCCXXVIII (Mar. 13, 1926), 601–02. (A & A)
484. ——. "Let Freedom 'Swing'," New York *Times*, Nov. 6, 1938, IX, 12 : 3. (J & C, Rad)
See: 227; 1323; 1461.
485. ——. "Let's Face It," *Time*, LIV (Sept. 26, 1949), 47–8. (Crit, Pers)
486. ——. "Life Goes to a Party to Listen to Benny Goodman and His Swing Band," *Life*, III (Nov. 1, 1937), 120–22; 124. (J & D, Ork, Pic)
487. ——. "Life Goes to a Party At the Hotel Lincoln in New York City to Hear Artie Shaw, Swing's Newest King," *Life*, VI (Jan. 23, 1939), 60–62. (J & D, Ork, Pic)
488. ——. "Links Concert and Jazz," New York *Times*, Apr. 13, 1924, II, 2 : 1. (Gen)
489. ——. "List and Addresses of Recording Firms," *Down Beat*, XIII (June 3, 1946), 14–15. (Disc)
490. ——. "List of Country's Leading Musicians," *Metronome*, LVII (Nov., 1941), 12–13. (Pers)
491. ——. "Look, Ma, Stan's Dancing Again!" *Down Beat*, XVII (Aug. 25, 1950), 1. (Ork)
492. ——. "Lopez on Jazz," *Musical Courier*, LXXXVIII (Jan. 24, 1924), 8. (Gen)
493. ——. "Lopez To Put Jazz Into Stock Market," New York *Times*, Jan. 10, 1925, 8 : 1. (Gen)
See: 287.
494. ——. "Jimmy Lord," *Jazz Hot*, 12 (Nov., 1936), 3. (Pers)
495. ——. "Louis the First," *Time*, LIII (Feb. 21, 1949), 52–8. (Hist, Pers)
See: 18; 1490; 1820; 2085.
496. ——. "Louis, Babe Ruth Go Hand in Hand," *Down Beat*, XVII (July 14, 1950), 10. (Pers)
497. ——. "Louis, Shearing On Same Bill Enrich Bop City Till," *Down Beat*, XVI (Oct. 7, 1949), 2. (Crit, Ork)
498. ——. "Louis Writes Life Story," *Down Beat*, XVII (May 5, 1950), 1. (Pers)
See: 859.
499. ——. "Low Taste," *Time*, XLVIII (Sept. 2, 1946), 41. (Ork)
500. ——. "Lutheran Church Bans Jazzy Organs," New York *Times*, Oct. 9, 1924, 23 : 4. (Inst)
501. ——. "Make Mine Music," *Life*, XX (Mar. 11, 1946), 56. (Pic)
502. ——. "Marche Funebre," *Etude*, XLIV (Aug., 1926), 558. (Gen)
503. ——. "Kaiser Marshall," *Record Changer*, VII (Mar., 1948), 12. (Pers)
504. ——. "Meadowbrook Opens Up For Fall With Woody Ork," *Down Beat*, XVII (Sept. 22, 1950), 1. (Ork)
505. ——. "A Medico On Jazz," *Musical Courier*, XCV (Aug. 11, 1927), 22. (Infl)

506. Anon. "Meet the Real Lena Horne," *Ebony*, III (Nov., 1947), 9–14. (Pers, Pic)
507. ——. "A Melodious Year," New York *Times*, Oct. 19, 1929, 18 : 4. (Gen)
508. ——. "Frank Melrose, Chi Pianist, Is Found Fatally Injured," *Down Beat*, VIII (Sept. 15, 1941), 6. (Pers)
509. ——. "Members of Krupa Crew Tell Their Lives, Interests," *Down Beat*, XVII (Aug. 25, 1950), 2. (Ork)
510. ——. "A Memorial Program," *Jazz Session*, 6 (Mar.-Apr., 1945), 6–8. (Pers, Rad)
511. ——. "Mengelberg Espouses Jazz," *Sheet Music Trade News*, II (Apr., 1924), 38. (Gen)
512. ——. "Johnny Mercer," *in* Anna Rothe (Ed). *Current Biography 1948*. New York: H. W. Wilson, 1949. pp. 445–46. (Pers)
513. ——. "The Merry Muses," New York *Times*, Apr. 13, 1926, 24 : 4. (A & A)
514. ——. "Metronome's Albums of the Year," *Metronome*, LXIII (Jan., 1947), 29. (Disc)
515. ——. "Metronome's All Stars (1946 Edition)," *Metronome*, LXIII (Jan., 1947), 24–5, 49. (Poll)
516. ——. "Metronome's All Stars," *Metronome*, LXIV (Jan., 1948), 24–5, 37–41. (Poll)
517. ——. "Metronome's Hall of Fame," A Series in *Metronome*: (Pers)

> "Louis Armstrong," LXIII (Jan., 1947), 26.
> "Mildred Bailey," LXIII (Mar., 1947), 18.
> "Will Bradley," LVI (Aug., 1940), 26.
> "Charlie Christian," LXIII (Aug., 1947), 27.
> "Roy Eldridge," LXIII (May, 1947), 25.
> "Duke Ellington," LXIII (Apr., 1947), 18.
> "Ziggy Elman," LVII (Apr., 1941), 22.
> "Benny Goodman," LXIII (Feb., 1947), 22.
> "Irving Goodman," LVII (Feb., 1941), 34.
> "Wolffe Taninbaum," LVII (Sept., 1941), 26.
> "Cootie Williams," LVII (June, 1941), 28.
> "Teddy Wilson," LXIII (July, 1947), 20.

518. ——. "Metronome's Records of the Year," *Metronome*, LXIII (Jan., 1947), 28–9. (Disc)
519. ——. "Mexican Students Ban Jazz As Aid in Spreading Our Rule," New York *Times*, Apr. 20, 1931, 7 : 2. (Gen, Infl)
520. ——. "The Mighty Mother of Jazz," New York *Times*, Jan. 8, 1923, 16 : 5. (Inst)
521. ——. "Glenn Miller," *in* Maxime Block (Ed). *Current Biography 1942*. New York: H. W. Wilson, 1943. pp. 597–99. (Pers)
522. ——. "Glenn Miller Commissioned a Captain," *Metronome*, LVIII (Oct., 1942), 5, 9. (Pers)
523. ——. "Million Dollar Band," *Look*, X (Feb. 5, 1946), 28–32. (Ork, Pic)
524. ——. "Mixed Reaction on Kenton Band's First N. Y. Job," *Down Beat*, IX (Mar. 15, 1942), 2. (Crit)
525. ——. "Montparnasse Jazz Is Stilled by Police," New York *Times*, Nov. 20, 1927, 2 : 5. (Gen, Geog)
526. ——. "More Good Swing and Sweet for V-Disc Listeners," *Metronome*, LXII (July, 1946), 46. (Disc)
527. ——. "More Hot and Dirty Breaks," *Etude*, XLV (May, 1927), 339. (Gen)
528. ——. "Mowing Down Mendelssohn: Swing Invades the Sacrosanct To Get Rugcutter Tunes," *Newsweek*, XIV (Sept. 18, 1939), 39. (J & D)
529. ——. "'Mr. A' Imports Jazz Band," New York *Times*, Aug. 15, 1926, 4 : 4. (Gen)

530. Anon. "Music and Dancing," New York *Times*, Oct. 21, 1926, 26 : 4. (Gen, J & D)
531. ——. "Music Clubs Against Jazzing of Classics," New York *Times*, Dec. 6, 1927, 29 : 2. (J & C)
532. ——. "Music is Music," *Time*, LV (May 22, 1950), 79. (Pers)
533. ——. "Musical Gossip," New York *Daily Tribune*, Apr. 15, 1900, III, 8 : 1. (Rag)
534. ——. "Musical Slang," *Etude*, LII (July, 1934), 393–94. (A & A, J & C)
535. ——. "Musician is Driven to Suicide by Jazz; Wouldn't Play It, Couldn't Get Employment," New York *Times*, Apr. 7. 1922, 1 : 2. (Infl)
536. ——. "Musician of the Year: Stan Getz," *in* Barry Ulanov and George Simon (Eds). *Jazz 1950.* New York: Metronome, 1950. p. 10. (Pers)
537. ——. "Musician of the Year: Lee Konitz," *in* Barry Ulanov and George Simon (Eds). *Jazz 1950.* New York: Metronome, 1950. p. 11. (Pers)
538. ——. "Musician of the Year: Lennie Tristano," *Metronome*, LXIV (Jan., 1948), 19. (Pers)
539. ——. "Musician 2/c," *New Yorker*, XIX (Dec. 25, 1943), 14–15. (Ork, Pers)
540. ——. "Musicians' Choice," *in* Barry Ulanov and George Simon (Eds). *Jazz 1950.* New York: Metronome, 1950. pp. 43–7. (Disc)
541. ——. "Musikers Unabridged Dictionary of Jazz Terms," *Metronome*, LII (Feb., 1936), 21, 61. (Lang)
542. ——. "N. E. Conservatory Starts Jazz Course," *Metronome*, LVIII (Aug., 1942), 7. (Ed)
543. ——. "N.Y.U. Will Teach Jazz," New York *Times*, July 15, 1937, 16 : 2. (Ed)
544. ——. "Fats Navarro Dies in NYC," *Down Beat*, XVII (Aug. 11, 1950), 1. (Pers)
545. ——. "Nazis Ban Concert by Bruno Walter... 'Negro Jazz' Prohibited..." New York *Times*, Mar. 17, 1933, 9 : 5 (Gen)
See: 547.
546. ——. "Nazis Ban Swing Music As Not Fit For Germans," New York *Times*, Nov. 27, 1938, 45 : 6. (Gen)
See: 635.
547. ——. "Nazis Reject Jazz, " New York *Times*, Mar. 18, 1933, 12 : 5. (Gen)
See: 545.
548. ——. "A Negro Explains Jazz," *Literary Digest*, LXI (Apr. 26, 1919), 28–9. (A & A, Hist)
549. ——. "Negroes," *Life*, V (Oct. 3, 1938), 58. (Pic)
550. ——. "New German Piano Now Jazzes Up Jazz," New York *Times*, June 8, 1924, II, 13 : 7. (Inst)
551. ——. "New Herd Sidemen Adept, Young, Solid," *Down Beat*, XV (Jan. 14, 1948), 4–5. (Pers)
552. ——. "New King," *Time*, XXXIV (Nov. 27, 1939), 56. (Pers)
553. ——. "New Orleans," *Ebony*, II (Feb., 1947), 26–31. (Pic, Rad)
554. ——. "New Orleans Memories," *Record Changer*, VII (Oct., 1948), 6–7. (Pic)
555. ——. "New Twist Marks Concert of Jazz," New York *Times*, Jan. 2, 1947, 23 : 5. (Crit)
556. ——. "New Word For Jazz Worth $1,000," *Down Beat*, XVI (July 15, 1949), 10. (Lang)
See:152.
557. ——. "New York Jazz Club," *Record Changer*, VII (Feb., 1948), 12–13. (Gen)
558. ——. "Newman Excoriates Jazz," *Musical America*, XLIV (Sept. 18, 1926), 16. (A & A)
See: 15; 17; 165; 168; 233; 559; 560; 2159; 2337; 3209.
559. ——. "Newman On Jazz," *Living Age*, CCCXXXII (Feb. 15, 1927), 362–63. (A & A)
See: 15; 17; 165; 168; 233; 558; 560; 2159; 2337; 3209.

560. Anon. "Newman Resumes Attack on Jazz," New York *Times*, Dec. 26, 1926, I, 30 : 3. (A & A)
    See: 15; 17; 165; 168; 233; 558; 559; 2159; 2337; 3209.
561. ——. "Nice Jumps," *Time*, LI (Mar. 8, 1948), 40. (Gen)
562. ——. "1945 Jazz Poll," *Jazz Session*, 7 (May-June, 1945), 3–15. (Poll)
563. ——. "1947's Musicmen," *Look*, XI (Jan. 7, 1947), 68. (Pers, Pic)
564. ——. "No Jazz on Russian Air," *Literary Digest*, CXIV (Aug. 27, 1932), 15–16. (Gen)
565. ——. "Noch Einmal: Jazzmusik," *Deutsche Musiker-Zeitung*, LXIII (Dec. 24, 1932), 622. (A & A)
566. ——. "Noise Upon Noise," New York *Times*, Dec. 29, 1938, 18 : 4. (Disc, Gen)
567. ——. "Non-Stop Flights of Jazz," New York *Times*, Dec. 16, 1927, 24 : 6. (Gen)
    See: 582.
568. ——. "N'Orlans Disclaims Honor as Jazz Parent," *Metronome*, LII (Nov., 1936), 27. (Hist)
569. ——. "Obituary—Thomas 'Papa Mutt' Carey," *Jazz Journal*, I (Nov., 1948), 10. (Pers)
570. ——. "Old Photographs," *in* George S. Rosenthal (Ed). *Jazzways*. Cincinnati: 1946. pp. 25–7. (Hist, Pic)
571. ——. "Old Ragtimer," *Time*, XXVI (Aug. 5, 1935), 54. (Pers, Rag)
572. ——. "On Swinging Spirituals," *Current History*, L (July, 1939), 52–3. (Infl)
573. ——. "On With the 'Charleston!'" *Literary Digest*, LXXXVI (Sept. 19, 1925), 40, 42. (J & D)
574. ——. "One For the Money, Two For the Show," *in* George S. Rosenthal (Ed). *Jazzways*. Cincinnati, 1946. pp. 95–7. (Pers)
575. ——. "One-Nighter Car Jump Kills Great Saxist Chu Berry," *Metronome*, LVII (Dec., 1941), 8. (Pers)
576. ——. "Opera and Concert Asides," New York *Times*, July 18, 1937, X, 5 : 8. (Ed)
577. ——. "Opera and Concert Asides," New York *Times*, Dec. 25, 1938, IX, 9 : 8. (Gen)
578. ——. "Opera and Concert Asides," New York *Times*, June 11, 1939, IX, 5 : 8. (Sw)
579. ——. "'Opera' on Ferryboats is Displaced by 'Swing'," New York *Times* Aug. 2, 1937, 9 : 2. (Gen)
580. ——. "An Opinion on 'Jazz' by Leopold Godowsky," *Metronome*, XXXVIII (June, 1922), 20. (Gen)
581. ——. "Orchestra Heads Name 'Jazz Czar'," New York *Times*, Feb. 6, 1927, 12 : 2. (Gen)
582. ——. "Orchestra Plays Jazz 33 Hours, Giving Poles the World Record," New York *Times*, Dec. 14, 1927, 23 : 2. (Gen)
583. ——. "Ordentling Salut," *Ekstrabladet*, Nov. 14, 1949, 6. (Crit)
584. ——. "Origin of 'Blues' Numbers," *Sheet Music News*, II (Oct., 1923), 8–9, 41. (Bl)
585. ——. "Origin of Rag-Time," *Brainard's Musical*, I (Autumn, 1899), 6. (Rag)
    See: 1174.
586. ——. "Origin of Rag-Time," *Metronome*, XVII (Aug., 1901), 7. (Rag)
587. ——. "The Origin of Ragtime," New York *Times*, Mar. 23, 1924, IX, 2 : 8. (Rag)
588. ——. "Origin of Term JAZZ," *Jazz Session*, 8 (July-Aug., 1945), 4–5. (Lang)
589. ——. "Origin of the Word Jazz Traced to West Africa by Princeton Men Preparing New Dictionary," New York *Times*, Oct. 15, 1934, 19 : 6. (Lang)
    See: 2604; 2953, 3159.

590. Anon. "Kid Ory Comes Back to Bizz," *Down Beat*, IX (Sept. 1, 1942), 2. (Pers)
591. ———. "Kid Ory, Famous Armstrong Trombonist, Returns to Active Duty," *Metronome*, LVIII (Sept., 1942), 7. (Pers)
592. ———. "Our Jazz Songs Rule in Venice," New York *Times*, Sept. 1, 1929, IX, 9 : 8. (Geog)
593. ———. "Our Jazz Symposium," *Music News*, XVI (Dec. 12, 1924), 3–5. (A & A, Gen)
594. ———. "Our Music Casts Much Influence," *Down Beat*, XVII (Sept. 22, 1950), 10. (Infl)
595. ———. "Philadelphia Hears First Complete Jazz Symphony," *Musical Courier*, XC (June 11, 1925), 5, 25. (Crit, J & C)
596. ———. "Philly Faculty Reads Like All-Star Band," *Down Beat*, XIV (Dec. 17, 1947), 14. (Ed)
597. ———. "Phuff?" *Time*, LIV (Oct. 31, 1949), 58. (Ork)
598. ———. "The Plain Truth About Jazz," *Musical Standard*, XXXVIII (June, 1932), 97. (A & A)
599. ———. "Poll Shows Effect of Dance Revival," *Down Beat*, XVII (Dec. 29, 1950), 12. (J & D, Poll)
600. ———. "Pollack Makes New Discovery," *Down Beat*, IX (Sept. 1, 1942), 6. (Pers)
601. ———. "Popular Music, A Symposium," in *Who's Who In Music*, Lee Stern, 1941. pp. 513–14. (Hist, Sw)
602. ———. *Popular Music as a Career*. Chicago: Institute for Research, 1940. 29 pp.
603. ———. "Chano Pozo Killed by 7 Shots," *Down Beat*, XV (Dec. 29, 1948), 1. (Pers)
604. ———. "Praises Broadway Music," New York *Times*, Jan. 11, 1926, 30 : 6. (Infl)
605. ———. "Predict Bright Future for Music Called Jazz," *Metronome*, XL (Apr., 1924), 79. (Gen)
606. ———. "Predicts Fall of Jazz," New York *Times*, Dec. 30, 1920, 3 : 2. (Gen)
607. ———. "Predicts National School of Music," New York *Times*, Jan. 2, 1925, 19 : 1. (Gen)
608. ———. "Primitive Savage Animalism, Preacher's Analysis of Jazz," New York *Times*, Mar. 3, 1922, 15 : 7. (A & A)
609. ———. "The Private Life of Billy Eckstine," *Ebony*, IV (Mar., 1949), 54–9. (Pers)
610. ———. "The Professional Amateur," *Time*, LIII (Jan. 31, 1949), 40–4. (Pers)
611. ———. "Professor Explains Bop," *Down Beat*, XVI (Feb. 25, 1949), 3. (A & A, Bop)
612. ———. "Professor of Jazz," *Newsweek*, XIX (May 11, 1942), 73. (Pers, Rad)
613. ———. "Puccini Wins Damages for 'Butterfly' Jazz," New York *Times*, Nov. 21, 1923, 21 : 7. (J & C)
614. ———. "Purifying American Jazz," New York *Times*, Apr. 7, 1927, 24 : 6. (Gen)
615. ———. "Putting Jazz in its Place," *Literary Digest*, LXXXII (July 5, 1924), 31–2. (A & A)
616. ———. "Quality in 'Blues'," *Metronome*, XXXIX (Sept., 1923), 140. (Bl)
617. ———. "The Quarries For Jazz," *Literary Digest*, LXXXIX (May 29, 1926), 27. (J & C)
618. ———. "Queen Mary Bars Jazz," New York *Times*, July 28, 1922, 3 : 6. (Gen)
619. ———. "Questions and Answers," *Eude*, XVI (Oct., 1898), 285; (Dec., 1898), 349; XVIII (Feb., 1900), 52. (Rag)
620. ———. "Radio Interests to Suppress Jazz," *Musical Courier*, XCIX (Dec. 14, 1929), 49. (Gen, Rad)
621. ———. "Radio's Policy on Swing," New York *Times*, Oct. 30, 1938, IX, 12 : 7. (J & C, Rad, Sw)
See: 94; 733; 742; 743.

622. Anon. "Raeburn Band Great, But Forced to Call It a Day," *Down Beat*, XVI (July 29, 1949), 13. (Ork)
623. —— —. "Rag-Time," *Musician*, V (Mar., 1900), 83. (Rag)
624. —— —. "Ragtime," London *Times*, Feb. 8, 1913, 11 : 3–4. (Rag)
625. —— —. "Rag Time and Program Making," *American Musician*, XXVIII (Aug. 10, 1912), 10. (Rag)
626. —— —. "Rag Time, New and Old," *Brainard's Musical*, I (Autumn, 1899), 2. (Rag)
627. —— —. "The Record Companies," *Metronome*, LXI (Oct., 1945), 23–5, 51. (Disc)
628. —— —. "Record Companies Go All Out For Dixieland," *Down Beat*, XVII (Apr. 7, 1950), 1. (Disc, Dix)
629. —— —. "Record Labels in Jazz History," *in* Orin Blackstone (Ed). *Jazzfinder '49.* New Orleans: Orin Blackstone, 1949. pp. 107–28. (Disc)
630. —— —. "Records of the Year," *Metronome*, LX (Jan., 1944), 24. (Disc)
631. —— —. "Records of the Year," *Metronome*, LXIV (Jan., 1948), 23. (Disc)
632. —— —. "Records of the Year: 49's Top 30," *in* Barry Ulanov and George Simon (Eds). *Jazz 1950.* New York: Metronome, 1950. p. 18. (Disc)
633. —— —. "Refuses to Decide Jazz Is a Nuisance," New York *Times*, Oct. 29, 1925, 11 : 3. (Gen)
634. —— —. "Reich Bars Radio Jazz to Safeguard 'Culture'," New York *Times*, Oct. 13, 1935, II & III, 3 : 7. (Gen)
635. —— —. "Reich City Bars 'Hot' Music," New York *Times*, Nov. 19, 1938, 2 : 4. (Gen) *See*: 546.
636. —— —. "Relax! The Battle of RPMs is Settled," *Down Beat*, XVII (Feb. 10, 1950), 3. (Disc)
637. —— —. "Remarks on Rag-Time," *Musical Courier*, LXVI (May 28, 1913), 22–3. (Rag)
638. —— —. "Respectablizing Jazz," *Literary Digest*, LXXIX (Nov. 24, 1923), 31. (A & A)
639. —— —. "Les Resultats du Referendum du H.C.B.," *Hot Club Magazine*, 10 (Oct., 1946), 10. (Poll)
640. —— —. "Reverend Satchelmouth," *Time*, XLVII (Apr. 29, 1946), 47–8. (Pers)
641. —— —. "Rex Spielt Bie Kerzenlicht," *Die Melodie*, III (1948/49), 5, 10. (Crit, Pers)
642. —— —. "Rhythm, Rhythm; 'Arthur Alberts' West African Documentary'," *Record Changer*, IX (Nov., 1950), 5–8, 17. (Disc)
643. —— —. "Rhythms In 'Jazz' Traced to Indians," New York *Times*, Dec. 28, 1936, 19 : 7. (Gen)
644. —— —. "The Riotous Return of Mr. Antheil," *Literary Digest*, XCIII (Apr. 30, 1927), 26–7. (Crit, J & C)
645. —— —. "'Round and Around," *Literary Digest*, CXXI (Apr. 4, 1936), 26. (Sw)
646. —— —. "Rugged Rugolo," *Metronome*, LXIII (Apr., 1947), 27, 46. (Pers)
647. —— —. "Charles Ellsworth (Pee Wee) Russell," *in* Anna Rothe (Ed). *Current Biography 1944.* New York: H. W. Wilson, 1945. pp. 569–71. (Pers)
648. —— —. "Sagfreren, Der Blev Altmuligmand," *Berlingske Tidende*, Oct. 22, 1949, 8–9. (Pers)
649. —— —. "'Satchelmouth' Symbol of Best Negro Music," *Down Beat*, V (Mar., 1938), 4. (Pers)
650. —— —. "Satchmo Comes Back," *Time*, L (Sept. 1, 1947), 32. (A & A, Bop, Pers)
651. —— —. "Satchmo Europe Trip Successful; Plan 2d Tour," *Billboard*, LXI (Oct. 22, 1949), 13. (Gen)
652. —— —. "'Satchmo' Hailed As King of Zulus at N.O. Mardi Gras," *Billboard*, LXI (Mar. 21, 1949), 23. (Pers) *See*: 18; 495; 1490; 1820; 2085.

653. Anon. "Satchmo Sock in Sweden; Italian Tour Mapped," *Variety*, CLXXVI (Oct. 19, 1949), 43. (Crit)

654. ———. "Say Jazz Will Live," New York *Times*, Dec. 23, 1923, VIII, 4 : 1. (A & A)

655. ———. "Says Autos and Jazz Ruin American Youth," New York *Times*, Oct. 11, 1924, 16 : 1. (Infl)
    See: 284.

656. ———. "Says Jazz Originated in Old French Music," New York *Times*, Mar. 25, 1928, 28 : 7. (A & A)

657. ———. "Says Jazz Rules Europe," New York *Times*, Jan. 23, 1925, 9 : 3. (Geog)

658. ———. "Says Jazz Threatens Christian Civilization," New York *Times*, Dec. 16, 1934, IV, 2 : 7. (Infl)

659. ———. "Says Jazz Will Play Itself Out," New York *Times*, Nov. 21, 1924, 16 : 1. (Gen)

660. ———. "School Outlaws Jazz as Travesty on Music," New York *Times*, Jan. 11, 1926, 1 : 6. (Gen)

661. ———. "Scoffs at Fear of Jazz," New York *Times*, Mar. 4, 1922, 9 : 1. (Gen)

662. ———. "Score Armistice Day of Jazz; British Want Quiet Celebration—Weary of American Rhythm," New York *Times*, Nov. 8, 1925, II, 2 : 5. (Gen)

663. ———. "Hazel Dorothy Scott," *in* Maxime Block (Ed). *Current Biography 1943*. New York: H. W. Wilson, 1944. pp. 677–79. (Pers)

664. ———. "Hazel Scott," *Look*, VI (Dec. 15, 1942), 46, 48–9. (Pers, Pic)

665. ———. "Raymond Scott," *in* Maxime Block (Ed). *Current Biography 1941*. New York: H. W. Wilson, 1942. pp. 763–65. (Pers)

666. ———. "Second Generation," *Time*, XLVII (June 24, 1946), 77. (Ork)

667. ———. "Seek to Purify Jazz," New York *Times*, Apr. 6, 1927, 20 : 6. (Gen)

668. ———. "Sees No American Opera," New York *Times*, Dec. 26, 1926, I, 24 : 7. (A & A, J & O)

669. ———. "Sees 'Swing' on Wane," New York *Times*, Sept. 14, 1939, 19 : 4. (Gen)

670. ———. "7,000 Jitterbugs at Swing Session," New York *Times*, Aug. 25, 1938, 13 : 1. (Gen)
    See: 138; 727.

671. ———. "Several Close Fights on at Midway Mark in Band Poll," *Down Beat*, XVII (Dec. 15, 1950), 1, 2, 19. (Poll)

672. ———. "Artie Shaw," *in* Maxime Block (Ed). *Current Biography 1941*. New York: H. W. Wilson, 1942. pp. 778–80. (Pers)

673. ———. "Shaw 'Through With Dance Bands'; To Play Longhair," *Down Beat*, XVI (Feb. 25, 1949), 1. (Pers)

674. ———. "Shaw's Swing Symphony," *Newsweek*, XVIII (Sept. 8, 1941), 74. (J & C, Pers)

675. ———. "George Shearing," *Metronome*, LXV (Oct., 1949), 13, 36. (Pers)

676. ———. "Shearing Proves Bop and Bach Combine Real Fine," *Down Beat*, XVI (June 17, 1949), 2. (Pers)

677. ———. "The Sheep in the Herman Herd," *Metronome*, LXI (Dec., 1945), 30–33. (Ork, Pers)

678. ———. "Showcase of Harlem," *Ebony*, IV (July, 1949), 13–18. (Pic)

679. ———. "Showman of the Year: Buddy Rich," *Metronome*, LXIII (Jan., 1947), 20. (Pers)

680. ———. "Showmen of the Year: Frankie Laine, Mel Torme," *Metronome*, LXIV (Jan., 1948), 21. (Pers)

681. ———. "Frank Sinatra," *in* Maxime Block (Ed). *Current Biography 1943*. New York: H. W. Wilson, 1944. pp. 700–02. (Pers)

682. ———. "Sincere Sounds," *Time*, XLVIII (Dec. 23, 1946), 73. (Pers)

683. ———. "Singer of the Year: Peggy Lee," *Metronome*, LXIII (Jan., 1947), 21. (Pers)

684. Anon. "Singer of the Year: Mary Ann McCall," *in* Barry Ulanov and George Simon (Eds). *Jazz 1950*. New York: Metronome, 1950. p. 14. (Pers)
685. ———. "Singers of the Year: Herb Jeffries, Sarah Vaughan," *Metronome*, LXIV (Jan., 1948), 20. (Pers)
686. ———. "Six New Jazz Messiahs," *Down Beat*, XV (Mar. 24, 1948), 14. (Ork)
687. ———. "Sixty Years," *Metronome*, LIX (Oct., 1943), 11. (Gen)
688. ———. "Bessie Smith," *Record Changer*, VII (Mar., 1948), 6–7. (Crit, Pers)
689. ———. "Willie Smith," *Ebony*, IV (June, 1949), 41–3. (Pers, Pic)
690. ———. "Soldier-Man Blues From Somewhere in France," *Literary Digest*, XCIII (June 18, 1927), 50, 52. (Bl)
691. ———. "Solo Man," *Time*, LIV (Dec. 5, 1949), 56, 58. (Pers)
692. ———. "Some Berlin Novelties," New York *Times*, Feb. 19, 1928, VIII, 8 : 3. (Ed)
693. ———. "Some Further Opinions on 'Jazz' by Prominent Writers," *Metronome*, XXXVIII (Aug., 1922), 27–8. (Infl)
694. ———. "Something to Dance To," *Time*, LV (Apr. 3, 1950), 72, 73. (Ork)
695. ———. "A Song Is Born," *Ebony*, III (May, 1948), 41–3. (Pic, Rad)
696. ———. "Songs of the Year," *Metronome*, LX (Jan., 1944), 28. (Gen)
697. ———. "Soprano Sax in Comeback," *Down Beat*, VII (Apr. 1, 1940), 2. (Inst)
698. ———. "Soulful Youths Buy Saxophones," New York *Times*, Jan. 25, 1925, VIII, 2 : 2. (Infl)
699. ———. "Sousa Expects Jazz to Wane; Denies It Is Truly American," New York *Times*, Apr. 26, 1928, 29 : 2. (Gen)
700. ———. "Sousa With a Floy Floy," *Time*, XLII (Sept. 6, 1943), 48–9. (Ork)
701. ———. "The Soviet Cult—Jazz Outlawed," New York Times, Jan. 8, 1928, VIII, 8 : 8. (Gen)
702. ———. "Specht Urges Ban on Foreign Artists," New York *Times*, Mar. 24, 1926, 5 : 1. (Gen)
See: 75.
703. ———. "Spirituals to Swing," *Time*, XXXIII (Jan. 2, 1939), 23–4. (Crit)
704. ———. "Staid Town Hall Resounds to Swing Music," New York *Times*, Dec. 15, 1938, 8 : 3. (Crit)
705. ———. "Stale Bread's Sadness Gave 'Jazz' to the World," *Literary Digest*, LXI (Apr. 26, 1919), 47–8. (A & A)
706. ———. "State Dept. Says 'Thanks, Louis'," *Down Beat*, XVII (July 14, 1950), 1. (Pers)
707. ———. "Staying Qualities of Jazz," *Pacific Coast Musical Review*, XLIV (Sept. 29, 1923), 3. (Gen)
708. ———. "The Stepin Fetchit of the Blues," *Metronome*, LIX (Sept., 1943), 20. (Pers)
709. ———. "Stowkowski Declares in Favor of 'Jazz'," *Musical Leader*, XLVII (Apr. 24, 1924), 400. (Gen)
710. ———. "Stokowski Defends Jazz," New York *Times*, May 16, 1924, 22 : 3. (A & A)
711. ———. "Straton Says Jazz is 'Agency of Devil'," New York *Times*, May 7, 1926, 10 : 3. (A & A)
712. ———. "Stravinsky as a 'Superman of Jazz' Is Local Commentator's View," New York *Times*, May 3, 1925, VIII, 6 : 6. (A & A)
See: 2209.
713. ———. "Students in Arms Against Jazz," *Literary Digest*, LXXII (Mar. 18, 1922), 35. (Gen)
714. ———. "Subject Index for Volume I," *Music and Rhythm*, I (Apr., 1941), 98–9. (Bibl)
715. ———. "A Subject of Serious Study," New York *Times*, Aug. 11, 1924, 12 : 6. (A & A)

716. Anon. "Success of the Year: Erroll Garner," *in* Barry Ulanov and George Simon (Eds). *Jazz 1950*. New York: Metronome, 1950. p. 16. (Pers)

717. ——. "Success of the Year: George Shearing," *in* Barry Ulanov and George Simon (Eds). *Jazz 1950*. New York: Metronome, 1950. p. 17. (Pers)

718. ——. "Success Story," *Time*, LVI (Oct. 23, 1950), 82, 85. (Pers)

719. ——. "Sufferers Before Our Time," New York *Times*, Nov. 20, 1927, III, 4 : 6. (Inst)

720. ——. "Sunday Jazz for London," New York *Times*, June 5, 1925, 20 : 1. (Gen)

721. ——. "Sweet Corn at Glen Island," *Time*, XLIX (June 2, 1947), 69–70. (Ork)

722. ——. "Swing," *Life*, V (Aug. 8, 1938), 50–60. (Pers, Pic, Sw)

723. ——. "Swing: Rhythmic Music Heedless of Tune, Time or Tradition," *Newsweek*, VII (Jan. 11, 1936), 27–8. (A & A, Sw)

724. ——. "Swing: Top Song Hits Are Tuneful, Sentimental," *Life*, XVII (Sept. 25, 1944), 39–40, 42. (Pers, Pic)

725. ——. "Swing Away from Swing," New York *Times*, Aug. 14, 1938, 10 : 3. (Gen)
     See: 1522; 1607.

726. ——. "Swing Bands Put 23,400 in Frenzy," New York *Times*, May 30, 1938, 13 : 2. (Crit, Gen)
     See: 443.

727. ——. "Swing Carnival Held to Benefit Charity," New York *Times*, June 13, 1938, 15 : 2. (Gen)
     See: 138; 670.

728. ——. "Swing Concert Tonight," New York *Times*, May 29, 1939, 19 : 2. (Gen).
     See: 729; 763.

729. ——. "Swing Convention Next Week," New York *Times*, May 22, 1939, 14 : 5 (Gen)
     See: 728; 763.

730. ——. "Swing Fiesta by Goodman," New York *Times*, May 22, 1938, II, 2 : 3. (Gen)

731. ——. "Swing is Art and is Becoming Great Art," *Science News Letter*, XXXVIII (Dec. 14, 1940), 377. (Sw)

732. ——. "'Swing' Is On the Way, But Up or Down? Embattled Experts Can't Agree," *Newsweek*, XII (July 25, 1938), 26–7. (A & A, Sw)

733. ——. "Swing It!" New York *Times*, Oct. 30, 1938, IV, 2 : 3. (J & C, Rad)
     See: 94; 621; 742; 743.

734. ——. "Swing Music Barred for St. Patrick March; Only Irish and American Tunes Permitted," New York *Times*, Feb. 27, 1938, II, 1 : 3. (Gen)

735. ——. "Swing Music for Skaters Barred by New Rochelle," New York *Times*, Jan. 28, 1939, 17 : 7. (Gen)

736. ——. "Swing Music Held Degenerated Jazz," New York *Times*, July 27, 1938, 19:5. (J & D, Sw)

737. ——. "Swing Music Produces These," *Life*, IV (Feb. 21, 1938), 4–7. (Infl, Pic)

738. ——. "'Swing Needs a New Name'—Says Stan Kenton," *Music and Rhythm*, II (Mar., 1942), 44. (A & A)

739. ——. "Swing Notes," *American Speech*, XIII (Apr., 1938), 158. (Lang)

740. ——. "Swing, Swing, Oh Beautiful Swing!" *Metronome*, LII (Feb., 1936), 19, 33. (Sw)

741. ——. "Swing Viewed as 'Musical Hitlerism'; Professor Sees Fans Ripe for Dictator," New York *Times*, Nov. 2, 1938, 25 : 3. (Infl)

742. ——. "'Swinging' Bach," New York *Times*, Oct. 30, 1938, IX, 7 : 1. (J & C, Rad)
     See: 94; 621; 733; 743.

743. ——. "'Swinging' Bach's Music on Radio Protested; FCC Is Urged to Bar 'Jazzing' of Classics," New York *Times*, Oct. 27, 1938, 1 : 4. (J & C, Rad)
     See: 94; 621; 733; 742.

744. Anon. "Symphonic Jazz," *Flutist*, VI (Feb., 1925), 25–7. (Crit, Ork)
745. ———. "A Symphony A Day," *Etude*, LVI (Nov., 1938), 705–06, 751, 766. (Gen)
746. ———. "Syncopated Melody Not Negro Music," *Music Trade Review*, XLVIII (Feb. 20, 1909), 15. (Rag)
747. ———. "Syncopation," *Brainard's Musical*, I (Autumn, 1899), 27. (Rag)
748. ———. "T.B. Kills Dick Wilson, Andy Kirk's Tenor Sax Ace," *Down Beat*, VIII (Dec. 15, 1941), 1, 34. (Pers)
749. ———. "Laurette Taylor Finds Jazz a Bane," New York *Times*, Feb. 20, 1922, 11 : 4. (Infl)
750. ———. "Tea and Jam," *Time*, XLVI (Dec. 3, 1945), 62. (Geog, Ork)
751. ———. "'That Good-Time Sound'," *Time*, LV (Mar. 6, 1950), 48–9. (Ork)
752. ———. "That 'Jazz' Wail Again," *Piano Trade Magazine*, XIX (Apr., 1922), 4. (Gen)
753. ———. "That Old Feeling," *Time*, XLIX (Mar. 31, 1947), 52. (Pers)
754. ———. "Theorist, Leader Raymond Scott Offers 88 Advice," *Down Beat*, XV (Apr. 21, 1948), 12. (A & A)
755. ———. "They Play the Lead," *Record Changer*, VIII (Oct., 1949), 6–7. (Pers)
756. ———. "They're Teaching Swing Over Philadelphia Air," *Metronome*, LVIII (Dec., 1942), 25. (Ed, Rad)
757. ———. "Thibaut Praises Jazz," New York *Times*, July 11, 1926, 24 : 2. (A & A)
758. ———. "Things to Come," *Metronome*, LXIV (Jan., 1948), 26–7. (A & A)
759. ———. "Thinks Ban on Jazz is Insult to U.S.," New York *Times*, June 1, 1924, II, 2 : 5. (Gen)
760. ———. "This Was Jazz in 1850," New York *Times*, June 22, 1924, IV, 15 : 3. (A & A)
761. ———. "Those Old Faces," *Time*, LI (Jan. 19, 1948), 51. (Gen, Pers)
762. ———. "The Three Flames," *Time*, L (July 28, 1947), 56. (Ork)
763. ———. "3,000 at Hippodrome For Swing Concert," New York *Times*, May 30, 1939, 13 : 2. (Gen)
See: 728; 729.
764. ———. "Tin Pan Alley Changes Tempo," *Business Week*, 32 (Apr. 16, 1930), 34. (Gen)
765. ———. "To Crusade Against Jazz," New York *Times*, Nov. 14, 1927, 21 : 3. (Gen)
766. ———. "'To Jazz' or 'To Rag'," *Literary Digest*, LXXIII (May 6, 1922), 37. (Rag)
767. ———. "To War on Jazz With Better Songs," *Playground*, XVI (Jan., 1923), 459–60. (Gen)
768. ———. "Top Tenorists Evaluate Coleman Contribution," *Down Beat*, XVII (Oct. 20, 1950), 3. (Pers)
See: 1809; 2052.
769. ———. "Dave Tough, 41, of Austin High Gang, Dies After Fall," *Down Beat*, XV (Dec. 29, 1948), 1. (Pers)
770. ———. "Tracking Jazz to Its Lair," *Musical America*, XL (June 14, 1924), 17. (Lang)
771. ———. "Frank Trumbauer Quits Music; Will Turn to Flying," *Down Beat*, VII (July 1, 1940), 13. (Pers)
772. ———. "Turkey's Jazz King Dies," New York *Times*, June 17, 1928, 6 : 1. (Pers)
773. ———. "Two Decades With the Duke," *Ebony*, I (Jan., 1946), 11–19. (Pers, Pic)
774. ———. "Undesirable Effects of Jazzmania," *Pacific Coast Musical Review*, XLIV (Apr. 28, 1923), 3, 4. (A & A, Infl)
775. ———. "V Discs Still Present Lusty Lists of Records," *Metronome*, LXII (Apr., 1946), 46–7. (Disc)

776. Anon. "Sarah Vaughan," *Ebony*, IV (Sept., 1949), 29–30. (Pers, Pic)

777. ——. "Joe Venuti," *Music and Rhythm*, II (Apr., 1942), 7. (Pers)

778. ——. "Victor Company Offers $40,000 in 3 Prizes for Native Symphonic and Jazz Compositions," New York *Times*, May 29, 1928, 16 : 3. (Gen)

779. ——. "Vienna is Alarmed by Inroads of Jazz," New York *Times*, Apr. 15, 1928, II, 2 : 4. (Geog, Infl, J & O)

780. ——. "Vipers, Tea and Jazz," *Newsweek*, XXVIII (Oct. 28, 1946), 88–9. (Pers, Rev)

781. ——. "Virtuoso of Jazz Favors New Rhythm," New York *Times*, Aug. 31, 1923, 15 : 4. (J & D)

782. ——. "A Virtuous Revolt Against Jazz," New York *Times*, Feb. 2, 1926, 28 : 6. (J & C)
See: 21.

783. ——. "Voliva Bans Jazz Records," New York *Times*, Jan. 11, 1921, 9 : 2. (Gen)

784. ——. "Voting Rules More Lenient as 1950 Band Poll Opens," *Down Beat*, XVII (Nov. 3, 1950), 1, 18. (Poll)

785. ——. "S. Wagner Attacks Jazz," New York *Times*, Dec. 7, 1925, 19 : 2. (A & A)

786. ——. "Thomas Wright (Fats) Waller," *in* Maxime Block (Ed). *Current Biography 1942*. New York: H. W. Wilson, 1943, pp. 862–64. (Pers)

787. ——. "Fats Waller Demonstrates Swing, Even Defines It," *Metronome*, LII (Feb., 1936), 19, 33. (A & A, Sw)

788. ——. "Wants Legislation to Stop Jazz As An Intoxicant," New York *Times*, Feb. 12, 1922, 1 : 2. (Infl)

789. ——. "War on Jazz Will Enlist Composers," *Musical Digest*, III (Oct. 31, 1922), 11. (Gen)

790. ——. "War on Rag-Time," *American Musician*, V (July, 1901), 4. (Rag)

791. ——. "Warns of Effects of 'Swing' on Youth," New York *Times*, Oct. 26, 1938, 20 : 8. (Infl)

792. ——. "Warns White Races They Must Drop Jazz," New York *Times*, Sept. 20, 1927, 4 : 3. (A & A, Infl)

793. ——. "Leo Watson, 52, Dies on Coast," *Down Beat*, XVII (June 16, 1950), 9. (Pers)

794. ——. "Waxeries Make Move to Cut Out 78 RPMs," *Down Beat*, XVII (Aug. 11, 1950), 1. (Disc)

795. ——. "Way Down Yonder," *Time*, LIII (Jan. 31, 1949), 39. (Dix, Ork)

796. ——. "Wedding March in Swing Barred," New York *Times*, Nov. 18, 1938, 22 : 7. (Gen)

797. ——. "Welcome," *Time*, LIV (Nov. 7, 1949), 44–6. (Pers)

798. ——. "Welsh Invoke Curfew Law As One Way to Stop Jazz," New York *Times*, Mar. 7, 1926, VIII, 12 : 4. (Geog, Infl)

799. ——. "What Is the Matter With Jazz?" *Musician*, XXXIII (Nov., 1928), 37. (A & A)

800. ——. "What Jazz Is," *Musical Courier*, LXXXV (Nov. 2, 1922), 21. (A & A, Gen)

801. ——. "What Los Angeles Thinks of Jazz," *Etude*, XLIII (May, 1925), 328. (A & A)

802. ——. "What Was Called For," *Time*, LIV (Nov. 28, 1949), 54–5. (Pers)

803. ——. "What's the Matter With Jazz?" *Etude*, XLII (Jan., 1924), 6. (A & A)

804. ——. "'What's Use of Goering?' Offered As A War Song," New York *Times*, Sept. 7, 1939, 17 : 4. (Sw)

805. ——. "When America Went Dance Mad," *Newsweek*, XIII (Apr. 3, 1939), 30–1. (J & D)

806. ——. "When European Composers Jazz," *Literary Digest*, XCVI (Mar. 17, 1928), 25–6. (J & C)

807. Anon. "When the Masters 'Jazz'," *Literary Digest*, XCVIII (Aug. 11, 1928), 23. (A & A)
See: 331; 843; 845; 2897.
808. ——. "Where the Etude Stands on Jazz," *Etude*, XLII (Aug., 1924), 515. (Gen)
809. ——. "Where Is Jazz Leading America?" *Etude*, XLII (Aug., 1924), 517–18, 520; (Sept., 1924), 595–96. (Infl)
810. ——. "Where Jazz Is Taking Us Musically," *Current Opinion*, LXXVII (Dec., 1924), 746–47. (Infl)
811. ——. "Joshua David (Josh) White," *in* Anna Rothe (Ed). *Current Biography 1944*. New York: H. W. Wilson, 1945. pp. 735–36. (Pers)
812. ——. "Paul Whiteman," *in* Anna Rothe (Ed). *Current Biography 1945*. New York: H. W. Wilson, 1946. pp. 671–74. (Pers)
813. ——. "A Whiteman Concert," New York *Times*, Apr. 22, 1924, 18 : 4. (Crit)
814. ——. "Paul Whiteman Eases Minds of the British," New York *Times*, Apr. 8, 1926, 27 :3. (Gen)
815. ——. "Paul Whiteman Im Zweilicht," *Die Melodie*, IV (June, 1949), 2. (Pers)
816. ——. "Whoa-ho-ho-ho-ho-ho!" *Time*, XXVII (Jan. 20, 1936), 30, 32, 34–5. (Sw)
817. ——. "Who's Got the Button?" *Musician*, XLIV (Mar., 1939), 54–5. (A & A, Sw)
818. ——. "Who's Who In the Critics Row," *Down Beat*, VII (Nov. 15, 1940), 2, 5; (Dec. 1, 1940), 6. (Pers)
819. ——. "Who's Who In the Music World," *Music and Rhythm*, II (Sept., 1941), 42; (Oct., 1941), 21; (Nov., 1941), 33; (Dec., 1941), 24; (Jan., 1942), 32; (Mar., 1942), 4; (Apr., 1942), 30. (Pers)
820. ——. "Why 'Jazz' Sends Us Back to the Jungle," *Current Opinion*, LXV (Sept., 1918), 165. (A & A)
821. ——. "Why Not Mix Jazz and Classics?" *Literary Digest*, XCI (Oct. 30, 1926), 29. (J & C)
822. ——. "Rudy Wiedoeft," *in* Maxime Block (Ed). *Current Biography 1940*. New York: H. W. Wilson, 1941. p. 869. (Pers)
823. ——. "Rudy Wiedoeft Dies in Flushing," New York *World Telegram*, Feb. 19, 1940, 19 : 2. (Pers)
824. ——. "Will Ragtime Save the Soul of the Native American Composer?" *Current Opinion*, LIX (Dec., 1917), 406–07. (Rag)
See: 1065; 1986; 2288.
825. ——. "Will South American Music Kill Jazz?" *Music and Rhythm*, II (Apr., 1942), 9–10, 48–9. (A & A)
826. ——. "Will War On Jazz With Better Songs," New York *Times*, Oct. 14, 1922, 16 : 2. (Gen)
827. ——. "Clarence Williams A Specialist on 'Blues'," *Metronome*, XXXIX (Sept., 1923), 78. (Bl, Pers)
828. ——. "Cootie Williams," *Look*, IX (May 15, 1945), 78. (Pers, Pic)
829. ——. "Wird der Walzer Wiederkommen?" *Zeitschrift für Musik*, XCVI (1929), 634–35. (Infl)
830. ——. "With Louis On the Danish Air," *Melody Maker*, XXV (Oct. 22, 1949), 9. (Crit)
831. ——. "With the Music Schools," *Musician*, XLVII (Feb., 1942), 31. (Ed)
832. ——. "Woody, Shearing Win '49 Poll," *Down Beat*, XVI (Dec. 30, 1949), 1, 12–13. (Poll)
833. ——. "Woody and TD Win, Ten New All-Stars," *Down Beat*, XIII (Jan. 1, 1946), 1, 5, 16. (Poll)
834. ——. "Woody's Blues Heaven," *Newsweek*, XXVI (Dec. 31, 1945), 76. (Ork, Pers)

835. Anon. "Wrong Way To Make Money On Dance Band Biz," *Down Beat*, XVII (Dec. 1, 1950), 10. (J & D)
836. ———. "Yazz und Grammophon im Gottesdienst," *Zeitschrift für Musik*, XCVI (Dec., 1929), 820–21. (Gen, Infl)
837. ———. "You Can't Tell the Players Without A Scorecard," *Down Beat*, XVII (Sept. 22, 1950), 1, 3. (Disc)
838. ———. "You'll Never Walk Alone; Not With the Miller Tag," *Down Beat*, XVI (June 17, 1949), 3. (Crit, Ork)
839. ———. "Young Man With A Horn," *Ebony*, V (Dec., 1949), 51–5. (Rad)
840. ———. "Youth and Today's Music," *Music Educators' National Yearbook*, XXX (1939–40), 63–8. (A & A)
See: 2542.
841. ———. Untitled. New York *Times*, Feb. 12, 1928, VIII, 8 : 6. (A & A)
842. Ansermet, Ernst-Alexandre. "Bechet and Jazz Visit Europe, 1919," *in* Ralph de Toledano (Ed). *Frontiers of Jazz*. New York: Oliver Durrell, 1947. pp. 115–22. (A & A, Ork)
843. Antheil, George. "American Folk Music," (lr) *Forum*, LXXX (Dec., 1928), 957–58. (A & A, J & C)
See: 331; 807; 845; 2897.
844. ———. "Jazz," *Querschnitt*, II (Summer, 1922), 172–73. (Gen)
845. ———. "Jazz Is Music," *Forum*, LXXX (July, 1928), 64–7. (A & A)
See: 331; 807; 843; 2897.
846. Anthony, Ray. "Job of Revival Rests with Leaders: Anthony," *Down Beat*, XVII (May 19, 1950) 16. (J & D, Pers)
847. Antrim, Doron K. "Josher and Jazzer. A Close-Up of Ben Bernie," *Metronome*, XLVII (July, 1931), 14, 40. (Pers)
848. ———. "The Ten Top Tunes of the Last Fifty Years," *Metronome*, L (Jan., 1934), 30–2. (Gen)
849. ———. "Tin Pan Avenue," *Scribner's* XCIX (Feb., 1936), 74–6. Condensed: *Readers' Digest*, XXVIII (Apr., 1936), 83–5. (Gen)
850. ———. *Paul Whiteman, Jimmy Dorsey, Rudy Vallee, Freddie Rich, Glen Gray, Frank Skinner, Enric Madriguera, Jimmy Dale, Merle Johnston, Guy Lombardo, Uriel Davis and Duke Ellington Give Their Secrets of Dance Band Success*. New York: Famous Stars, 1936. 87 pp.
851. Apold, Felix. "Die Jazzmusik," *Signale*, LXXXVII (Mar. 27, 1929), 428–30. (A & A)
852. Arendt, Hans. "Triumphator Jazz?" *Deutsche Musiker-Zeitung*, LXIII (Dec. 10, 1932), 598–99. (A & A)
853. Armitage, Jack. "Billie Holiday," *Jazz Hot*, IV (June-July, 1938), 9. (Pers)
854. Armitage, Merle (Ed). *George Gershwin*. New York: Longmans, Green, 1938. 252 pp. (Pers)
855. Armstrong, Lil. "Lil Tells of 1st Time She Met Louis," *Down Beat*, XVII (July 14, 1950) 18. (Pers)
856. Armstrong, Louis. "'Berigan Can't Do No Wrong'..." *Down Beat*, VIII (Sept. 1, 1941), 7. (Pers)
857. ———. "Bunk Didn't Teach Me," *Record Changer*, IX (July-Aug., 1950), 30. (Hist, Pers)
858. ———. "Care of the Lip," *Record Changer*, IX (July-Aug., 1950), 30. (Gen)
859. ———. "Europe—With Kicks," *Holiday*, VII (June, 1950), 8, 9, 10, 11, 12, 14, 16, 18, 20, 22. (Pers)
See: 498.
860. ———. "From Louis' Photo Album," *Record Changer*, IX (July-Aug., 1950), 28–9. (Pers, Pic)
861. ———. "Les Hite et Son Orchestre," *Jazz Hot*, IV (Dec.-Jan., 1937/38), 7. (Pers)

862. Armstrong, Louis. "Louis on the Spot," *Record Changer*, IX (July-Aug., 1950), 23-4, 44. (Pers)
863. —— —. "My Best On Wax," *Down Beat*, XVII (Apr. 7, 1950), 11. (Disc)
864. —— —. "King Oliver Is Dead," *Jazz Hot*, IV (Apr.-May, 1938), 9. (Pers)
865. —— —. "Joe Oliver Is Still King," *Record Changer*, IX (July-Aug., 1950), 10-11. (Pers)
866. —— —. "60-Year-Old 'Bunk' Johnson, Louis' Tutor, Sits In the Band," *Down Beat*, VIII (Aug. 15, 1941), 11. (Pers)
867. —— —. "Storyville," *True*, XXI (Nov., 1947), 32-3, 100-05. (Hist)
868. —— —. *Swing That Music*. New York: Longmans, Green, 1936. 136 pp. (Pers)
869. —— —. "Swing That Music," (Extract From Book of Same Title) *in* Elie Siegmeister. *The Music Lover's Handbook*. New York: William Morrow, 1943. pp. 711-18. (Pers)
870. —— —. "Ulceratedly Yours; Louis Armstrong," *Down Beat*, XVII (July 14, 1950), 1, 19. (Pers)
871. Armstrong, Lucille. "Louis' Favorite Dish," *Record Changer*, IX (July-Aug., 1950), 18. (Gen, Pers)
872. Arntzenius, L.M.G. *Amerikaansche Kunstindrukken*. Amsterdam: A. de Lange, 1927. 190 pp.
873. Artero, J. "Sobre el Jazz-Band y la Orquesta Moderna," *Vida Musical*, I (June, 1923), 5-6. (A & A, Inst)
874. Asbury, Herbert. "Congo Square," *in* Herbert Asbury. *The French Quarter*. Garden City: Garden City Pub., 1938. pp. 237-53. (Gen)
875. —— —. "Storyville," *in* Herbert Asbury. *The French Quarter*. Garden City: Garden City Pub., 1938. pp. 424-55. (Hist, Ork)
876. Asman, James and Bill Kinnell. *American Jazz No. 1*. Chilwell Notts.,England: Jazz Appreciation Society, 1945. 22 pp.
877. —— —. *American Jazz No. 2*. Chilwell Notts., England: Jazz Appreciation Society, 1946. 22 pp.
878. —— —. *Jazz*. Chilwell Notts., England: Jazz Appreciation Society, 1944. 20 pp.
879. —— —. *Jazz On Record*. Chilwell Notts., England: Jazz Appreciation Society, 1944. 20 pp.
880. —— —. *Jazz To-Day*. Chilwell Notts., England: Jazz Appreciation Society, 1945. 24 pp.
881. Aurthur, Bob. "Gentleman Jacques," *Jazz Record*, 6 (May 1, 1943), 3. (Pers)
882. Austin, Alex. "Dancers," *in* Charles Harvey (Ed). *Jazz Parody*. London: Spearman, 1948. pp. 21-6. (Fict)
883. Austin, Cecil. "Jazz," *Music and Letters*, VI (July, 1925), 256-68. (A & A)
884. Autolycus. "'Rag-Time' On Parnassus," *Musical Opinion*, XXXVI (Feb., 1913), 328-29. (J & C, Rag)
885. Avakian, Al. "Sidney Bechet, Musical Father to Bob Wilbur," *Jazz Record*, 56 (June, 1947), 5-6. (Pers)
886. Avakian, George M. "How I Found the Unissued Armstrongs," *Jazz Information*, II (Dec. 6, 1940), 17, 24. (Disc)
887. —— —. "'I Mean the Jeebies'," *Record Changer*, IX (July-Aug., 1950), 22. (Disc)
888. —— —. "Paul Mares: New Orleans Rhythm King," *Record Changer*, VIII (Nov., 1949), 17, 31. (Disc, Pers)
889. —— —. "The Safety Valve," *Jazz Information*, II (Mar. 21, 1941), 16-17, 30. (Disc)
890. —— —. "Bessie Smith On Records," *Jazz Record*, 58 (Sept., 1947), 5, 25-7. (Disc, Pers)
891. —— —. "Why Bury O'Brien?" *Jazz Information*, II (Aug. 23, 1940), 12-13. (Pers)
892. —— —. "Windy City Reunion," *Record Changer*, VIII (July, 1949), 5-6, 17-18. (Disc, Hist)

893. Bach, Bob. "Babs' Three Bips and a Bop," *Metronome*, LXIII (May, 1947), 26. (Ork)
894. ——. "Will Bradley Hasn't Quit," *Metronome*, LXIII (Aug., 1947), 36–7. (Pers)
895. ——. "Don't Forget Larry!" *Metronome*, LXIII (Oct., 1947), 34–5. (Pers)
896. ——. "He's Capitol!" *Metronome*, LXII (Aug., 1946), 18, 34–6, 40. (Pers)
897. ——. "Hoagy: From Bix to Boyd," *Metronome*, LXIII (Jan., 1947), 27. (Pers)
898. ——. "Mel Is Well!" *Metronome*, LXIII (Aug., 1947), 25, 45–6. (Pers)
899. ——. "Quiet Riot!" *Metronome*, LXIII (Oct., 1947), 13–14, 32. (Pers)
900. ——. "Wha' Hoppeen, Noro? Rhumbop!" *Metronome*, LXIII (July, 1947), 22, 49. (Ork)
901. ——. "You Gotta Swing! Says the Count," *Metronome*, LXIII (May, 1947), 19, 46. (A & A)
902. Back, Jack. *Triumph des Jazz*. Vienna: Alfa-Edition, c. 1949. 239 pp.
903. Bacon, Paul. "The High Priest of Be-Bop: The Inimitable Mr. Monk," *Record Changer*, VIII (Nov., 1949), 9–11, 26. (Bop, Pers)
904. ——. "One Man's Panorama," *Record Changer*, IX (Feb., 1950), 9, 14. (Disc)
905. ——. "To Be or Not to Bop: Nard Griffin," *Record Changer*, VII (Nov., 1948), 15. (Rev)
906. Bagar, Robert. "Condon Says Hot Jazz Has Future," New York *World Telegram*, July 1, 1944, 8 : 6–8. (Pers)
907. ——. "Fats Waller in Carnegie Hall," New York *World Telegram*, Jan.15, 1942 14 : 4–6. (Crit)
908. Baihle, Gaston. "Jazz—In 'Cap and Gown'," *School Musician*, II (Jan., 1931), 14, 45. (Pers)
909. Baker, Dorothy. *Young Man With A Horn*. New York: Houghton, Mifflin, 1938. 243 pp.; New York: Readers Club, 1943. 243 pp.; New York: Editions for the Armed Services, 1943. 224 pp.; London: Victor Gollancz, 1938. (Fict)
910. Baker, John H. "Some Georgia and Texas Jazz," *Jazzfinder*, I (June, 1948), 18. (Disc)
911. Ball, E. D. "This Joyous Jazz," *Musical Opinion*, LVI (July, 1933), 852. (A & A)
912. Ball, John Jr. *The Phonograph Record Industry*. Boston: Bellman, 1947. 47 pp.
913. Ballanta-Taylor, Nicholas George Julius. "American Jazz Is Not African," New York *Times*, Sept. 19, 1926, X, 8 : 1. Reprinted: *Metronome*, XLII (Oct. 1, 1926), 21. (A & A)
914. ——. "Jazz Music and Its Relation to African Music," *Musical Courier*, LXXXIV (June 1, 1922), 7. (A & A)
915. Ballard, Eric. "Dixieland to the Duke," *Swing Music*, 14 (Autumn, 1936), 16–17, 94–6. (A & A, Hist)
916. Bankhead, Tallulah. "Louis the End—and Beginning—Tallulah," *Down Beat*, XVII (July 14, 1950), 1, 19. (Pers)
917. ——. "Satchmo; An Appreciation of Louis Armstrong," *Flair*, I (Nov., 1950), 36–7, 107. (Pers)
918. Banks, Dave. "Be-Bop Called Merely the Beginning of a New Creative Music Form," *Down Beat*, XV (Feb. 11, 1948), 16. (A & A, Bop)
919. ——. "Jazz in Kansas City," *Metronome*, LXIII (Apr., 1947), 48–9. (Geog)
920. ——. "Radio Announcer Looks at Jazz," *Down Beat*, X (Feb. 1, 1943), 12. (Rad)
921. Bannister, Lawrence H. (Ed). *International Jazz Collectors Directory*. Worcestershire: Lawrence H. Bannister, 1948. 78 pp.
922. Barbour, Harriot B. and Warren S. Freeman. "Music of the Day," *in* Harriot B. Barbour and Warren S. Freeman. *How to Teach Children to Know Music*. New York: Smith & Durrell, 1942. pp. 180–96. (Disc)
923. Baresel, Alfred. "…and His Boys. Das Moderne Orchester und Seine Musik," *Die Musik*, XXIV (May, 1932), 580–83. (A & A)

924. Baresel, Alfred. "Jazz als Rittung," *Auftakt*, VI (1926), 213–16. (A & A)
925. ———. "Kunst-Jazz," *Melos*, VII (July, 1928), 354–57. (A & A, J & C)
926. ———. *Das Neue Jazzbuch*. Leipzig: W. Zimmermann, 1929. 98 pp.
927. Barnard, Eunice Fuller. "Jazz Is Linked to the Factory Wheel," *New York Times*, Dec. 30, 1928, V, 4–5. (Infl)
928. Barnet, Charlie. "'My Band Does Not Imitate Duke's'," *Down Beat*, VIII (June 15, 1941), 2, 19. (Ork)
929. ———. "You Made a Bad Error, Mix," *Down Beat*, XVI (July 15, 1949), 1, 19. (Gen)
    See: 2061; 3270.
930. Barron, Blue. "Sweet Music Will Play at the Funeral of Swing!" *Music and Rhythm*, II (Jan., 1942), 17. (A & A, Sw)
931. Barron, Ray. "Flanagan Debut in Boston Ballroom Pulls Full House," *Down Beat*, XVII (Apr. 21, 1950), 1, 19. (Ork)
932. Bath, Gomer. "The Spirit of Jazz," *Jacobs' Orchestra Monthly*, XX (June, 1929), 6–7. (A & A)
933. Bauduc, Ray. "All Jazz Comes From the Blues," *Down Beat*, VII (June 1, 1940), 19. (A & A, Bl)
934. Bauer, Marion. "L'Influence du 'Jazz Band'," *Revue Musicale*, V (Apr., 1924), 31–6. (A & A, Infl, J & C)
935. ———. "Jazz and American Music," *in* Marion Bauer. *Twentieth Century Music*. New York: G. P. Putnam's Sons, 1933. pp. 270–77. (J & C)
936. ———. "A New American Idiom," *Musical Leader*, LVIII (Mar. 13, 1930), 6. (A & A, J & C)
937. ———. "New Light on 'Jazz'," *Musical Leader*, LI (Sept. 18, 1926), 6. (A & A)
938. ———. "Orchestra Plays Jazz Suite by Gruenberg," *Musical Leader*, LVIII (Mar. 13, 1930), 6. (J & C)
939. ———. "Tradition: Real and Imported," *Musical Leader*, XLVIII (Aug. 21, 1924), 181. (J & C)
940. Beall, George E. "Forgotten Giants," *Jazz Information*, II (Dec. 20, 1940), 12–20. (Disc, Pers)
941. ———. "The New Orleans Rhythm Kings," *in* Ralph de Toledano (Ed). *Frontiers of Jazz*. New York: Oliver Durrell, 1947. pp. 82–90. (Ork)
942. ———. "Whoopee Makers," *Jazz Hot*, III (Aug.-Sept., 1937), 7–8. (Disc, Ork)
943. Bechet, Sidney, and others. "In Praise of Satchmo," *Record Changer*, IX (July-Aug., 1950), 12–13. (Pers)
944. Beeler, Bruce. "A New Light on Jazz," *Etude*, LV (June, 1937), 406. (A & A)
945. Bel, Andre de and Marcel Cumps. "Dizzy in Belgium," *Hot Club Magazine*, 25 (Mar., 1948), 5–7. (Crit, Pers)
946. Belaiev, Victor. "Stravinsky, Weill and Jazz," *Christian Science Monitor*, May 18, 1929, 6. (J & C)
947. Beliard, Octave. "Defense et Illustration du Jazz," *Les Annales Politiques et Litteraires*, CIV (Dec. 10, 1934), 255–58. (A & A)
948. Bell, Clive. "'Plus de Jazz'," *New Republic*, XXVIII (Sept. 21, 1921), 92–6. Reprinted: Clive Bell. *Since Cezanne*. New York: Harcourt, Brace, 1928. pp. 213–30. (A & A)
949. Bell, Leslie R. "Music Education and Jazz," *School*, XXXI (May, 1943), 759–62. (Ed)
950. Bellson, Louie. "The Musical Drummer," *Down Beat*, XVII (July 28, 1950), 16; (Sept. 8, 1950), 18; (Oct. 6, 1950), 18; (Nov. 3, 1950), 16; (Dec. 1, 1950), 16. (Inst)
951. Beneke, Tex. "Swing Was Never King," *Metronome*, LXIII (Feb., 1947), 20–1, 37. (Sw)
    See: 2171.

952. Bennett, Rodney. "The Ubiquitous Rag," *Sackbut*, VI (Nov., 1925), 99–101. (Rev)
953. Benny, Milton. "California, Here I Come," *Metronome*, LIX (Oct., 1943), 39, 43. (Hist)
954. Benoist-Mechin, J. (Trans: Samuel Putnam). "Jazz Band," *Musical Courier*, LXXXVIII (Feb. 21, 1924), 12. (A & A)
955. Berend, Dave. *Swing Style for the Piano.* New York: Amsco Music Sales, 1937. 63 pp.
956. Berg, Arne. "Scandinavia in Ferment," *in* Orin Blackstone (Ed). *Jazzfinder '49.* New Orleans: Orin Blackstone, 1949. pp. 40–4. (Geog)
957. Berger, Francesco. "A Jazz Band Concert," *Monthly Musical Record*, XLIX (Aug., 1919), 174–75. (Crit, Infl)
958. ——. "Some English Observations Upon A First Hearing of a Jazz Band Concert," *Metronome*, XXXVIII (Oct., 1922), 84–5. (Crit)
959. Berger, Morroe. "Jazz: Resistance to the Diffusion of a Culture Pattern," *Journal of Negro History*, XXXII (Oct., 1947), 461–94. (A & A)
960. ——. "Jazz Pre-History—and Bunk Johnson," *in* Ralph de Toledano (Ed). *Frontiers of Jazz.* New York: Oliver Durrell, 1947. pp. 91–103. (A & A, Hist, Pers)
961. Bergh, Øivind. *Moderne Dansemusikk.* Oslo: Musikk-Huset, 1945. 146 pp.
962. Bergman, Dorothy. "Jazz, the Expression of the Age," *Musician*, XXXV (Sept., 1930), 12. (A & A)
963. Bergman, Lewis. "Small-Time Musician," New York *Times*, Sept. 10, 1939, VII, 12, 16. (Pers)
964. ——. "Swinging the Classics," New York *Times Magazine*, Jan. 14, 1940, 17. (J & C)
965. Bernhard, Edmond and Jacques DeVergnies. *Apologie du Jazz.* Brussels: Les Presses de Belgique, 1945. 234 pp.
966. Bernhard, Paul. "The German Side of Jazz," *Living Age*, CCCXXX (Sept. 11, 1926), 580–85. (Geog, Hist, Inst)
967. ——. *Jazz, Eine Musikalische Zeitfrage.* München: Delphin-Verlag, 1927. 109 pp.
968. Bernie, Ben. "How I Choose My Men," *Metronome*, XLV (June, 1929), 19, 28. (Ork)
969. Bernstein, Leonard. "Jazz Forum: Has Jazz Influenced the Symphony? Yes," *Esquire*, XXVII (Feb., 1947), 47, 152–53. (A & A, Infl, J & C)
    See: 1990.
970. Berr de Turique, Stephane. "Quelques Mots Sur le Jazz," *Monde Musical*, XL (Mar. 31, 1929), 92. (A & A)
971. Berry, R. E. "Home of the Blues," New York *Times Magazine*, May 5, 1940, 21. (Bl, Hist)
972. Berton, Ralph. "Blesh, Jazz, and Metronome," *Jazz Record*, 35 (Aug., 1945), 6–8, 14. (Gen)
973. Bettonville, Albert. "L'Arbre du Jazz," *Jazz* (Brussels), I (Aug., 1945), 3–5.
974. ——. "Autour de la Disparition du Major Glenn Miller," *Jazz* (Brussels), I (June, 1945), n. p. (Pers)
975. ——. "Les Bebopers," *Hot Club Magazine*, 17 (May, 1947), 6–7. (Bop, Pers)
976. ——. "The Best Belgian Recordings," *Hot Club Magazine*, 15 (Mar., 1947), 6–7. (Disc)
977. ——. "Les Blues de Bessie Smith," *Hot Club Magazine*, 7 (July, 1946), 11. (Pers)
978. ——. "Rudy Bruder, Un Grand Pianiste," *Music* (Brussels), XV (Feb., 1939), 25. (Pers)
979. ——. "Don Byas," *Hot Club Magazine*, 12 (Dec., 1946), 8–9. (Pers)
980. ——. "Chicago Jazz, au Temps des Gangsters..." *Hot Club Magazine*, 6 (June, 1946), 6–7, 9. (Chi)

981. Bettonville, Albert. "Le King Cole Trio," *Hot Club Magazine*, 11 (Nov., 1946), 8–9. (Ork)
982. ——. "Collectionneurs et Amateurs," *Hot Club Magazine*, III (Aug., 1948), 9, 10, 11. (Disc)
983. ——. "Concerts Rex Stewart," *Hot Club Magazine*, 26 (Apr., 1948), 7–8. (Crit, Ork)
984. ——. "La Danse et le Jazz," *Jazz* (Brussels), I (Sept., 1945), 14, 15. (J & D)
985. ——. "En 1860, 'Blind Tom' Etait l'Ancetre des Pianistes de Jazz," *Hot Club Magazine*, 1 (Jan., 1946), 13. Reprinted: "En 1860 'Blind Tom' Era el Antepasado de los Pianistas de Jazz," *Ritmo y Melodia*, IV (Sept., 1947), n. p. (Hist, Pers)
986. ——. "Raoul Faisant," *Hot Club Magazine*, 5 (May, 1946), 11. (Pers)
987. ——. "Feuille de Temperature," *Hot Club Magazine*, 14 (Feb., 1947), 14. (Gen)
988. ——. "Nick Frerar et Son Big Band," *Hot Club Magazine*, 13 (Jan., 1947), 7. (Ork)
989. ——. "Lionel Hampton," *Jazz* (Brussels), I (Feb., 1946), 3, 4, 5. (Pers)
990. ——. "Coleman Hawkins," *Hot Club Magazine*, 8 (Aug., 1946), 6–7. (Pers)
991. ——. "Coleman Hawkins," *Ritmo y Melodia*, V (May-June, 1948), n. p. (Pers)
992. ——. "Erskine Hawkins," *Jazz* (Brussels), I (Mar., 1945), 7. (Pers)
993. ——. "The Herman Herd," *Jazzology*, I (July, 1946), 5–7. (Ork)
994. ——. "Woody Herman 1946," *Hot Club Magazine*, 3 (Mar., 1946), 11, 13. (Pers)
995. ——. "Bib Hillman," *Music* (Brussels), XV (July, 1939), 107; (Aug., 1939), 107. (Pers)
996. ——. "Billie Holiday," *Jazz* (Brussels), I (July, 1945), 3–4. (Pers)
997. ——. "Billie Holiday 'Fruit Etrange'," *France-Belgique*, I (Dec. 22, 1944), 1, 8. (Pers)
998. ——. "Le Jazz," *Music* (Brussels), XIV (Oct., 1938), 147. (A & A)
999. ——. "Jazz Pele-Mele," *Hot Club Magazine*, 9 (Sept., 1946), 6; 10 (Oct., 1946), 8–9. (Disc)
1000. ——. "Freddy Johnson," *Music* (Brussels), XIV (Apr., 1938), 3. (Pers)
1001. ——. "Jimmy McPartland, Dans l'Ombre de Bix," *Jazz* (Brussels), I (Apr., 1945), 3, 4. (Pers)
1002. ——. "Madame Louis… Lil Hardin… Armstrong," *Hot-Revue*, I (June, 1946), 13–16. (Pers)
1003. ——. "Marginales," *Hot Club Magazine*, 16 (Apr., 1947), 6–7. (Gen)
1004. ——. *Paranoia du Jazz*. Brussels: Cahiers du Jazz, 1939. 40 pp.
1005. ——. "La Parole Est a Bunk Johnson," *Jazz* (Brussels), I (Dec., 1945), 6, 7. (Pers)
1006. ——. "Premier Souvenir de Jazz… Sam Wooding and His Chocolate Dandies," *Hot Club Magazine*, 7 (July, 1946), 7–8. (Ork)
1007. ——. "Bob Shaw's New Orleans Band," *Jazz Hot* XV (June, 1949), 33. (Ork)
1008. ——. "Muggsy Spanier," *Jazz* (Brussels), II (Mar., 1946), 7, 8. (Pers)
1009. ——. "Toots Thielemans Trio," *Jazz Hot*, XV (May, 1949), 17, 35. (Ork)
1010. ——. "Vicky Thunus, Pianiste," *Jazz* (Brussels), I (Nov., 1945), 14, 15. (Pers)
1011. ——. "Fats Waller: Portrait," *Jazz* (Brussels), I (Mar., 1945), 14. (Pers)
1012. ——. "Anny Xhofleer, Chanteuse de Jazz," *Music* (Brussels), XIV (Mar., 1938), 49. (Pers)
1013. Betz, Betty. "Be-Bop, BG, and a Box of Bubble Gum," *Down Beat*, XVI (Aug. 26, 1949), 2. (Geog)
1014. Bickart, Roger. "La Musique Par Disques," *Musique*, I (Oct. 15, 1927), 35–7. (Disc)
1015. Bickford, Myron A. "Something About Ragtime," *Cadenza*, XX (Sept., 1913), 13; (Nov., 1913), 10–11. (Rag)
1016. Bie, Oskar. *Das Rätsel der Musik*. Leipzig: Durr & Weber, 1922. 100 pp.
1017. Biedermann, Felix. *Jazz, Wiener Roman*. Wien: E. Strache, 1925. 325 pp. (Author's pseudonym, Felix Dormann, at head of title)

1018. Biemiller, Carl L. "Armstrong and His Hot-Noters Point A Trend," *Holiday*, IV (Oct., 1948), 13–14, 16. (Ork)

1019. Birchard, Clarence C. "America... A Treasure House of Folk Music," *Musician*, XXXVI (Sept., 1931), 7–8. (Gen)

1020. Black, Douglas C. *Matrix Numbers—Their Meaning and History*. Melbourne: Australian Jazz Quarterly, 1946. 24 pp.

1021. ——. (Ed: William H. Miller). *Matrix Numbers*. Melbourne: Australian Jazz Quarterly, 1946. 24 pp.

1022. Blackstone, Orin. "Big Eye Louis," *Jazz Information*, II (Dec. 20, 1940), 6–10. (Pers)

1023. ——. "Bix and Carmichael," *Jazzfinder*, I (Mar., 1948), 18. (Disc)

1024. ——. *Index to Jazz*. New Orleans: Gordon Gullickson, 1947. 4 vols.

1025. ——. "Modern Record Research," *in* Orin Blackstone (Ed). *Jazzfinder '49*. New Orleans: Orin Blackstone, 1949. pp. 142–50 (Disc)

1026. ——. (Ed). *The Jazzfinder '49*. New Orleans: Orin Blackstone, 1949. 152 pp.

1027. Blesh, Rudi. *America's Contribution to Jazz*. Bombay: United States Information Service, 1949. 7 pp.

1028. ——. "Louis Armstrong Plays With Concert Group in Carnegie Hall 'Pops'," New York *Herald Tribune*, May 4, 1948, 19: 1. (Crit)

1029. ——. "Claude Bolling; New French Sensation," *Record Changer*, VIII (Feb., 1949), 7, 20. (Pers)

1030. ——. "In Reply to Charles Delaunay," *Record Changer*, VIII (Apr., 1949), 9. (Gen)
    See: 1241; 1446.

1031. ——. "Jazz Begins," *in* George S. Rosenthal (Ed). *Jazzways*. Cincinnati, 1946. pp. 9–15, 116–18, 120. (A & A, Hist)

1032. ——. "Willie Bunk Johnson, Last of the Olympians," *Record Changer*, VIII (Sept., 1949), 12. (Pers)

1033. ——. "Jelly Roll Morton's Washington Documentary," *Jazz Record*, 56 (June, 1947), 24–5. (Disc)

1034. ——. "On the Riverboats," *Record Changer*, IX (July-Aug., 1950), 9, 43, 44. (Pers, Hist)

1035. ——. "Shake That Thing," *Record Changer*, VII (June, 1948), 6. (A & A, J & D)

1036. ——. *Shining Trumpets, A History of Jazz*. New York: Alfred A. Knopf, 1946. 365 pp.

1037. ——. "Some Thoughts on the Jazz Revival," *Record Changer*, VII (Nov., 1948), 14, 23. (A & A, NO)

1038. ——. *This is Jazz*. San Francisco: Privately Printed, 1943. 36 pp. Reprinted: London: Jazz Music Books, 1943. 34 pp.

1039. ——. "What is New Orleans Style?" *Record Changer*, VII (Mar., 1948), 11, 16. (A & A, NO)

1040. ——. and Harriet Janis. *They All Played Ragtime*. New York: Alfred A. Knopf, 1950. 338 pp. (Rag)

1041. Blom, Eric. "The American Intoxicant," *Sackbut*, VII (Apr., 1927), 264–67. (A & A)
    See: 1178.

1042. ——. "Jazz in the Concert Hall," *Musical Opinion*, XLIX (Feb., 1926), 485–86. (Crit, A & A)

1043. ——. "Musical Hope for Musical Comedy," *Christian Science Monitor*, Sept. 10, 1927, 8. (Gen)

1044. Bloom, Mickey. "The World's Pace Setters on Swing Trumpet," *Metronome*, LII (Mar., 1936), 17, 60. (Pers)

1045. Bluthner, Hans. "Stegreif-Musik: Jazz," *Dionysos*, 18 (Oct. 1, 1948), 5. (A & A, NO)

1046. Boatfield, Graham. "Mr. Morton Meets the Rhythm Clubs," *Jazz Music*, II (Feb.-Mar., 1944), 119–20. (Disc, Pers)

1047. Bolgen, Kaare A. "An Analysis of the Jazz Idiom," *Music Teachers' Review*, XI (Sept.-Oct., 1941), 3–9. (A & A, Infl)

1048. Bonavia, F. "Recent Works at Oxford and London... Jazz," New York *Times*, Aug. 16, 1931, 6 : 6. (Gen)

1049. Bonneau, Pierre. "Originalite du Jazz," *Hot Club Magazine*, 5 (May, 1946), 3, 5. (A & A)

1050. Bookman, J. "One Night Tour," *Collier's*, CVIII (Nov. 1, 1941), 22–3, 42–3. (Ork)

1051. Borel, Claude. "Connaissance du Jazz," *Hot Club Magazine*, 17 (May, 1947), 15–16. (A & A)

1052. Borneman, Ernest. "Again French Elan Drowns Out Jazz But Daunts None," *Down Beat*, XV (June 16, 1948), 1–2. (Gen)

1053. ——. "'Bop Will Kill Business Unless It Kills Itself First'—Louis Armstrong," *Down Beat*, XV (Apr. 7, 1948), 2–3. (A & A Bop)

1054. ——. "Both Schools of Critics Wrong," *Down Beat*, XIV (July 30, 1947), 16; (Aug. 13, 1947), 16. (Crit)

1055. ——. *A Critic Looks at Jazz*. London: Jazz Music Books, 1946. 53 pp. Originally published in the *Record Changer* in serial form under title: "Anthropologist Looks at Jazz."

1056. ——. "Diary—68 Hours Without Sleep," *Down Beat*, XV (Aug. 25, 1948), 6–7. (Pers)

1057. ——. "Hussah! Hot Club's Quintet Rides Again," *Down Beat*, XIV (Dec. 17, 1947), 14. (Crit, Ork)

1058. ——. "Jazz Cult: I. Intimate Memoirs of an Acolyte. II. War Among the Critics," *Harper's*, CXCIV (Feb.-Mar., 1947), 141–47, 261–73. (A & A, Hist) *See*: 3081.

1059. ——. "Nice Fete Melange of Fights, Gaiety, Occasionally Jazz," *Down Beat*, XV (Mar. 24, 1948), 16–17. (Crit)

1060. ——. "Rex Wows Parisians," *Down Beat*, XV (Jan. 14, 1948), 3. (Crit)

1061. ——. *Tremolo*. New York: Harper, 1948. 224 pp. London: Jarrolds, 1948. (Author's pseudonym, Cameron McCabe, at head of title). (Fict)

1062. Borsky, Arthur. "'Ripplin' Rhythm, Yes; But Why Apologise For Legitimate Jazz'" *Down Beat*, VIII (Oct. 15, 1941), 18. (A & A)

1063. Bowles, Paul. "Anatomy of Jazz," *Modern Music*, XVI (May-June, 1939), 281–85. (Rev)

1064. ——. "Once Again, Le Jazz Hot," *Modern Music*, XX (Jan.-Feb., 1943), 140–42. (Rev)

1065. Bowman, James Cloyd. "Anti-Ragtime," (lr) *New Republic*, V (Nov. 6, 1915), 19. (Rag) *See*: 824; 1986; 2288.

1066. Boyce, David. "Special Arrangement," *in* Charles Harvey (Ed). *Jazz Parody*. London: Spearman, 1948. pp. 50–6. (Fict)

1067. Boyer, Richard O. "Bop," *New Yorker*, XXIV (July 3, 1948), 28–32, 34–7. (Bop, Pers)

1068. ——. "The Hot Bach," *New Yorker*, XX (June 24, 1944), 30–4, 37–8, 40, 42, 44; (July 1, 1944), 26–32, 34; (July 8, 1944), 26–31. (Ork, Pers)

1069. Bragaglia, Anton Giulio. *Jazz Band*. Milan: Edizioni Corbaccio, 1929. 292 pp.

1070. Braggiotti, Mary. "King of Jazz and His New Throne," New York *Post*. Nov. 2, 1943, 29 : 1–3. (Pers)

1071. Brand, Pat. "Headlines! Headlines!" *in* Charles Harvey (Ed). *Jazz Parody*. London: Spearman, 1948. pp. 5–20. (Fict)

1072. Breck, Flora E. "Robert Harkness Deplores Jazz," *Choir Leader*, XXXVIII (June, 1931), 101–02. (A & A)

1073. Brennan, William. "Artie Shaw is Now a Symphonic Sender," New York *World Telegram*, Feb. 14, 1941, 16 : 1–4. (Pers)
1074. Breslaw, Lillian. "Swing: A Defense," (lr) New York *Times*, Feb. 26, 1939, IV, 9 : 7. (Sw)
1075. Brock, H. I. "Jazz Is to Do a Turn in Grand Opera," New York *Times*, Feb. 14, 1926, IV, 5 : 1. (J & D)
1076. Brockway, Howard. "Jazz," *Review*, I (May 24, 1919), 46. (A & A)
1077. Brody, Iles. "Man the Kitchenette," *Esquire*, XXI (Feb., 1944), 93, 149. (Gen)
1078. Bronner, Ed. "Star Studded Shellac," *Record Changer*, VIII (May, 1949), 11, 21. (Disc)
     See: 2137.
1079. Broome, John. "On the Feather in Esquire's Bonnet," *Jazz Record*, 35 (Aug., 1945), 4–5. (Gen)
1080. Brown, Ken, Ralph Venables and Jackson D. Hale. *Collectors' Catalog*. Glasgow: Ken Brown, 1943. 24 pp.
1081. Brown, Sterling A. "The Blues as Folk Poetry," *in* B. A. Botkin (Ed). *Folk-Say, A Regional Miscellany*. Norman: University of Oklahoma Press, 1930. (Bl)
1082. ——. "Blues, Ballads and Social Songs," *in 75 Years of Freedom*. Washington, D. C.: Library of Congress, 1940. pp. 17–25. (Bl)
1083. ——. "A Few Stray Notes on Jazz," *Vassar Brew* (Dec., 1945), 6–7, 20; (June, 1946), 15. (A & A)
1084. ——. "Ma Rainey," *in* Sterling A. Brown. *Southern Road*. New York: Harcourt, Brace, 1932. pp. 62–4. (Poet)
1085. Brown, William E. "Driving Out Jazz," *Musical Courier*, CII (Mar. 28, 1931), 38–9. (A & A)
1086. Broyles, B. J. "Hails Jeri Southern As New Star," *Down Beat*, XVII (Feb. 10, 1950), 2. (Pers)
1087. Brubeck, Dave. "Jazz' Evolvement As Art Form," *Down Beat*, XVII (Jan. 27, 1950), 12, 15; (Feb. 10, 1950), 13, 18. (A & A)
1088. Bruynoghe, Yannick. "Defense du Duke," *Hot Club Magazine*, 6 (June, 1946), 14–15. (Disc, Pers)
     See: 1229; 1230.
1089. ——. "52nd Re-Bop Street," *Hot Club Magazine*, 20 (Oct. 1, 1947), 10. (Bop)
1090. ——. "New-Orleans", *Hot Club Magazine*, 5 (May, 1946), 7. (Gen, NO)
1091. ——. "Gertrude 'Ma' Rainey," *Hot Club Magazine*, 7 (July, 1946), 14. (Pers)
1092. Bruyr, Jose. "Un Entretien Avec . . . Darius Milhaud," *Guide du Concert*, XVI (Oct. 18, 1929), 55–8. (J & C)
1093. Buchanan, Charles L. "Gershwin and Musical Snobbery," *Outlook*, CXLV (Feb. 2, 1927), 146–48. (A & A, J & C)
1094. ——. "The National Music Fallacy: Is American Music to Rest On a Foundation of Ragtime and Jazz?" *Arts and Decoration*, XX (Feb., 1924), 26, 62. (A & A, J & C)
1095. ——. "Ragtime and American Music," *Opera Magazine*, III (Feb., 1916,) 17–19, 25. (J & C, Rag)
1096. ——. "Two Views of Ragtime. II. Ragtime and American Music," *Seven Arts*, II (July, 1917), 376–83. (Rag)
     See: 2289.
1097. Bukofzer, Manfred. "Soziologie des Jazz, *Melos*, VIII (Aug.–Sept., 1929), 387–91. (A & A)
1098. Burian, E. F. *Jazz*. Praha: Aventinum, 1928. 208 pp.
1099. ——. "Jazz-Requiem," *Auftakt*, VIII (1928), 20–1. (J & C)
1100. Burk, John N. "Ragtime and Its Possibilities," *Harvard Musical Review*, II (Jan., 1914), 11–13. (Rag)

1101. Burg, John N. "Ragtime Has Its Possibilities," *Opera Magazine*, II (June, 1915), 24–5. (Rag)
1102. Bushkin, Joe. "Ole Satchmo, the Gourmet," *Down Beat*, XVII (July 14, 1950), 12. (Pers)
1103.′ Butler, Henry F. "Accursed Jazz," *Baton*, III (Apr., 1924), 10. (A & A)
1104.′ Byrne, John P. "Dancing Dublin Keeps Low-Paid Orks Working," *Down Beat*, XV (Aug. 25, 1948), 2. (Geog)
1105. C. S. "Schoenberg and Jazz," *Musical Courier*, LXXXVIII (Apr., 1924), 6. (Gen)
1106. Cadman, B. Meredith. "Hot and Hybrid," *Etude*, LVII (June, 1939), 374. (Rev)
1107. — —. "Music for 'Jam Sessions'," *Etude*, LXVI (Feb., 1948), 73. (Rev)
1108. Cadman, Charles Wakefield. "Rag-Time," (lr) *Musical Courier*, LXIX (Aug. 12, 1914), 31. (Rag)
1109. Cain, Noble. "Choral Fads and Jitterbug Fancies," *Music Educator's National Yearbook*, XXX (1939/40), 339–42. Reprinted: *Music Educator's Journal*, XXVI (Sept., 1939), 26–7. (Ed, Infl)
1110. Calloway, Cab. *The New Cab Calloway's Hepsters Dictionary*. New York: C. Calloway, 1944. 15 pp. (Lang)
1111. Campbell, E. Simms. "Blues Are the Negroes' Lament," *Esquire*, XII (Dec. 1939), 100, 276–80. Reprinted: Frederic Ramsey, Jr. and Charles Edward Smith (Eds). *Jazzmen*. New York: Harcourt, Brace, 1939. pp. 101–17. (Bl)
1112. — —. "Homeland of Happy Feet," *Esquire*, V (Feb., 1936), 101–03. (J & D, Pic)
1113. — —. "Jam in the Nineties," *Esquire*, X (Dec., 1938), 102, 200, 202, 207. (Hist)
1114. — —. "Swing, Mr. Charlie!" *Esquire*, V (Feb., 1936), 100, 183. (J & D)
1115. Campbell, S. Brunson. "Early Great White Ragtime Composers and Pianists," *Jazz Journal*, II (May, 1949), 12–11. (Pers, Rag)
1116. — —. "Looking Backwards," *Jazz Journal*, II (June, 1949), 9–10. (Hist)
1117. — —. "Ragtime," *Jazz Journal*, II (Apr., 1949), 9–10. (Rag)
1118. — —. "Ragtime Begins," *Record Changer*, VII (Mar., 1948), 8, 18. (Hist, Pers, Rag)
1119. Canfield, Mary Cass. "Great American Art," *in* Mary Cass Canfield. *Grotesques and Other Reflections*. New York: Harper, 1927. pp. 36–47. (Infl)
1120. Caraceni, Augusto. *Il Jazz Dalle Origini ad Oggi*. Milan: Edizioni Suvini e Zerboni, 1937. 179 pp. Reprinted: *Jazz*. Roma: Zampardi, 1945. 173 pp.
1121. Carew, Roy J. "Assorted Rags," *Record Changer*, VIII (Feb., 1948), 6. (Hist, Rag)
1122. — —. "Historic Corner," *Jazz Forum*, 4 (Apr., 1947), 9. (Hist)
1123. — —. "New Orleans Recollections," *Record Changer*, VII (Dec., 1948), 12. (Hist, Pers)
1124. — —. "Random Recollections," *Jazz Forum*), 3 (Jan., 1947), 1–2, 32. (Hist)
1125. — —. "Those Jelly Roll Songs," *Jazzfinder*, I (Aug., 1948), 3–4. (Pers)
1126. Carlile, Tom. "Prodigy Drummer in Kneepants," *Pageant*, II (Nov., 1946), 93. (Pers
1127. Carmichael, Hoagy. *The Stardust Road*. New York: Rinehart, 1946. 156 pp.
1128. Carpenter, John Alden. "Jazz Is Assuming Prominence as an American Music Idiom," *Musical Digest*, XI (Nov. 23, 1926), 3. (A & A, Infl, J & C)
1129. Carter, Benny. "My Nine Lives," *Swing Music*, (May–June, 1936), 55, 71. (Pers)
1130. Carter, Elliot. "Once Again Swing; Also 'American Music'," *Modern Music*, XVI (Jan.-Feb., 1939), 99–100. (Sw)
1131. Casella, Alfredo. "Alfredo Casella Discusses Jazz," *Musical Courier*, C (Jan. 4, 1930), 7. (A & A)

1132. Casella, Alfredo. "Casella on Jazz," *Musical Courier*, LXXXVII (July 12, 1923), 22. (A & A)
1133. ——. "Jazz," *Christian Science Monitor*, Dec. 11, 1926, 10. (A & A)
1134. ——. "La Vita Musicale Negli Stati Uniti," *Critica Musicale*, 5–6 (May-June, 1922), 121, 122, 123, 124, 125, 126, 127. (Gen)
1135. Castillo, Lloyd G. del. "Jazz—Is It Music or Something Else?" *Jacobs' Orchestra Monthly*, XV (June-July, 1924), 8–9. (A & A)
1136. Castro, Fernando. "One Night in Havana," *Metronome*, LIII (Feb., 1937), 20, 22; (Mar., 1937), 29, 46. (Geog)
1137. Cayton, Horace R. "Social Significance in Jazz Louses Good Stuff Up," *Down Beat*, XIII (Dec. 16, 1946), 8. (A & A)
1138. Cerrai, Vittoris. *Guida Practica di Instrumentazience per Jazz*. Roma: Officina d'Arte, 1934.
1139. Cerri, Livio. *Jazz, Musica d'Oggi*. Milan: Rodolfo Malfasi, 1948. 270 pp.
1140. Cesana, Otto. "Have Dance Orchestras Reached Their Peak?" *Down Beat*, IX (Mar. 1, 1942), 9. (A & A)
1141. ——. "Swing Is—Well It's Here," *Metronome*, LII (June, 1936), 14. (A & A, Sw)
1142. Chandler, Ted. "Back Bay Shuffle," *Jazz Quarterly*, II (Summer, 1944), 14–15, 24. (Ork)
1143. Chasdel, J. "Swing from Paris," *Hot Club Magazine*, 1 (Jan., 1946), 10–11. (Crit, Geog)
1144. Chenette, Ed. "Town Clef Topics," *Metronome*, XXXIX (Mar., 1923), 35. (A & A)
1145. Chop, Max. "Jazz als Lehrfach," *Signale*, LXXXVI (Jan. 11, 1928), 43–4. (Ed, Infl)
1146. Chotzinoff, Samuel. "Jazz: A Brief History," *Vanity Fair*, XX (June, 1923), 69. (Hist)
1147. Ciardi, Anthony P. "The c-r-dex System for the Filing and Indexing of Phonograph Records," *Record Changer*, VIII (Feb., 1949), 11–12. (Disc)
1148. Clamer, Guilliam. "Freddy Moore," *Record Changer*, IX (Dec., 1950), 9, 10, 18. (Pers)
1149. Clark, Dave. "Educated Cat Stole My Mute Idea—Joe Oliver," *Down Beat*, VII (Mar. 1, 1940), 8. (Pers)
1150. ——. "Little Brother Montgomery Alive, Still Playing 88," *Down Beat*, VII (Nov. 15, 1940), 10. (Pers)
1151. Clark, Kenneth S. (lr) *Musical Courier*, LXXXV (Nov. 16, 1922), 47, 54. (Gen) *See*: 482.
1152. Clark, Robert. "Music Education vs. Radio and Dance-Hall Rhythm," *Music Educator's Journal*, XXIII (May, 1937), 33–4. (Infl)
1153. Clarke, Francis. "Beastly Tunes," *London Mercury*, III (Mar., 1921), 510–20. (A & A)
1154. Clinton, Larry. "Swing Grows Up," *Good Housekeeping*, CVII (Oct., 1938), 13, 92. (J & D, Sw)
1155. Clyne, Anthony. "Jazz," *Sackbut*, VI (Aug., 1925), 12–14. (A & A)
1156. Coeuroy, Andre. *Histoire Generale du Jazz*. Paris: Editions Denoel, 1942.
1157. ——, and Andre Schaeffner. *Le Jazz*. Paris: C. Aveline, 1926. 150 pp.
1158. Coffey, Jere. "Platter Stirs Memories of 'Ol' Tom Cat of Keys'," *Down Beat*, XII (Dec. 15, 1945), 5. (Pers)
1159. Coleman, Bill. "Accompanying Bessie Smith," *Jazz Hot*, IV (Dec.-Jan., 1937/38), 5. (Pers)
1160. Collet, Henri. "Jazz et Musique," *Menestrel*, XCII (Oct. 10, 1930), 427. (Gen)
1161. ——. "Le Jazz Revelateur," *L'Edition Musicale Vivante*, IV (Oct., 1931), 7–9. (Gen)

1162. Combe, Edouard. "Jazz and Guitar," *Living Age*, CCCXXVIII (Feb. 6, 1926), 326–30. (A & A, Inst)
1163. Comfort, Iris Tracy. "Sauce for the Classicists," *Etude*, LXIV (Feb., 1946), 80, 113. (Gen)
1164. Condon, Eddie. "The Blue Blower," *Record Changer*, VII (May, 1948), 7. (Pers)
1165. ——. "How Bands Are Made," *Saturday Review of Literature*, XXX (Aug. 30, 1947), sup. 8, 22. (Rev)
1166. ——. *We Called It Music*. New York: Henry Holt, 1947. 341 pp. (Narration by Thomas Sugrue).
1167. —— and Thomas Sugrue. "Brother Jazz," *Colliers'*, CXX (Aug. 23, 1947), 11–13, 38–40; (Aug. 30, 1947), 20–1, 56–7; (Sept. 6, 1947), 16–17, 68–9. (Pers)
1168. Connell, Tom. "B. G.: The King of Swing Abdicates," *Metronome*, LXII (Aug., 1946), 41. (Pers)
1169. Cons, Carl. "Bunny Berigan Teams Up With Bix," *Music and Rhythm*, II (July, 1942), 50. (Pers)
1170. ——. "The Jargon of Jazz," (lr) *American Mercury*, XXXVIII (May, 1936), sup. 10. (Lang)
1171. ——. "What Music and Rhythm Stands For," *Music and Rhythm*, II (May, 1942), 49. (Gen)
1172. —— and George von Physter. *Destiny*. Chicago: Down Beat Publishing 1938. n. p.
1173. Considine, Jim. "I'm Away Ahead of Peck Kelley," *Down Beat*, VII (July 15, 1940), 9. (Pers)
1174. Converse, C. Crozat. "Rag-Time Music," *Etude*, XVII (June, 1899), 185; (Aug., 1899), 256. (Rag)
   See: 585.
1175. Cook, Will Marion. "'Spirituals' and 'Jazz'," (lr) New York *Times*, Dec. 26, 1926, VII, 8 : 2. (A & A)
1176. Cooper, Gypsie. "Can Women Swing?" *Metronome*, LII (Sept., 1936), 30. (Gen)
1177. Copland, Aaron. "El Interludio del Jazz," *in* Aaron Copland. (Trans: Nestor R. Ortiz Oderigo). *Musica y Musicos Contemporaneos*. Buenos Aires: Editorial Losada, 1945. pp. 96–101. (A & A)
1178. ——. "Jazz Structure and Influence," *Modern Music*, IV (Jan.-Feb., 1927), 9–14. (A & A)
   See: 1041.
1179. Cort, Willy de. "Le Referendum du H. C. B.," *Hot Club Magazine*, 7 (July, 1946), 21. (Poll)
1180. Cosmetto, Cleon. *La Vraie Musique de Jazz*. Lausanne: J. F. Chastellain, 1945. 50 pp.
1181. Covarrubias. "Impossible Interview; Fritz Kreisler vs. Louis Armstrong," *Vanity Fair*, XLV (Feb., 1936), 33. (Gen)
1182. Cowell, Henry. "Jazz Today," *Trend*, II (Nov., 1934), 162–64. (A & A)
1183. Crane, Burton. "Coda on Japan," *Metronome*, LIII (Jan., 1937), 17, 53. (Geog)
1184. Creelman, Eileen. "Harry James, Idol of the Paramount's Jitterbugs, Talks of Swing and of the Movies," New York *Sun*, May 11, 1943, 19 : 1–5. (Sw)
1185. Cresser, Lord. "Calypso and Jazz," *Jazz Journal*, II (Feb., 1949), 2–3, 9. (A & A)
1186. Cressy, Paul. *The Taxi-Dance Hall*. Chicago: University of Chicago Press, 1932. 300 pp.
1187. Crichton, Kyle. "Peel that Apple!" *Collier's*, C (Dec. 4, 1937), 22, 48. (J & D)
1188. Criel, Gaston. *Swing: Presentation de Jean Cocteau et Charles Delaunay*. Paris: Editions Universitaires Francaises, 1948. 92 pp.

1189. Crosby, Bing. "My Ten Favorite Vocalists," *Music and Rhythm*, II (Mar., 1942), 8–9. (Pers)
1190. Crosby, Ted. *The Story of Bing Crosby*. Cleveland: World, 1946. 239 pp.
1191. Csida, Joseph. "Why Victor Launched Dance Ork Series," *Down Beat*, XVII (May 19, 1950), 1, 27. (Disc, J & D)
1192. Cumps, Marcel. "Rex Stewart a Bruxelles," *Hot Club Magazine*, 26 (Apr., 1948), 9. (Crit, Ork)
1193. Cundall, Tom. "Spotlight on Spike," *Jazz Journal*, I (Oct., 1948), 2–3. (Pers)
1194. Cuney-Hare, Maud. "Negro Idiom and Rhythm," *in* Maud Cuney-Hare. *Negro Musicians and Their Music*, Washington: Associated, 1936. pp. 131–156. (Gen)
1195. Cunliffe, Ronald. "How to Treat Jazz-Mania," *Music Teacher*, VIII (Oct., 1929), 567–68; (Nov., 1929), 645. (Infl)
1196. — —. "The Jazz-Mad Pupil," *Music Teacher*, VIII (June, 1929), 331–32. (Infl)
1197. Cunningham, J. M. "Tilts at Carl Engel Over Jazz," (lr) *Musical America*, XXXVI (May 13, 1922), 41. (A & A)
1198. Curran, Dale. "Vic Dickenson—Trombone," *Jazz Record*, 22 (July, 1944), 4–5, 11. (Pers)
1199. — —. *Dupree Blues*. New York: Alfred A. Knopf, 1948. 228 pp. (Fict)
1200. — —. "Hear That Ragtime Band," *Jazz Record*, 18 (Mar., 1944), 6–7. (Hist, Pers)
1201. — —. *Piano In the Band*. New York: Reynal & Hitchcock, 1942. 261 pp. (Fict)
1202. — —. "Three Brass, Four Rhythm," *in* George S. Rosenthal (Ed). *Jazzways*. Cincinnati, 1946. pp. 18–24, 103–04. (Hist)
1203. Cuthbert, Clifton. *The Robbed Heart*. New York: L. B. Fischer, 1945. 219 pp. (Fict)
1204. D. J. 'For Better or For Worse," *Musical Digest*, V (Feb. 5, 1924), 15. (A & A)
1205. Dabinett, Ward. "Not Commercial," *in* Charles Harvey (Ed). *Jazz Parody*. London: Spearman, 1948. pp. 62–8. (Fict)
1206. DaCapo. "Jazz," *Musical News and Herald*, LVII (Oct. 4, 1924), 281. (A & A)
1207. Daems, Jacques F. "A Propos de In the Mood," *Hot Club Magazine*, 4 (Apr., 1946), 15. (Disc)
1208. — —. "Considerations Sur les Sections Rhythmiques," *Hot Club Magazine*, 22 (Dec. 1, 1947), 14–15. (Disc, Inst)
1209. — —. "Le Jazz et la Critique," *Hot Club Magazine*, 13 (Jan., 1946), 16. (A & A)
1210. Dahlgren, Claes. "Sweden Spawning Top Modern Jazzmen," *Down Beat*, XVII (Nov. 17, 1950), 3. (Geog)
1211. Dameron, Tadd. "The Case for Modern Music," *Record Changer*, VII (Feb., 1948), 5, 16. (A & A, Bop)
1212. Damon, S. Foster. "American Influence on Modern French Music," *Dial*, LXV (Aug. 15, 1918), 93–5. (J & C, Rag)
1213. Dana, Robert W. "Cab Calloway," New York *Herald Tribune*, Aug. 11, 1943, 14 : 4. (Pers)
1214. Dance, Stanley F. "The Emperor Montezuma, Mr. Jelly Lord, and Others," *Jazz Music*, II (Feb.-Mar., 1944), 117–18. (Disc)
1215. — —. "Towards Criteria," *Jazz Forum*, 1 (n. d.), 2–5. (Crit)
1216. — —. James Asman and Bill Kinnell (Eds). *Jazz Notebook*. Chilwell Notts., England: Jazz Appreciation Society, n. d. 24 pp.
1217. Daniels, Mike. "Musician of the Year: Artie Shaw," *Metronome*, LX (Jan., 1944), 18–20. (Pers)
1218. Dare, Alan D. "Care of Records," *Record Changer*, IX (Nov., 1950), 9, 12. (Disc)
1219. — —. "Some Notes on Use and History: Cornet and Trumpet," *Record Changer*, IX (Oct., 1950), 9. (Inst)

1220. Dare, Alan D. (with technical advice by C. S. Woodworth, IV). "The Relation of Phono-Pickups to Record Wear," *Record Changer*, VIII (Apr., 1949), 11. (Tech)

1221. —— and C. S. Woodworth, IV. "The Loudspeaker, Its Proper Function," *Record Changer*, VIII (Dec., 1949), 8, 19. (Tech)

1222. ——. "The Proper Application of Tone Controls," *Record Changer*, VIII (Oct., 1949), 11, 16. (Tech)

1223. ——. "The Relation of the Amplifier to Good Reproduction," *Record Changer*, VIII (June, 1949), 7. (Tech)

1224. Darrell, R. D. "All Quiet on the Western Jazz Front," *Disques*, III (Sept., 1932), 290–94. (A & A, Hist)

1225. ——. "Black Beauty," *Disques*, III (June, 1932), 152–61. (Disc, Pers)

1226. ——. "Jacob and Isaac (and Daniel)," *Disques*, III (Apr.. 1932), 64–8. (Pers)

1227. David, Hans Th. "Abschied vom Jazz," *Melos*, IX (Oct., 1930), 413–17. (A & A)

1228. David, Jean. *Le Jazz et Les Hommes d'Aujourd'hui*. Brussels: Editions de l'Onyx, 1946. 80 pp.

1229. Davies, Ron. "Lettre Ouverte aux Modernistes," *Hot Club Magazine*, 5 (May, 1946), 8–9. (Ork)
See: 1088; 1230.

1230. ——. "Nous Avons Encore Besoin d'Espoir," *Hot Club Magazine*, 8 (Aug., 1946), 11. (Pers)
See: 1088; 1229.

1231. ——. "Muggsy Spanier; Sa Vie et Ses Disques," *Hot Club Magazine*, 7 (July, 1946), 3–5; 8 (Aug., 1946), 3–5; 9 (Sept., 1946), 3–4; 10 (Oct., 1946), 3–4. (Disc, Pers)

1232. ——. "Clarence Williams; A Suggested Discography," *Jazzfinder*, I (June, 1948), 8–15; (July, 1948), ?; (Aug., 1948), 9–18. (Disc)

1233. Davison, Wild Bill. "Wild Bill Calls Tough 'Little Bludgeon Foot', Defends Old Jazzmen," *Down Beat*, XIV (Mar. 26, 1947), 11. (Gen)
See: 1595; 1597.

1234. Decsey, Ernst. "Jazz In Vienna," *Living Age*, CCCXXXIV (Mar. 1, 1928), 441–45. (J & O)

1235. Degrois, Andre. "De l'Evolution du Gout des Blancs Pour les Musiciens de Leur Race," *Hot Club Magazine*, 20 (Oct. 1, 1947), 11–12. (Gen, Pers)

1236. Deiro, Pietro. (Ed: Elvera Collins). "Swing Music in Accordian Playing," *Etude*, LX (July, 1942), 491, 495. (Inst, Sw)

1237. Deitch, Gene and George Avakian. *The Cat*. New York: Record Changer, 1948. 32 pp.

1238. De Jonge, H. "Harry James," *Jazz Hot*, IV (Oct.-Nov., 1938), 11. (Pers)

1239. Delage, Maurice. "La Musique de Jazz," *Revue Pleyel*, 31 (Apr., 1926), 18–20. (A & A)

1240. Delaunay, Charles. "As I See It," *Jazz Record*, 55 (May, 1947), 14–16. (Crit)

1241. ——. "An Attack on Critical Jabberwocky," *Record Changer*, VIII (Mar., 1949), 13–14. (Crit)
See: 1031; 1446.

1242. ——. *De La Vie et du Jazz*. Paris: Editions Hot Jazz, 1939. 95 pp. Reissued: Lausanne: Editions de l'Echiquier, c. 1947.

1243. ——. *Hot Discography*. Paris: Hot Jazz, 1936. 271 pp. Reprinted in 1938 and 1940 under same title. 1940 edition reprinted under same title, New York: Commodore Records, 1943. 416 pp. Reprinted as *Hot Discographie, 1943*. Paris: Collection du Hot Club de France, 1944. 538 pp. (Disc)

1244. ——. "Jazz Abroad: France," *Jazz Forum*, I (n. d.), 13–14. (Geog)

1245. ——. (Trans: Walter E. Schaap). "Jazz 1939," *Jazz Hot*, 31 (Apr.-May, 1939), 3–5. (A & A)

1246. Delaunay, Charles. "Jazz 1946," *Hot Club Magazine*, 2 (Feb., 1946), 9–10. (Gen)
1247. ——. (Eds: Walter E. Schaap and George Avakian). *New Hot Discography*. New York: Criterion, 1948. 608 pp. (Disc)
1248. Demeuldre, Leon. "Luis Russell," *Hot Club Magazine*, 21 (Nov. 1, 1947), 9. (Pers)
1249. ——. "Swing Drummers Blancs," *Hot Club Magazine*, 12 (Dec., 1946), 7. (Pers)
1250. ——. "Swing Drummers Noirs," *Hot Club Magazine*, 9 (Sept., 1946), 9, 11. (Pers)
1251. DeSantis, Tony. "Can't Make Loot on Jazz, Says Op," *Down Beat*, XVII (May 19, 1950), 3. (J & D)
1252. Desmond, John. "Making Catnip for the Hepcats," New York *Times*, June 20, 1943, VI, 16–17, 37. (Ork)
1253. Deutsch, Hermann. "Louis Armstrong," *Esquire*, IV (Oct., 1935), 70, 138. (Fict, Pers)
1254. Dexter, Bruce. "Bunny Berigan: Giant of the Swing Era," *Record Changer*, VIII (Nov., 1949), 7, 26. (Pers)
1255. Dexter, Dave, Jr. "Alto Comes Back; Tenor Men Take a Back Seat," *Down Beat*, VII (May 15, 1940), 19. (Inst)
1256. ——. "Meyer Davis Made Dance Music a 'Big Business'," *Down Beat*, VIII (Mar. 1, 1941), 8–9, 11. (Pers)
1257. ——. "J. Dorsey, Bing Top 1941 Record Peddlers," *Down Beat*, VIII (Dec. 15, 1941), 6, 35. (Disc)
1258. ——. "'I Didn't Want to Set the World on Fire'—Powell," *Music and Rhythm*, II (Dec., 1941), 30. (Pers)
1259. ——. "'I Want to Interpret, Not Improvise'—Scott," *Down Beat*, VII (Sept. 1, 1940), 6. (Ork)
1260. ——. *Jazz Cavalcade*. New York: Criterion, 1946. 258 pp.
1261. ——. "Jump for Joy!" *Music and Rhythm*, II (Nov., 1941), 20–1. (Crit)
1262. ——. "Men Behind the Bands: Bill Borden," *Down Beat*, VIII (June 1, 1941), 9. (Pers)
1263. ——. "Men Behind the Bands: Jimmy Dale," *Down Beat*, IX (Feb. 15, 1942), 17. (Pers)
1264. ——. "Men Behind the Bands: Bob Mersey," *Down Beat*, IX (Jan. 1, 1942), 17. (Pers)
1265. ——. "Moten and Lee Are Patron Saints of Kansas City Jazz," *Down Beat*, VIII (Jan. 1, 1941), 8, 18; (Jan. 15, 1941), 8, 13. Pt. II entitled "Kaycee Local 627 Prospered During 1930 Boom Days." (KC, Ork, Pers)
1266. ——. "Story of Emmet Hardy Told by New Orleans Musicians," *Down Beat*, VII (May 15, 1940), 8–9, 11; (June 1, 1940), 8–9. Pt. II entitled "Hardy Welcomed Death by Playing the Blues." (Pers)
1267. ——. "The Year's Best Records," *Down Beat*, IX (Jan. 1, 1942) 14. (Disc)
1268. ——. "Your Band Can Make Money If Your Manager Knows How," *Music and Rhythm*, I (Nov., 1940), 84–6. (Pers)
1269. Dick, Gretchen. "American Ideas Adopted at Paris Theatres," *Musical Leader*, XLVI (Aug. 9, 1923), 123–24. (Geog)
1270. Dickerson, Reed. "Hot Music: Rediscovering Jazz," *Harper's*, CLXXII (Apr., 1936), 567–74. (A & A)
1271. Doc. "N. Clark Jazz Will Lose Its 'King' When Lee Goes," *Down Beat*, XV (Dec. 15, 1948), 3. (Pers)
1272. Dodge, Roger Pryor. "Louis Armstrong," *Jazz* (New York), I (Dec., 1943), 5. (A & A, Pers)
1273. ——. "Harpsichords and Jazz Trumpets," *Hound and Horn*, VII (July–Sept., 1934), 587–608. Reprinted: Ralph de Toledano (Ed). *Frontiers of Jazz*. New York: Oliver Durrell, 1947. pp. 13–31. (A & A)

1274. Dodge, Roger Pryor. "The Hot Solo," *Atlantic Monthly*, CLXXIV (July, 1944), 120. (A & A)
1275. ——. "Identification," *Jazz* (New York), I (June, 1942), 27–9. (A & A)
1276. ——. "Negro Jazz," *Dancing Times*, n. s. 229 (Oct., 1929), 32–5. (A & A)
1277. ——. "The Psychology of the Hot Solo," *Jazz Forum*, I (n. d.), 7–9. (A & A)
1278. Dor, Nicolas. "A la Recherche du Jazz Perdu," *Hot Club Magazine*, 4 (Apr., 1946), 11. (Gen)
1279. Dorsey, Jimmy. "My Twelve Favorite Altomen," *Music and Rhythm*, II (Sept., 1941), 12–13. (Pers)
1280. Dorsey, Tommy. "Tommy Dorsey on Trombonists," *Metronome*, LIX (Oct., 1943), 28. (Pers)
1281. ——. "The Ten Greatest Trombone Players," *Music and Rhythm*, II (June, 1942), 14. (Pers)
1282. Douglas, Gilbert. *Lost Chords, the Diverting Story of American Popular Songs.* Garden City: Doubleday, Doran, 1942. 377 pp.
1283. Douglas, Paula. "Nichols Pennies and Jazz," *Record Changer*, IX (Apr., 1950), 5, 18. (Ork)
1284. Douglass, Archie. "Mrs. Hopkins Pays A Call," *in* Charles Harvey (Ed). *Jazz Parody.* London: Spearman, 1948. pp. 86–91. (Fict)
1285. Downes, Olin. "An American Composer," *Musical Quarterly*, IV (Jan., 1918), 23–36. (Rag)
1286. ——. "American Popular Music in Europe," New York *Times*, Aug. 1, 1926, VII, 5 : 1. (A & A, Pers)
1287. ——. "Concerning 'Modern American Music'," New York *Times*, Nov. 23, 1924, VIII, 6 : 1. (Crit)
1288. ——. "A Concert of Jazz," New York *Times*, Feb. 13, 1924, 16 : 1. (Crit)
1289. ——. "Goodman Is Heard In 'Swing' Concert," New York *Times*, Jan. 17, 1938, 11 : 4. (Crit)
See: 308.
1290. ——. "A Piano Concerto in the Vernacular to Have Its Day With Damrosch," New York *Times*, Nov. 29, 1925, VIII, 6 : 1. (J & C)
1291. ——. "A Study of Jazz," New York *Times*, May 21, 1939, X 5 : 1. (Rev)
1292. ——. "Truths About Composers—More Discussion of Jazz," New York *Times*, Oct. 3, 1926, VIII, 6 : 1. (A & A)
See: 15; 17; 165; 168; 233; 558; 559; 560; 2159; 2337; 3210.
1293. Downs, Judy. "Bud Wilson: Trombone In a Million," *Jazz Quarterly*, II (Summer, 1944), 8–10, 23–4. (Pers)
1294. Downs, Karl E. "Duke Ellington; Aristocrat of Jazz," *in* Karl E. Downs. *Meet the Negro.* Pasadena: Login, 1943. pp. 82–3. (Pers)
1295. ——. "Lena Horne; Hollywood Star," *in* Karl E. Downs. *Meet the Negro.* Pasadena: Login, 1943. pp. 130–31. (Pers)
1296. ——. "Jimmy Mundy; Whiteman Arranger," *in* Karl E. Downs. *Meet the Negro.* Pasadena: Login, 1943. pp. 122–23. (Pers)
1297. Drew, Peter. "Bertha's Blues," *Record Changer*, VII (Apr., 1948), 11. (Pers)
1298. ——. "The Castle Jazz Band," *Record Changer*, VII (Apr., 1949), 10. (Ork)
1299. ——. "Inside Pee Wee," *Record Changer*, IX (Feb., 1950), 5. (Pers)
1300. ——. "Jazz at Tanglewood," *Record Changer*, IX (Oct., 1950), 6. (Ed)
1301. ——. "The Professional Viewpoint," *Record Changer*, IX (July-Aug., 1950), 31, 46, 47. (A & A, Pers)
1302. Drexel, Constance. "Bananas Across the Sea," *Collier's*, LXXIII (Mar. 1, 1924), 31. (Geog)
1303. Dufour, Elise and Edgcumb Pinchon. "The Song of the Body," *Oeverland*, LXXXIII (Feb., 1925), 50–3, 90–1; (Mar., 1925), 107–08, 129. Pt. II entitled "Jazz—The Bad Genius." (J & D)

1304. Dugan, James. "Jazz Archives," *New Masses*, XXXII (Aug. 15, 1939), 28. (Disc)
1305. — —. "Old Man Jiver," *Collier's*, CXVII (Feb. 9, 1946), 27, 51–2. (Pers)
1306. Dunlap, Orrin E., Jr. "Ragtime to Radio," New York *Times*, Apr. 25, 1937, X, 12 : 1. (Hist, Rad)
1307. — —. "Seen From a Podium," New York *Times*, Mar. 26, 1939, X, 12 : 2. (A & A, Sw)
1308. Durand, Andre. "The Hot Club Quintet," *Swing Music*, 14 (Autumn, 1936), 28–9. (Ork)
1309. Dutton, William S. "We've Got Rhythm," *American Magazine*, CXIX (Mar., 1935), 52–3, 126–28. (Ork)
1310. Ebel, Bud. "'Old Wolverines Couldn't Read So I Pulled Out'," *Down Beat*, IX (June 15, 1942), 5. (Ork)
1311. Edwards, Eddie. "Once Upon a Time," *Jazz Record*, 55 (May, 1947), 5–6, 34. (Hist)
1312. Edwards, Paul. *Notions Elementaires Sur le Jazz*. Belgium: 1940. 75 pp.
1313. Egan, Jack. "Kenton Plan Seeks Spots Exclusively for Modern Jazz," *Down Beat*, XV (Dec. 15, 1948), 1, 5. (Gen)
1314. — —. "New Curricula Covers Biz, But Not the Vital School of Hard Knocks," *Down Beat*, XVI (July 29, 1949), 18. (Ed)
1315. — —. "Talk of Wee-Hour Band Travel Ban Causes Dither," *Down Beat*, XV (Aug. 25, 1948), 1. (Gen)
1316. — —. "Webster in Royal Return to Duke," *Down Beat*, XV (Dec. 1, 1948), 1. (Crit)
1317. Egg, Bernhard. *Jazz-Fremdwörterbuch*. Leipzig: W. Ehrler, 1927. 47 pp.
1318. Ehrlich, Evelyn. "Carnegie Concert Has Below Par Ellington," *Down Beat*, XIII (Jan. 28, 1946), 3. (Crit)
1319. — —. "Here's News Capsule of Music World for 1945," *Down Beat*, XIII (Jan. 1, 1946), 3. (Gen)
1320. Elbaum, Evalyn. "Billie Rogers Discusses Horns," *Down Beat*, X (Mar. 15, 1943), 12. (Pers)
1321. Eldridge, Roy. "Roy Eldridge on Trumpeters," *Metronome*, LIX (Oct., 1943), 27. (Pers)
1322. Eldridge, Thomas R. "Jazzing Classical Music," (lr) New York *Times*, Mar. 7, 1932, 16 : 7. (J & C)
1323. Eldridge, Zachary. "Comment on Swinging Bach," New York *Times*, Nov. 6, 1938, IX, 8 : 2. (J & C).
      See: 227; 484; 1461.
1324. Ellington, Duke. "By Duke Ellington," *Needle*, I (July, 1944), 10. (Crit)
      See: 1325; 2207; 2701.
1325. — —. "Defense of Jazz," *American Mercury*, LVIII (Jan., 1944), 124. (A & A)
      See: 1324; 2207; 2701.
1326. — —. "Duke Ellington on Arrangers," *Metronome*, LIX (Oct., 1943), 35. (Pers)
1327. — —. (Ed. Gunnar Asklund). "Interpretations in Jazz," *Etude*, LXV (Mar., 1947), 134, 172. (A & A)
1328. Elliot, Gilbert, Jr. "The Doughboy Carries His Music With Him," *New Music Review*, XVIII (Aug., 1919), 236–39. (Gen)
1329. Ellis, Norman. *Instrumentation and Arranging for the Radio and Dance Orchestra*. New York: Roell, 1936. 209 pp.
1330. Emge, Charles. "Band Tieups Next TV Trend?" *Down Beat*, XVII (Apr. 21, 1950), 6. (Rad)
1331. — —. "Battlefront Trip Easier Than a U.S. One-Nighter Tour: Brown," *Down Beat*, XVII (Dec. 15, 1950), 2. (Pers)
1332. — —. "Billy, Shearing Opener Hits Jackpot," *Down Beat*, XVII (Oct. 20, 1950), 1, 19. (Crit, Ork, Pers)

1333. Emge, Charles. "Jimmy Blanton Takes Last Ride," *Down Beat*, IX (Aug. 15, 1942), 12. (Pers)

1334. —— ——. "Dixie Jubilee Once More Proves Boxoffice Bonanza," *Down Beat*, XVII (Nov. 17, 1950), 1, 13. (Crit, Dix)

1335. —— ——. "Good Jazz Film Will Be Made When Story Found," *Down Beat*, XVII (Jan. 27, 1950), 8. (Rad)

1336. —— ——. "Gray Palladium Date to Affect West Coast's Dance Biz Future," *Down Beat*, XVII (Aug. 25, 1950), 1. (Crit, Ork)
See: 266.

1337. —— ——. "Jazz Names Spotted in Studio Orchestras," *Down Beat*, XV (Feb. 25, 1948), 8. (Pers)

1338. —— ——. "Kenton to Debut in 'Workshop Concert'," *Down Beat*, XVII (Jan. 13, 1950), 1. (Ork)

1339. —— ——. "Kenton Unveils Ork at Preview Concert," *Down Beat*, XVII (Mar., 1950), 1, 16. (Crit, Ork)

1340. —— ——. "Kenton Winds Up 1st 'Innovations' Tour," *Down Beat*, XVII (July 14, 1950), 5. (Crit, Pers)

1341. —— ——. "'Me A Showman?—Hell, Yes!'—Krupa," *Music and Rhythm*, II (Jan 1942), 20, 48. (Pers)

1342. —— —-. "Red Norvo Producing Fine Music With New Trio," *Down Beat*, XVII (Aug. 11, 1950), 1, 19. (Ork, Pers)

1343. —— ——. "Seriously Ill, Jelly Roll Fights an Unfriendly World," *Down Beat*, VIII (Apr. 1, 1941), 13. (Pers)

1344. —— ——. "Showing of Jazz Movies Arouses Big Storm in L. A.," *Down Beat*, XVII (Nov. 17, 1950), 9. (Rad)

1345. —— ——. "Thornhill Cold to Video Programs from Ballrooms," *Down Beat*, XVII (June 2, 1950), 4. (Rad)

1346. —— ——. "Venuti Part of 'Golden Era' of Jazz," *Down Beat*, XVII (Dec. 1, 1950), 3. (Hist, Pers)

1347. —— ——. "'YMWH' Film Has Pretty Incoherent Slant on Jazz," *Down Beat*, XVII (Mar. 10, 1950), 15. (Rad)

1348. Enefer, Douglas S. *Jazz In Black and White*. London: Alliance, 1945. 63 pp.

1349. Engel, Carl. "Jazz," in Carl Engel. *Discords Mingled*. New York: Alfred A. Knopf, 1931. pp. 140–50. (A & A)

1350. —— ——. "Jazz: A Musical Discussion," *Atlantic Monthly*, CXXX (Aug., 1922), 182–89. Reprinted: Herbert S. Mallory. *Backgrounds of Book Reviewing*. Ann Arbor: George Wahr, 1931. pp. 343–51. (A & A)
See: 351.

1351. —— ——. "Jazz, In the Proper Light," *Journal of Proceedings of the Fifteenth Annual Meeting of the Music Supervisors' National Conference*, Mar. 20–24, 1922. pp. 137–44. (A & A)

1352. —— ——. "Views and Reviews," *Musical Quarterly*, XII (Apr., 1926), 306. (Hist)

1353. Ertegun, Nesuhi. "Benny Carter," *Record Changer*, VII (May, 1948), 5–6. (Pers)

1354. —— ——. "New Orleans on the Air," *Jazz Record*, 20 (May, 1944), 6–7. (Rad)

1355. Esterre, Neville d'. "A Syncopated Apology," *British Musician*, IV (Sept., 1928), 174–77; (Oct., 1928), 202–04. (Gen)

1356. Estes, Stephen A. "The 'New' Jazz," *Music Lover's Magazine*, I (Sept., 1922), 7. (J & C)

1357. Evans, C. S. "Life and Letters: Jazz Poetry," *Music Teacher*, II (Apr., 1923), 391. (Gen)

1358. Evans, Paul (Doc). "Dixieland, Twin City Style," *Jazz Record*, 35 (Aug., 1945), 10–11, 14. (Hist)

1359. Evans, Robert. "The Jazz Age," in Charles Harvey (Ed). *Jazz Parody*. London: Spearman, 1948. pp. 27–31. (Fict)

1360. Evans, Robert. "There's A Great Day," *in* Chalres Harvey (Ed). *Jazz Parody*. London: Spearman 1948. pp., 77–85. (Fict)

1361. Ewen, David. *Men of Popular Music*. Chicago: Ziff-Davis, 1944. 213 pp. New York: Editions for the Armed Services, 1944. 192 pp.

1362. ——. *The Story of George Gershwin*. New York: Holt, 1943. 211 pp. Reprinted as: *George Gershwin*. Buenos Aires: Editorial Estuardo, 1947. 249 pp. (Pers)

1363. ——. "What Is This Thing Called Jazz?" *Musical Courier*, CIV (Feb. 20, 1932), 7, 30. (A & A, Hist)

1364. Ewing, Annemarie. *Little Gate*. New York: Rinehart, 1947. 278 pp. (Fict)

1365. Exideuil, P. d'. "Adieu a Louis Armstrong," *Europe Nouvelle*, XVI (Apr. 22, 1933), 371–2. (A & A)

1366. F. R. S. "Jazz and German Musicians," *Jacobs' Orchestra Monthly*, XV (Mar., 1924), 30–1. (Geog)

1367. Fairchild, Leslie. "Horse-Sense and Horse-Play in Music," *Outlook*, CXXXIX (Jan. 14, 1925), 59–60. (A & A, Hist, Infl)

1368. Farber, Manny. "New Orleans Survival," *New Republic*, CX (Feb. 21, 1944), 242–43. (A & A, Disc, Ork, Pers)

1369. Farjeon, Harry. "Rag-Time," *Musical Times*, LXV (Sept., 1924), 795–97. (Rag)

1370. ——. "Rag-Time," *New Music Review and Church Music Review*, XXIII (Nov., 1924), 513–15. (J & C, Rag)

1371. Farmer, Harcourt. "The March Funebre of 'Jazz'," *Musical America*, XXXII (June 19, 1920), 42. (A & A)

1372. Farmer, Henry George. "The Arab Influence on Music in the Western Sudan, Including References to Modern Jazz," *Musical Standard*, XXIV (Nov. 15, 1924), 158–59. (A & A)

1373. Farnsworth, Ken. "Specht's 'Jass' Played a Big Part in Progress of Swing," *Down Beat*, VII (Sept. 1, 1940), 7. (Hist, Pers)

1374. Farres, Enrique. "El Jazz, la Musica Progresista y el Publica," *Club de Ritmo*, 41 (Sept., 1949), 5. (A & A, Bop)

1375. Faulkner, Anne Shaw. "Does Jazz Put the Sin in Syncopation?" *Ladies' Home Journal*, XXXVIII (Aug., 1921), 16, 34. (A & A, Infl, J & D)

1376. Feather, Leonard G. "All-American Jazz Ballot, 1945," *Esquire*, XXIII (Feb., 1945), 28–9, 102. (Poll)

1377. ——. "'Be-Bop??!!—Man, We Called It Kloop-Mop!!'," *Metronome*, LXIII (Apr., 1947), 21, 44–5. (Bop, Pers)

1378. ——. "Boniface Faces the Future," *Metronome*, LXIII (July, 1947), 15, 42. (Pers)

1379. ——. "Esquire's All-American Jazz Band, 1946," *Esquire*, XXV (Feb., 1946), 56–9. (Poll)

1380. ——. "Europe Goes Dizzy," *Metronome*, LXIV (May, 1948), 18–19, 35. (Ork)

1381. ——. "Facts About Max," *Metronome*, LXIV (Nov., 1948), 26–8. (Pers)

1382. ——. "Leonard Feather Says..." *Metronome*, LX (Jan., 1944), 48. (Crit) *See*: 2826.

1383. ——. "Goffin: He Knocks Himself Out On History, Ichthyology and Jazz, Works With the Underground and Takes the A Train," *Metronome*, LX (Feb., 1944), 18, 31. (Pers)

1384. ——. "Heil Hammond," *Jazz* (New York), I, no. 8 (n. d.), 14, 20. (Crit, Pers) *See*: 1670; 3061.

1385. ——. *Inside Be-Bop*. New York: J. J. Robbins, 1949. 103 pp. (Bop)

1386. ——. "Javanese Jive Man," *Metronome*, LIX (Dec., 1943), 16, 29. (Pers)

1387. ——. "Jazz in Europe: Slow But Pure," *Metronome*, LIX (Oct., 1943), 46–7. (Geog)

1388. ——. "Jazz Is Where You Find It," *Esquire*, XXI (Feb., 1944), 35, 129–30. (A & A, Sw)

1389. Feather, Leonhard G. "Lombardo Grooves Louis!" *Metronome*, LXV (Sept., 1949), 18. (Pers)
1390. —— —. "Louis: King of the Zulus," *Melody Maker*, XXV (Mar. 26, 1949), 3. (Pers)
   See: 18; 28; 495; 1490; 2085.
1391. —— —. "Men Behind the Bands: William Moore, Jr.," *Down Beat*, VIII (Feb. 15, 1941), 12. (Pers)
1392. —— —. "Men Behind the Bands: Jiggs Noble," *Down Beat*, VII (Oct. 15, 1940), 7. (Pers)
1393. —— —. "Men Behind the Bands: Eddie Sauter," *Down Beat*, VII (Mar. 1, 1940), 17. (Pers)
1394. —— —. "Men Behind the Bands: Lou Singer," *Down Beat*, VIII (Nov. 15, 1941), 19. (Pers)
1395. —— —. "New Horns For Old," *in* Barry Ulanov and George Simon (Eds). *Jazz 1950*. New York: Metronome, 1950. pp. 23–6. (Inst)
1396. —— —. "Pettiford-of-the-Month," *Metronome*, LIX (Nov., 1943), 18. (Pers)
1397. —— —. "Pops Pops Top on Sloppy Bop," *Metronome*, LXV (Oct., 1949), 18, 25. (Bop)
1398. —— —. "The Rhythm Section," *Esquire*, XXV (Feb., 1946), 102, 145. (Gen)
   See: 1399; 1400; 1410; 2262; 2263; 2264; 2877.
1399. —— —. "The Rhythm Section: Dizzy, 21st Century Gabriel," *Esquire*, XXIV (Oct., 1945), 90–1. (Bop, Pers)
   See: 1398; 1400; 1410; 2262; 2263; 2264; 2877.
1400. —— —. "The Rhythm Section: Red Norvo, Hot Prototype," *Esquire*, XXIV (Aug., 1945), 96–7. (Pers)
   See: 1398; 1399; 1410; 2262; 2263; 2264; 2877.
1401. —— —. "The Street Comes Back to Charlie Ventura," *Metronome*, LXIII (May, 1947), 20, 48–9. (Pers)
1402. —— —. "Tempo Di Jazz," *Musician*, XLVI (May, 1941), 97; (June, 1941), 113; (July-Aug., 1941), 129; (Sept., 1941), 144; (Oct., 1941), 162; (Nov., 1941), 178; (Dec., 1941), 192; XLVII (Jan., 1942), 12; (Feb., 1942), 28; (Mar., 1942), 45; (Apr., 1942), 59; (May-June, 1942), 76; (July, 1942), 99; (Aug., 1942), 124; (Sept.-Oct., 1942), 144; (Dec., 1942), 172. (A & A)
1403. —— —. "Three Years Behind the Blindfold," *Metronome*, LXV (Nov., 1949), 28–9, 56–7. (Disc)
1404. —— —. "Trumpeter's Jubilee," New York *Times*, Oct. 26, 1941, IX, 6: 5–6. (Pers)
1405. —— —. "Sara Vaughan," *Metronome*, LXII (July, 1946), 21, 48–9. (Pers)
1406. —— —. "What's Happened to Benny Goodman?" *Esquire*, XXV (Apr., 1946), 100, 179–80. (A & A, Pers)
1407. —— —. "When Bill Harasses His Horn the Sound Is Uncommon, A Real Phenomenon," *Metronome*, LXI (Dec., 1945), 27, 45. (Pers)
1408. —— —. "Woody Was A Natural," *Metronome*, LXI (Dec., 1945), 23–5. (Pers)
1409. —— —. "Yardbird Flies Home," *Metronome*, LXIII (Aug., 1947), 14, 43–4. (Pers)
1410. —— —, and Paul Eduard Miller. "The Rhythm Section," *Esquire*, XXI–XXIV (June, 1944–Dec., 1945), (Gen)
   See: 1398; 1399; 1400; 2262; 2263; 2264; 2877.
1411. Featheringill, Evelyn. "The Harlem Hamfats," *Jazz Quarterly*, II (Summer, 1944), 4–7, 20–2. (Ork, Pers)
1412. Fell, John L. "Four Years in 4/4," *Saturday Review of Literature*, XXXIII (Aug. 26, 1950), 41–2. (Disc)
1413. Fensterwald, Ralph. "Smith's Fabulous Pork Chop," *Jazz Record*, 58 (Sept., 1947), 12–13. (Pers)
1414. Ferand, Ernst Thomas. *Die Improvisation In der Musik*. Zürich: Rheinverlag, 1938. 464 pp.

1415. Ferguson, Otis. "Breakfast Dance, In Harlem," *New Republic*, LXXXVI (Feb. 12, 1936), 15–16. (Gen, Hist)
1416. —— ——. "John Hammond," *H. R. S. Society Rag*, 2 (Sept., 1938), 1–7. (Pers)
1417. —— ——. "Jazz At Random," *New Republic*, CIV (Feb. 24, 1941), 277–78. (Gen)
1418. —— ——. "The Man With the Blues in His Heart," *New Republic*, XCI (July 14, 1937), 277–79. (Pers)
1419. —— ——. "Man... You're Jiving Me Crazy," *H. R. S. Society Rag*, 3 (Jan., 1939), 8–10. (A & A, Crit, Lang)
1420. —— ——. "A Mild Ribbing," (lr) *New Republic*, LXXXVI (Mar. 11, 1936), 140. (Gen)
       See: 2361.
1421. —— ——. "The Piano in the Band," *New Republic*, XCIII (Nov. 24, 1937), 68–70. Reprinted: Ralph de Toledano (Ed). *Frontiers of Jazz*. New York: Oliver Durrell, 1947. pp. 162–69. (Pers)
1422. —— ——. "Records; A Start on Jazz," *New Republic*, CVI (Feb. 9, 1942), 205–07. (Disc)
1423. —— ——. "Speaking of Jazz," *New Republic*, XCIX (Aug. 2, 1939), 363; C (Aug. 16, 1939), 48. (Rev)
1424. —— ——. "The Spirit of Jazz," *New Republic*, LXXXIX (Dec. 30, 1936), 269–71. (Ork, Pers)
1425. —— ——. "Young Man With a Horn," *New Republic*, LXXXVII (July 29, 1936), 354. (Pers)
1426. —— ——. "Young Man With a Horn Again," *New Republic*, CIII (Nov. 18, 1940), 693–95. (Pers)
1427. Ferroud, Pierre Octave. "L'Evolution du Jazz," *L'Edition Musicale Vivante*, II (Feb., 1929), 9–12; (Mar., 1929), 9–11; (Apr., 1929), 9–11. (A & A, Hist)
1428. Festissime. "In Praise of Jazz," *Irish Monthly*, LXII (Mar., 1934), 133–43. (A & A)
1429. Fillmore, Henry. *Henry Fillmore's Jazz Trombonist for Slide Trombone Bass Clef*. Cincinnati: Fillmore Music House, 1919.
1430. Filmer, Vic. *Vic Filmer's Guide to Buskers*. London: V. Filmer's Music Advice Bureau, 1944. 24 pp. 2nd Edition, 1944.
1431. —— ——. *Jive and Swing Dictionary*. Penzance, England, 1947. 20 pp. (Lang)
1432. Finck, Henry T. "Jazz—Lowbrow and Highbrow," *Etude*, XLII (Aug., 1924), 527–28. (A & A, J & C)
1433. Fingerman, Charles. "Jazz, the Imposter," *Crescendo*, XXIV (Oct., 1931), 14. (A & A)
*1444. Finkelstein, Sidney. *Jazz: A People's Music*. New York: Citadel, 1948. 278 pp.
1445. —— ——. "Jazz Reaches a Turning Point," *in* Orin Blackstone (Ed). *Jazzfinder '49*. New Orleans: Orin Blackstone, 1949. pp. 5–14. (A & A)
1446. —— ——. "Peace In the Ranks," *Record Changer*, VIII (Mar., 1949), 11–12. (Crit)
       See: 1030; 1241.
1447. —— ——. "The Relation of the Blues to Bop," *Record Changer*, VIII (Nov., 1949), 15–16. (A & A, Bl, Bop)
1448. Finlayson, H. Ross. "Reeds and Wind," *Esquire*, V (May, 1936), 119, 138. (Inst)
1449. Fischer, Peter. "Lionel Hampton," *in* George S. Rosenthal (Ed). *Jazzways*. Cincinnati, 1946. pp. 52–3. (Pers)
1450. Fischer, T. "Jazz-Band," *Deutsche Musiker-Zeitung*, LVI (Apr. 18, 1925), 385–86. (A & A)
1451. Flanagan, Ralph. "Flanagan Tosses Roses at Men Behind Scenes," *Down Beat*, XVII (May 19, 1950), 17. (Pers)

---

* Ten numbers have been inadvertently skipped between 1433 and 1444.

1452. Fleischmann, Hugo R. "The First Jazz Opera and Operetta," *Chesterian*, IX (Mar., 1928), 152–55. (J & O)
1453. Fletcher, George. "Jazz In Hollywood," *Record Changer*, VII (May, 1948), 14–15. (Gcog, Pic)
1454. — —. "Lu Watters' Yerba Buena Jazz Band," *Record Changer*, VII (Apr., 1948), 12–13. (Ork, Pic)
1455. Fletcher, Robert. "Big Sidney Catlett Says He Likes Snare Drum Best," *Music and Rhythm*, I (Apr., 1941), 74–5. (Pers)
1456. Fonollosa, Jose Maria. "El Jazz, Musica Sin Snobs," *Club de Ritmo*, 41 (Sept., 1949), 3. (A & A)
1457. Fouad, Pierre and Hugues Panassie. (Trans: Ian Munro Smyth). "Alix Combelle," *Jazz Hot*, III (Mar.-Apr., 1937), 8–9. (Pers)
1458. Fox, Charles. "'Got the World In a Jug, Lawd!'" *in* Charles Harvey (Ed). *Jazz Parody*. London: Spearman, 1948. pp. 99–110. (Fict)
1459. — —. "The Claude Hopkins Orchestra," *Jazz Forum*, 3 (Jan., 1947), 7–8, 9. (Ork)
1460. Fox-Strangways, A. H. "The Spirit of Jazz," *British Musician*, VII (June, 1931), 120–22. (A & A)
1461. Franco, Johan. "Against All 'Arrangements'," (lr) New York *Times*, Nov. 13, 1938, IX, 8 : 3. (J & C)
See: 227; 484; 1323.
1462. Frank, Stanley. "Now I Stash Me Down to Nod," *Esquire*, XXI (June, 1944), 53, 168–70. (Lang)
1463. Frank, Waldo. "Jazz and Folk Art," *New Republic*, XLIX (Dec. 1, 1926), 42–3. Reprinted: Waldo Frank. *In the American Jungle*. New York: Farrar and Rinehart, 1937. pp. 119–23. (A & A)
1464. Frankenstein, Alfred V. "Jazz Arrives at the Opera," *Review of Reviews*, LXXIX (Mar., 1929), 138, 140. (J & O)
1465. — —. *Syncopating Saxophones*. Chicago: R. O. Ballou, 1925. 103 pp.
1466. Frazier, George. "The All-Time All-Star Jazz Band," *Pageant*, V (Feb., 1950), 95–101. (Pers)
1467. — —. "The Banjo Is Dead! Why Isn't It Buried?" *Music and Rhythm*, II (June, 1942), 23, 27. (Inst)
1468. — —. "'Benny's New Band Is Too Much Like Benny's Old Band,'" *Down Beat*, VIII (Mar. 15, 1941), 6. (Crit)
1469. — —. "Crosby Band 'My Pet, But Dissipates Talent'," *Down Beat*, VIII (Aug. 15, 1941), 8. (Ork)
1470. — —. "Frazier Foams At the Mouth at Paying $1.50 for Sidney Bechet," *Down Beat*, VIII (May 15, 1941), 7. (Crit, Disc)
1471. — —. "Bobby Hackett Is A Great Cornet Player," *Music and Rhythm*, II (Jan., 1942), 27. (Pers)
1472. — —. "'Stan Kenton's Band Will Devastate 'Em and Nothing Can Be Done About It'," *Down Beat*, IX (Apr. 1, 1942), 9. (Crit, Ork)
1473. — —. "Andy Kirk Band Sends Me ..." *Down Beat*, VIII (Oct. 15, 1941), 13. (Ork)
1474. — —. "Norvo Unappreciated Genius—Frazier," *Down Beat*, VIII (Feb. 15, 1941), 6. (Pers)
1475. — —. "Swing Critics," *Jazz Hot*, 10 (July, 1936), 3–6. (Pers)
1476. — —. "Those Wonderful Early Days," *Music and Rhythm*, II (Oct., 1941), 42. (Hist)
1477. — —. "Why I Hate Glenn Miller's Music," *Music and Rhythm*, II (Mar., 1942), 7, 46, 48. (A & A)
1478. — —. "'You Can Have Kenton, I'll Take Muggsy Any Day'," *Down Beat*, IX (Feb. 1, 1942), 5. (A & A, Pers)

1479. Frederick, Lewis. "Why Glen Miller's Music Gets the Girls," *Liberty*, XVII (Oct. 26, 1940), 45–6. (Infl, Ork)

1480. Freedman, Marvin. "Black Music's On Top; White Jazz Stagnant," *Down Beat*, VII (Apr. 1, 1940), 7, 20. (A & A)

1481. —— ——. "Wingy Declares: 'Musicians Today Are Just Kidding'," *Down Beat*, VII (Oct. 15, 1940), 8. (Pers)

1482. Freeman, Don. "Big City Blues," *PM Magazine*, May 9, 1943, 14 : 1–4, 15 : 1–4. (Fict)

1483. —— ——. "'I'll Lead Strings in My New Band,' Says Barnet," *Down Beat*, XVII (Dec. 29, 1950), 1. (Pers)

1484. Freese, Myron V. "What Jazz Has Done to the Fretted Instruments," *Cadenza*, XXXI (Feb., 1924), 3–7. (Infl)

1485. Fry, Alderson Francis, Max Kaplan and William C. Love. *Who's Who In Jazz Collecting*. Nashville: Hemphill, 1942. 52 pp.

1486. Fulling, Virgil. "Amateur Night on Beale Street," *Scribner's*, CI (May, 1937), 58–61. Abr: *Readers' Digest*, XXX (June, 1937), 79–81. (Gen)

1487. Fulton, Jack. "Swing: Agent of Peace," (lr) New York *Times*, Oct. 16, 1938, IV, 9 : 7. (Infl)

1488. Furness, Clement. "Monotonous Musical Fare," New York *Times*, Jan. 6, 1927, 28 : 7. (Gen)

1489. Gabler, Milt. "Hot Renaissance of Dixieland Jazz," New York *Times Magazine*, Sept. 24, 1950, 26–7, 38. (Dix)

1490. Gagliano, Nick. "King Louis' Triumph Tempered," *Down Beat*, XVI (Apr. 8, 1949), 18.
See: 18; 28; 495; 1820; 2085.

1491. Galpin, Benjamin E. "'Pep' In Music," *Etude*, LIV (Nov., 1936), 686. (Gen)

1492. Ganfield, Jane. *Books and Periodicals On Jazz From 1926 to 1932*. Unpublished MS, New York Public Library, 1933. 11 pp. (Bibl)

1493. Garbett, Arthur S. "Why You Like Jazz," *Sunset*, LII (Mar., 1924), 21–3, 62–4. (A & A)

1494. Garceau, Phil. "The Price of Swing," *in* Charles Harvey (Ed). *Jazz Parody*. London: Spearman, 1948. pp. 69–76. (Fict)

1495. Gardner, Martin. "The Devil and the Trombone," *Record Changer*, VII (May, 1948), 10. (Fict)

1496. —— ——. "The Trouble With Trombones," *Record Changer*, VII (Oct., 1948), 10. (Fict)

1497. Gardner, Paul. "Jazz in Iceland Nice and Icy," *Metronome*, LX (Jan., 1944), 47. (Geog)

1498. Garroway, Dave. "Everyone Owes Debt to Louis, Says Garroway," *Down Beat*, XVII (July 14, 1950), 1, 19. (Pers)

1499. Gates, W. F. "Ethiopian Syncopation—the Decline of Ragtime," *Musician*, VII (Oct., 1902), 341. (Rag)

1500. Gautier, Madeleine. (Trans: Ian Munro-Smyth). "Notes Sur l'Improvisation Collective," *Jazz Hot*, 8 (May, 1936), 7. (A & A)

1501. —— ——. (Trans: Walter E. Schaap). "Bessie Smith," *Jazz Hot*, 22 (Dec.-Jan., 1937/38), 3, 5. (Pers)

1502. —— ——. (Trans: Ian Munro Smyth). "Swing Bassistes," *Jazz Hot*, 12 (Nov., 1936), 9–10. (Pers)

1503. —— ——. (Trans: Walter E. Schaap). "'Fats' Waller," *Jazz Hot*, 32 (July-Aug., 1939), 11. (Pers)

1504. Gayer, Dixon. "Chicago, Chicago ..." *Metronome*, LIX (Oct., 1943), 37–8. (Chi, Hist)

1505. —— ——. "'Chicago Style All Bunk Bud Freeman Asserts, Ain't No Such Animal'," *Down Beat*, IX (Dec. 1, 1942), 4. (Chi)
See: 1509.

1506. Gayer, Dixon. "Gotta Feel the Blues To Play 'Em, Asserts T-Bone," *Down Beat*, IX (Oct. 15, 1942), 5. (Bl, Pers)
1507. ———. "Meet Mr. Moore," *Ebony*, I (Dec., 1945), 40–5. (Pers, Pic)
1508. ———. "Strings Are the Bunk, Says Beat's New Critic," *Down Beat*, IX (Aug. 15, 1942), 4. (Inst)
1509. ———. "There Is a Chicago Style!—Mares," *Down Beat*, X (Feb. 15, 1943), 4. (Chi)
See: 1505.
1510. ———. "Whom Is Roger Telling About Jazz?" *Down Beat*, IX (Sept. 15, 1942), 23. (A & A)
See: 2926.
1511. Gaze, Richard and Dorothy Gaze. (Ed: William H. Miller). *George Brunies: His Story.* Melbourne: William H. Miller, 1946. 8 pp. (Pers)
1512. Gee, John (Ed). *That's A Plenty.* Hemel, Hempstead, Herts.: Society for Jazz Appreciation in the Younger Generation, 1945. 32 pp.
1513. ———. *Waller and Johnson.* Hemel, Hempstead, Herts.: Society for Jazz Appreciation in the Younger Generation, 1945. 24 pp. (Pers)
1514. ——— and Michael Wadsley. *Jazzography.* Tring, Herts.: Society for Jazz Appreciation in the Younger Generation, 1944. 24 pp.
1515. Gerigk, Herbert. "Was Ist Mit der Jazzmusik?" *Die Musik*, XXX (July, 1938), 686. (Gen)
1516. Gershwin, George. "The Composer in the Machine Age," *in* Olivier M. Sayler. *Revolt in the Arts.* New York: Brentano's, 1930. pp. 264–69. (J & C)
1517. ———. "Does Jazz Belong to Art?" *Singing*, I (July, 1926), 13–14. (A & A)
See: 1518; 1987.
1518. ———. "Mr. Gershwin Replies to Mr. Kramer," *Singing*, I (Oct.,1926),17–18. (A & A)
See: 1517; 1987.
1519. ———. "The Relation of Jazz to American Music," *in* Henry Cowell (Ed). *American Composers on American Music.* Stanford: Stanford University Press, 1933. pp. 186–87. Reprinted: Elie Siegmeister. *The Music Lover's Handbook.* New York: William Morrow, 1943. pp. 728–29. (A & A)
1520. ———. "When We Have Jazz Opera," *Musical Canada*, VI (Oct., 1925), 13–14. (J & C, J & O)
1521. Gibbons, Frank J. "Pre-Jazz, Jazz, Post-Jazz," *Metronome*, XXXIX (Sept., 1923), 81, 88, 155. (A & A, Hist)
1522. Gilbert, Gama. "Higher Soars the Swing Fever," New York *Times*, Aug. 14, 1938, VII, 6–7, 19. (Lang, Sw)
See: 725; 1607.
1523. ———. "Swing," New York *Times*, Nov. 19, 1939, VII, 14, 19. (A & A, Hist, Sw)
1524. ———. "Swing: What Is It?" New York *Times*, Sept. 5, 1937, X, 5:1. (A & A, Hist, Sw)
1525. ———. "Swing It! And Even In a Temple of Music," New York *Times*, Jan. 16, 1938, VIII, 7. (A & A, Hist, Sw)
1526. Gilbert, Henry F. "Concerning Jazz," *New Music Review*, XXI (Dec., 1922), 438–41. (A & A)
1527. ———. "Concerning the Jazz Question," *Etude*, LIII (Feb., 1935), 74. (A & A)
1528. Gilbert, Will G. *Jazzmuziek.* 's-Gravenhage: J. Philip Kruseman, 1939. 116 pp. (with C. Poustochkine)
1529. Giles, Richard Y. "Jazz Comes of Age," *Scholastic*, XXVII (Oct. 19, 1935), 7–8. (Hist, Inst)
1530. Gillespie, James F. with Wesley Stout. "Hot Music," *Saturday Evening Post*, CCIV (Mar. 19, 1932), 10–11, 83, 86, 88. (Hist, Ork)

1531. Gillespie, Kyrle. "Jazz Interest Increased in Wartime Britain," *Metronome*, LVIII (Feb., 1942), 24, 44. (Geog)

1532. Gistucci, Paul. "Autour Du Jazz," *Guide du Concert*, XII (Feb. 12, 1926), 521. (A & A)

1533. Gleason, Ralph J. "'Basie Will Always Have a Swinging Band'," *Down Beat*, XVII (Nov. 17, 1950), 1, 2. (Ork, Pers)

1534. ——. "Biz Needs New Personal Managers, Says Christy," *Down Beat*, XVII (Nov. 3, 1950), 7. (Gen, Pers)

1535. ——. "Bunk's An Amazing Story," *Down Beat*, XVI (Aug. 26, 1949), 6–7. (Pers)

1536. ——. "Dizzy Getting a Bad Deal From Music Biz; Gleason," *Down Beat*, XVII (Nov. 17, 1950), 14. (Pers)

1537. ——. "Frisco Dixiecats Rise in Protest Against Spanier," *Down Beat*, XVII (Dec. 15, 1950), 16. (Dix, Pers)

1538. ——. "Louis Bash Doesn't Blow Up Storm; Weather Does," *Down Beat*, XVII (Feb. 24, 1950), 18. (Crit, Ork)

1539. ——. "A Short Analysis of Hot Jazz Record Collecting," *Hobbies*, XLVI (May, 1941), 35–6. (Disc)

1540. ——. "What Are They Doin' to Satchmo?" *Down Beat*, XIV (Sept. 24, 1947), 7. (Disc, Ork)

1541. ——. "Woody Reorganizes: To Go After Dance Crowd," *Down Beat*, XVII (May 5, 1950), 1. (J & D, Ork)

1542. Globus, Rudo S. "Pops," *Audio Engineering*, XXXIV (Jan., 1950), 26, 27, 33, 34, 35. (Disc, Tech)

1543. ——. "Pops," *Audio Engineering*, XXXIV (Feb., 1950), 22, 37, 38, 39. (Disc, Tech)

1544. ——. "Pops," *Audio Engineering*, XXXIV (June, 1950), 30, 39, 40, 41, 42, 43. (A & A, Disc, Ork)

1545. ——. "Pops," *Audio Engineering*, XXXIV (July, 1950), 30, 32, 33, 35. (Disc, Tech)

1546. ——. "Pops," *Audio Engineering*, XXXIV (Aug., 1950), 24, 33, 34, 35, 36. (Disc, Gen)

1547. ——. "Pops," *Audio Engineering*, XXXIV (Sept., 1950), 22, 40, 41. (A & A, J & C)

1548. ——. "Pops," *Audio Engineering*, XXXIV (Nov., 1950), 34, 66, 67, 68. (Gen, Tech)

1549. ——. "Pops," *Audio Engineering*, XXXIV (Dec., 1950), 36, 38, 39. (Pers, Tech)

1550. ——. "Pops; Recording Criteria," *Audio Engineering*, XXXIV (Mar., 1950), 28, 29, 30, 31, 39; (Apr., 1950), 38, 39, 40, 41, 42; (May, 1950), 24, 26, 28, 30, 31. (Disc, Tech)

1551. Goffin, Robert. *Louis Armstrong, Le Roi du Jazz*. Paris: Pierre Seghers, 1947. 304 pp. (Pers)

1552. ——. "L'Avenir du Jazz," *Hot Club Magazine*, 16 (Apr., 1947), 3–5. (Extrait de 'Histoire du Jazz'). (A & A)

1553. ——. "The Best Negro Jazz Orchestras," *in* Nancy Cunard (Ed). *Negro*. London: Wishart, 1934. pp. 291–93. (Ork, Pers)

1554. ——. "Bix at Lake Forest," *Esquire*, XXI (Mar., 1944), 59, 144–45. (Pers)

1555. ——. "Du Blues au Swing," *Hot Club Magazine*, 3 (Mar., 1946), 3, 5; 4 (Apr., 1946), 3, 5. (Extrait de 'Histoire du Jazz'). (Lang)

1556. ——. "Esquire's All-American Jazz Band," *Esquire*, XXI (Feb., 1944), 28–9. (Poll)

1557. ——. "La Famille Bechet," *Hot Club Magazine*, 15 (Mar., 1947), 3–4, 16. (Extrait de 'La Nouvelle-Orleans'). (Pers)

1558. Goffin, Rob. *Aux Frontieres du Jazz*. Paris: Editions du Sagittaire, 1932. 256 pp.
1559. —— —. (Trans: James F. Bezou). *Horn of Plenty; The Story of Louis Armstrong.* New York: Allen, Towne & Heath, 1947. 304 pp. (Pers)
1560. —— —. "Hot Jazz," *in* Nancy Cunard (Ed). *Negro.* London: Wishart, 1934. pp. 378–79. (A & A, Hist)
1561. —— —. *Jazz From the Congo to the Metropolitan.* Garden City: Doubleday, 1946. 254 pp.; New York: Editions for the Armed Services, 1943. 384 pp. Reprinted as: *Histoire du Jazz.* Montreal: Parizeau, 1945.
1562. —— —. "Jazzmen's Greatest Kicks," *Esquire*, XXII (Aug., 1944), 61, 142–43. (Gen)
1563. —— —. "Milneburg," *Hot Club Magazine*, 13 (Jan., 1947), 4–6. (Extrait de 'La Nouvelle-Orleans'). (Gen)
1564. —— —. *Nouvelle Histoire du Jazz.* Bruxelles: L'Ecran du Monde, 1948. 334 pp.
1565. —— —. *La Nouvelle-Orleans, Capitale du Jazz.* New York: Editions de la Maison Francaise, 1946. 269 pp.
1566. —— —. "Where Jazz Was Born," *Pageant*, I (Feb., 1945), 93–5. (Hist)
1567. —— — and Charles Delaunay (Eds). *Jazz 47.* Paris: Societe Intercontinentale du Livre, 1947. 76 pp.
1568. Gogh, Rupert van. "The Evolution of Jazz," *West African Review*, VI (Mar., 1935), 15–17. (A & A)
1569. Goldberg, Isaac. "Aaron Copland and His Jazz," *American Mercury*, XII (Sept., 1927), 63–5. (A & A, J & C)
1570. —— —. *George Gershwin and American Music.* Girard: Haldeman-Julius, 1936. 32 pp. (Pers)
1571. —— —. *George Gershwin, A Study in American Music.* New York: Simon & Schuster, 1931. 305 pp. (Pers)
See: 1576.
1572. —— —. "Jazz," *Forum*, LXXXVII (Apr., 1932), 232–36. Reprinted: Louis W. Jones and others (Eds). *These United States.* New York: R. Long and Richard R. Smith, 1933. pp. 548–57. (A & A)
1573. —— —. *Jazz Music; What It Is and How To Understand It.* Girard: Haldeman-Julius, 1927. 62 pp.
1574. —— —. "Jazzo-Analysis," *Disques*, I (Dec., 1930), 394–98. (A & A, Pers)
1575. —— —. "More Jazzo-Analysis," (lr) *Disques*, I (Feb., 1931), 535. (A & A)
1576. —— —. "Music by Gershwin," *Ladies' Home Journal*, XLVIII (Feb., 1931), 12–13, 149, 151; (Mar., 1931), 20, 208–10, 212–13; (Apr., 1931), 25, 198–99. (Pers) *See:* 1571.
1577. —— —. *Tin Pan Alley.* New York: John Day, 1930. 341 pp.
1578. Goldman, Elliott. *Clarence Williams Discography.* London: Jazz Music Books, 1947. 24 pp. (Disc)
1579. Goldman, John. "Meade Lux Lewis," *Swing Music*, 14 (Autumn, 1936), 62–3. (Pers)
1580. Goldsen, Mort. "Jazz Club Francais," *Metronome*, LXI (Oct., 1945), 27. (Geog)
1581. Gombosi, Otto. "The Pedigree of the Blues," *in* Theodore M. Finney (Ed). *Volume of Proceedings of the Music Teachers National Association, Fortieth Series.* Pittsburg: The Association, 1946. pp. 382–89. (A & A, Bl, BW)
1582. Gonzales, Babs and Paul Weston. *Boptionary: What Is Bop?* Hollywood: Capitol Records, 1949. 8 pp. (Bop)
1583. Goodbrod, R. M. "Conquering the Jazz Craze of Young Pianists," *Etude*, LII (Feb., 1934), 82. (J & C)
1584. Goodman, Benny. "Jam Session," *Pictorial Review*, XXXIX (May, 1938), 15. (Lang, Sw)
1585. —— —. "Now Take the Jitterbug," *Collier's*, CIII (Feb. 25, 1939), 11–13. (As told to Ted Shane). (J & D, Sw)

1586. Godman, Benny. "When Swing Meets the Classics," *Scribner's Commentator*, IX (Mar., 1941), 90–2. (Pers)
1587. ——, and Irving Kolodin. *The Kingdom of Swing*. New York: Stackpole Sons, 1939. 265 pp. (Pers)
1588. ——. "The Kingdom of Swing," *in* Elie Siegmeister (Ed). *The Music Lover's Handbook*. New York: William Morrow, 1943. pp. 718–28. (Extract from book of same title). (Pers)
1589. Goodrich, A. J. "Syncopated Rhythm vs. 'Rag-Time'," *Musician*, VI (Nov., 1901), 336. (Rag)
1590. Goodrich, Marti. "Criticising the Critics," *Jazz Session*, 7 (May-June, 1945), 18, 30. (Crit)
1591. Gordon, Gray. "Experiment in Dance Music," New York *Times*, May 2, 1939, 22 : 7. (J & D)
1592. Gordon, H. S. "The Jazz Myth," *Sackbut*, VI (Nov., 1925), 116–17. (A & A)
1593. Gordon, James. "Honey in the Jive," *American Magazine*, CXXXVIII (Aug., 1944), 28–9. (Pers)
1594. Gorki, Maxim. (Trans: Marie Budberg). "The Music of the Degenerate," *Dial*, LXXXV (Dec., 1928), 480–84. (A & A)
1595. Gottlieb, Bill. "Change Guard at Condon's Village Club," *Down Beat*, XIV (Feb. 12, 1947), 1. (Gen)
    See: 1233; 1597.
1596. ——. "Chubby Plays 5th Dimensional Jazz," *Down Beat*, XIV (Apr. 23, 1947), 14. (Ork)
1597. ——. "Condon Raps Tough for 'Re-Bop Slop'," *Down Beat*, XIII (Oct. 7, 1946), 4, 17. (Bop)
    See: 1233; 1595.
1598. ——. "Dance Music, Harmony Included in Curriculum," *Down Beat*, XIV (July 2, 1947), 6. (Ed)
1599. ——. "Delaunay Escapades With Gestapo Related," *Down Beat*, XIII (Sept. 9, 1946), 13. (Pers)
1600. ——. "From Heebie Jeebies to Bebop," *Saturday Review of Literature*, XXXI (Oct. 30, 1948), 50–1. (Inst)
1601. ——. "'I'm Not Slipping'—Duke Ellington," *Down Beat*, XIII (June 17, 1946), 4, 14. (A & A, Ork)
1602. ——. "Lion Tracked to His Lair—Or Willie Smith's Story," *Down Beat*, XIV (Jan. 1, 1947), 14. (Pers)
1603. ——. "Louis Center of New Commotion," *Down Beat*, XIV (July 2, 1947), 3. (Pers)
1604. ——. "Mezz Blows Mess of Mellow Words," *Down Beat*, XIII (Nov. 4, 1946), 4–5. (Rev)
1605. ——. "Thelonius Monk—Genius of Bop," *Down Beat*, XIV (Sept. 24, 1947), 2. (Bop, Pers)
1606. ——. "Tricky Sam Nanton, 42, Dies On Tour With Duke," *Down Beat*, XIII (Aug. 12, 1946), 9. (Pers)
1607. Gould, Jack. "News of the Night-Clubs—The Decline of Swing," New York *Times*, Aug. 7, 1938, IX, 8 : 4. (Gen)
    See: 725; 1522.
1608. Goursat, Georges Marie. *La Ronde de Nuit*. Paris: A. Fayard, 1923. 126 pp. (Author's pseudonym, "Sem," at head of title).
1609. Grace, Harvey. "Jazz Goes Modern," *Musical Times*, LXXVI (Dec., 1935). 1094–97. (A & A) (Author's pseudonym, "Feste," at head of title)
1610. Graener, Paul. "Nie wieder Niggermusik," *Neues Musikblatt*, XV (Jan., 1936). 3–4. (Gen)

1611. Grainger, Percy A. "Jazz," *Musikblätter des Anbruch*, VII (Apr., 1925), 210–12. (A & A)

1612. ——. "Jazz and the Music of the Future," *in* James Francis Cooke. *Great Men and Famous Musicians on the Art of Music*. Philadelphia: Theo. Presser, 1925. pp. 308–13. (A & A)

1613. ——. "Never Has Popular Music Been As Classical As Jazz," *Metronome*, XLII (July 1, 1926), 10. (A & A)

1614. ——. "What Effect Is Jazz Likely to Have Upon the Music of the Future?" *Etude*, XLII (Sept., 1924), 593–94. (A & A, Infl, Inst)

1615. Graner, Georg. "Ein Buch von Jazz," *Allgemeine Musik-Zeitung*, LV (Feb. 10, 1928), 141–43. (Rev)

1616. ——. "Jazz-Glosse," *Allgemeine Musik-Zeitung*, LIII (Feb. 12, 1926), 121–122. (A & A)

1617. ——. "Der Jazzrausch," *Deutsche Musiker-Zeitung*, LVI (June 27, 1925), 649. (A & A)
See: 2609.

1618. Grauer, Bill. "Dixieland Clarinet," *Record Changer*, VII (Aug., 1948), 11–12. (Pers)

1619. ——. "Editorial," *Record Changer*, IX (July-Aug., 1950), 6–7, 43. (Pers)

1620. ——. "In Defense of Label Collecting," *Record Changer*, IX (May, 1950), 7, 20. (Disc)

1621. ——. "Blind Willie Johnson," *Record Changer*, VIII (June, 1949), 6. (Disc, Pers)

1622. ——. "Louis Today," *Record Changer*, IX (July-Aug., 1950), 27. (Pers)

1623. ——. "Kid Punch," *Record Changer*, VII (June, 1948), 10, 25. (Pers)

1624. ——. "The Record Changer's Jazz Band Contest: The Winner!" *Record Changer*, IX (Jan., 1950), 7, 16. (Ork, Poll)

1625. Gray, Glen. "Casa Loma Made Swing Commercial," *Down Beat*, VII (May 15, 1940), 3, 14. (Ork, Sw)

1626. Gray-Clark, G. F. and Eric S. Tonks. *Deep Henderson*. Newark, Notts.: Jazz Appreciation Society, 1944. 24 pp.

1627. Green, Abel. "Benny Goodman; The Cosmopolite of the Month," *Cosmopolitan*, CXVI (Mar., 1944), 8, 12–13. (Pers)

1628. Greenbaum, Lucy. "Saga of 'Satchmo'," *New York Times*, May 4, 1947, VII, 32:3. (Rev)

1629. Greene, Maude. "The Background of the Beale Street Blues," *Tennessee Folklore Society Bulletin*, VII (Mar., 1941), 1–10. (Hist)

1630. Greene, Robert S. "Bix: He Was An Emotion More than Anything Else," *Record Changer*, VIII (May, 1949), 8, 20. (Pers)

1631. ——. "The Firehouse Five *plus* Two," *Record Changer*, VIII (Sept., 1949), 7–11. (Ork)

1632. Grew, Eva Mary. "On Jazz and Choric Recitals," *Sackbut*, X (July, 1930), 325–28. (Poet)

1633. Grezzi, Juan Rafael. "Hoagy Carmichael," *Swing Music*, (May-June, 1936), 69–70. (Disc, Pers)

1634. Griffin, Nard. *To Be or Not to Bop*. New York: Leo B. Workman, 1948. 24 pp. (Bop)

1635. Grove, Mary and Thurman Grove. "New Stars in the Making," *in* Orin Blackstone (Ed). *Jazzfinder '49*. New Orleans: Orin Blackstone, 1949. pp. 15–24. (Pers)

1636. Gruenberg, Louis. "Der Jazz Als Ausgangspunkt," *Musikblätter des Anbruch*, VII (Apr., 1925), 196–99. Reprinted as: "Jazz As the Starting Point," *Metronome*, XLII (Jan. 1, 1926), 15, 56. (A & A, Infl)

1637. ——. "Vom Jazz und andern Dingen," *in* Hans Heinsheimer and Paul Stefan (Eds). *25 Jahre Neue Musik*. Wien: Universal-Edition, 1926. pp. 229–36. (Gen)

1638. Guilliams, A. E. "Detrimental Effects of Jazz on Our Younger Generation," *Metronome*, XXXIX (Feb., 1923), 59. (Infl)
1639. Guillod, Eric. "Lester Young," *Hot Club Magazine*, 15 (Mar., 1947), 10–11. (Pers)
1640. Guiterman, Arthur. "Jazz," *in* Arthur Guiterman. *The Light Guitar*. New York: Harper, 1923. pp. 96–9. (Poet)
1641. Gullickson, Gordon. *Numerical Index to Delaunay's Hot Discography*. Washington: G. Gullickson, 1941. 28 pp. (Disc)
1642. Gurwitch, Andy. "Continental Jazz Works Examined," *Down Beat*, XV (Apr. 7, 1948), 22. (Rev)
1643. — —. "Jazz Returns to Europe," *Metronome*, LXIII (Feb., 1947), 25, 43–5. (Geog)
1644. — —. "What Europeans Write About Jazz," *Down Beat*, XIV (Aug. 13, 1947), 10–11. (Rev)
1645. — —. "Works of Panassie Are Discussed," *Down Beat*, XV (Feb. 11, 1948), 15. (Rev)
1646. Gutman, Hanns. "Mechanisierung und Jazz," *Musikblätter des Anbruch*, VIII (Oct.-Nov., 1926), 407–08. (Gen)
1647. H. A. "A Jazz Orchestra," *Musical News and Herald*, LXV (July 21, 1923), 57. (Crit)
1648. H. B. B. "Jazz," *Living Age*, CCCVI (July 31, 1920), 280–81. (A & A)
1649. Hagen, Milt. *The Magic of Music*. New York: 1931. 51 pp.
1650. Haggin, B. H. "Gershwin and Our Music," *Nation*, CXXXV (Oct. 5, 1932), 308–09. (A & A, J & C)
1651. — —. "Improvised Jazz," *in* B. H. Haggin. *Music On Records*. New York: Oxford University Press, 1938. pp. 131–40. (Disc)
1652. — —. "Music," *Nation*, CXLVIII (June 3, 1939), 653–54. (Rev)
1653. — —. "Music," *Nation*, CLXIII (July 27, 1946), 110. (Rev)
1654. — —. "Music In the 20's," *Saturday Review of Literature*, VI (May 17, 1930), 1046–47. (A & A)
1655. — —. "The Pedant Looks at Jazz," *Nation*, CXXI (Dec. 9, 1925), 685–88. (A & A)
1656. — —. "Records," *Nation*, CLXIII (July 20, 1946), 80–1. (A & A)
1657. — —. "Two Parodies," *Nation*, CXXII (Jan. 13, 1926), 40. (A & A, J & C)
1658. Hahn, George. "America and Its Music," *Melody*, VI (Apr., 1922), 5–7. (Gen)
1659. Haig, Kenneth. "Bury the Dead," *Jazz Information*, II (Aug. 9, 1940), 17–18. (A & A, NO)
1660. Hall, Henry. "British Bands Cannot Feel Swing," *Metronome*, LI (Oct., 1935), 17, 33. (Geog, Sw)
1661. Hallock, Ted. "Bop Jargon Indicative of Intellectual Thought," *Down Beat*, XV (July 28, 1948), 4. (Lang)
1662. — —. "Kenton's Music 'Greatest Ever'," *Down Beat*, XVII (Mar. 24, 1950), 1, 16, 18. (Crit, Ork)
1663. — —. "'Man, Tatum Is Jazz'—Big Tea," *Down Beat*, IX (July 1, 1942), 11. (Pers)
1664. — —. "Two Chicago Bands Amaze Critic!" *Down Beat*, XV (Mar. 10, 1948), 3. (Ork)
1665. — —. "'Won't Pull a Thornhill': Skitch," *Down Beat*, XVII (Mar. 10, 1950), 2. (Pers)
1666. Hamblett, Charles. "Music—Sm-o-oth & Boppy: New Fashion in Rhythm," *Illustrated Weekly of India*, Dec. 19, 1948, 38–9. (Bop)
1667. Hame, Olli. *Rytmin Voittokulku—Kirja Tanssimusiikista*. Helsinki: Frazer's Musicstore, 1949. 222 pp.

1668. Hamilton, Clarence G. "Jazz and Its Effects," *Etude*, XLII (Aug., 1924), 531. (Infl)

1669. Hammond, John. "Bunny Was Never Happy," *Music and Rhythm*, II (July, 1942), 17. (Pers)

1670. —— ——. "Is the Duke Deserting Jazz?" *Jazz* (New York), I, no. 8 (n. d.), 15. (Crit, Pers)
See: 1384; 3061.

1671. —— ——. "The Story of Duke's Boss," *Music and Rhythm*, II (June, 1942), 22–3. (Pers, Ork)

1672. —— ——. "Why Has Benny Goodman Changed?" *Music and Rhythm*, II (June, 1942), 13, 33. (A & A, Pers)

1673. —— ——, and James Dugan. "Swat that Jitterbug," *Theatre Arts Committee Magazine*, I (Jan., 1939), 10–11. (J & D)

1674. Handy, W. C. (Ed). *Blues, An Anthology*. New York: A. &. C. Boni, 1926, 180 pp. Reprinted as: *A Treasury of the Blues*. New York: Charles Boni, 1949. 258 pp. (Bl)

1675. —— ——. *Father of the Blues*. New York: Macmillan, 1941. 317 pp. (Pers)

1676. —— ——. (Ed: Myles H. Fellowes). "The Heart of the Blues," *Etude*, LVIII (Mar., 1940), 152, 193, 211. (A & A, Bl))

1677. Hansen, Millard. "Coleman Hawkins Discusses Tenor Sax," *Music and Rhythm*, II (June, 1941), 80–1. (Inst, Pers)

1678. Hapke, Walter. "Im Spiegel des Jazz," *Zeitschrift für Musik*, XCVIII (Oct., 1931), 888–89. (J & C)

1679. Harap, Louis. "The Case for Hot Jazz," *Musical Quarterly*, XXVII (Jan., 1941), 47–61. Reprinted: Ralph de Toledano (Ed). *Frontiers of Jazz*. New York: Oliver Durrell, 1947. pp. 3–12. (A & A)

1680. Harman, Carter. "Friday Evenings of Hot Jazz on Second Avenue," New York *Times*, Oct. 15, 1950, II, 7 : 1–4. (Gen)

1681. —— ——. "Revival of Interest in Dixieland Style and Swing Noted in Current Trend," New York *Times*, May 14, 1950, II, 6 : 1–2. (Disc)

1682. Harris, H. Meunier. "A Jazz Bibliography," *in* Orin Blackstone (Ed). *Jazzfinder '49*. New Orleans: Orin Blackstone, 1949. pp. 129–42. (Bibl)

1683. —— ——. "Portrait de George Lewis," *Hot Club Magazine*, 12 (Dec., 1946), 3–6. (Disc, Pers)

1684. Harris, Markham. "Jazz," *in Encyclopedia Americana*, Vol. XV. New York: Americana, 1941. pp. 768–70. (A & A)

1685. Harris, Pat. "Average Lawrence Sideman Philly-Born, 22, Loyal to Elliot," *Down Beat*, XV (Feb. 11, 1948), 12. (Ork, Pers)

1686. —— ——. "Can't Make Money As A Jazz Singer: Starr," *Down Beat*, XVII (Dec. 15, 1950), 6. (Pers)

1687. —— ——. "Dorothy Collins 'Most Underrated'," *Down Beat*, XVI (Dec. 30, 1949), 18. (Pers)

1688. —— ——. "Diz Sacrifices Spark to Get His 'Bop With Beat'," *Down Beat*, XVII (Jan. 13, 1950), 8. (Crit, Ork)

1689. —— ——. "Drummers Should Be Musicians, Too: Tiny Kahn," *Down Beat*, XVII (Apr. 7, 1950), 3. (A & A, Inst, Pers)

1690. —— ——. "Hyams, Like Shearing, 'Refreshing'," *Down Beat*, XVI (Dec. 2, 1949), 19. (Pers)

1691. —— ——. "I Didn't Know What I Was Getting Into: Little Smack," *Down Beat*, XVII (Jan. 13, 1950), 6. (Pers)

1692. —— ——. "'I Sing Like A Man,' Says Farrell," *Down Beat*, XVII (June 16, 1950), 3. (Pers)

1693. —— ——. "Jazz Book A Good Survey," *Down Beat*, XVI (Jan. 14, 1949), 10. (Rev)

1694. Harris, Pat. "'Jazz Dead,' Says Teddy Powell, Trying Comeback," *Down Beat*, XVII (June 16, 1950), 7. (Crit, Ork)

1695. ———. "Let There Be No Further Despair," *Down Beat*, XVI (Feb. 25, 1949), 6. (Ork, Pers)

1696. ———. "Red Mitchell 'An Amazing Bassist'," *Down Beat*, XVII (Apr..21, 1950), 2. (Pers)

1697. ———. "Nothing But Bop? 'Stupid,' Says Miles," *Down Beat*, XVII (Jan. 27, 1950), 18–19. (Pers)

1698. ———. "Oscar Pettiford Now on Cello Kick," *Down Beat*, XVII (Dec. 29, 1950), 20. (Inst, Pers)

1699. ———. "Pres Talks About Himself, Copycats," *Down Beat*, XVI (May 4, 1949), 15. (Pers)

1700. ———. "Russo, With Great Crew, Still Just Experimenting," *Down Beat*, XVI (June 3, 1949), 4–5. (Ork)

1701. ———. "Scott Musicians Make Long Story Short," *Down Beat*, XV (May 5, 1948), 2. (Ork)

1702. ———. "Stravinsky, Bird, Vibes Gas Roach," *Down Beat*, XVI (June 3, 1949), 6. (Pers)

1703. ———. "Studies Bop, Returns to Original Love, Dixieland," *Down Beat*, XVII (Apr. 21, 1950), 4. (Pers)

1704. ———. "Think I'm Pioneering: Billy Bauer," *Down Beat*, XVII (Jan. 27, 1950), 6–7. (Pers)

1705. ———. "'Unknown' Haynes Sparks Bird's Strings," *Down Beat*, XVII (Dec. 1, 1950), 2. (Pers)

1706. ———. "Woody, Basie Work With Small Units, Explain Why," *Down Beat*, XVII (Mar. 24, 1950), 5, 6, 7. (Ork)

1707. Harrison, Richard G. "How Great A Jazzman Was Bunny Berigan?" *Down Beat*, XIV (Mar. 12, 1947), 12. (A & A, Pers)

1708. ———. "Room For Two Schools of Jazz Thought Today," *Down Beat*, XIII (Nov. 4, 1946), 10, 13. (A & A)

1709. Harrison, Sidney. "Jazz—The Music of Exile," *Etude*, LIX (Mar., 1941), 150. (A & A)

1710. Harrisson, Mark. "Belgian Jive," *Hot Club Magazine*, 3 (Mar., 1946), 15. (Lang)

1711. Hart, Floyd T. "A Guide to Evaluating Jazz," *Music Educator's Journal*, XXIX (Nov.-Dec., 1942), 43. (A & A)

1712. ———. "The Relation of Jazz Music to Art," *Music Educator's Journal*, XXVI (Sept., 1939), 24–5, 73. (A & A)

1713. Hart, James D. "Jazz Jargon," *American Speech*, VII (Apr., 1932), 241–54. (Lang)

1714. Hartmann, Hans H. "HCF," *Die Melodie*, III, no. 9 (1948), 7, 10. (Gen)

1715. Harvey, Charles (Ed). *Jazz Parody—An Anthology of Jazz Fiction*. London: Spearman, 1948. 110 pp. (Fict)

1716. Harvey, Holman. "It's Swing!" *Delineator*, CXXIX (Nov., 1936), 10–11. Abr: *Reader's Digest*, XXX (Jan., 1937), 99–102. (Hist, Lang, Sw)

1717. Haskell, Arnold L. "'Nigger Heaven'," in Arnold L. Haskell. *Balletomania*. New York: Simon & Schuster, 1934. pp. 280–91. (J & D)

1718. Hauck, Udo Ralph and Barry Ulanov. "Musik Oder Atombombe?" *Die Melodie*, III, no. 10 (1948), 5, 12. (A & A, Ork)

1719. Hauser, Richard. "U.S. Conquest: Hot 'Yahtz'," New York *Times Magazine*, Aug. 20, 1950, 26. (Geog)

1720. Haynes, Dale and Don Haynes. "Blesh's 'Shining Trumpets' A Sadly Misguided Commentary," *Down Beat*, XIV (Feb. 12, 1947), 15. (Rev)

1721. Haynes, Don C. "Bunk's 2nd Try Proves His Horn the Real Thing," *Down Beat*, XIII (Oct. 7, 1946), 19. (Crit, Pers)

1722. Haynes, Don C. "Cow Cow Davenport," *Jazz Information*, II (Oct. 25, 1940), 8–10. (Pers)
1723. —— ——. "Duke Draws Sell-Out Crowd Who Sit On Hands," *Down Beat*, XIII (Feb. 11, 1946), 1, 12–13. (Crit)
1724. —— ——. "Productive Year For Musicians on Records," *Down Beat*, XIII (Jan. 1, 1946), 12. (Disc)
1725. Hazel, Monk. "He Got Ideas Strictly From Emmet Hardy," *Down Beat*, IX (Mar. 1, 1942), 8. (A & A, Pers)
  See: 2636; 2637.
1726. Hearne, Will Roy. "Gennett Records," *Record Changer*, IX (Dec., 1950), 12–13. (Disc)
1727. Helander, Olle. *Jazzens Vag, En Bok Om Blues Och Stomps.* Stockholm: Nordiska Musikforlaget, 1947. 346 pp.
1728. Henderson, Fletcher. "He Made the Band Swing," *Record Changer*, IX (July-Aug., 1950), 15–16. (Hist, Pers)
1729. —— ——. "Henderson 'Had To Get Louis' For Roseland Ork," *Down Beat*, XVII (July 14, 1950), 4, 5. (Hist, Pers)
1730. Henderson, Harry and Sam Shaw. "And Now We Go Bebop!" *Collier's*, CXXI (Mar. 20, 1948), 16–17, 88. (Bop)
1731. Henderson, W. J. "Ragtime, Jazz, and High Art," *Scribner's*, LXXVII (Feb., 1925), 200–03. (A & A, J & C, Rag)
  See: 283.
1732. Henry, Leigh. "Jazz In Relation to Chamber Music," *in* Walter Willson Cobbett (Ed). *Cobbett's Cyclopedic Survey of Chamber Music.* London: Oxford University Press, 1930. Vol. II, pp. 31–4. (A & A, J & C)
1733. —— ——. "The Nature and Function of Jazz," *Musical News and Herald*, LXVII (Aug. 2, 1924), 92. (A & A)
1734. —— ——. "What's Wrong With Jazz?" *Musical Opinion*, L (Nov., 1926), 151–53. (A & A)
1735. Henry, Lewis. "Is Jazz An Art?" *Canon*, III (Jan., 1950), 353–55. (A & A)
1736. Henshaw, Laurie. "Europe Is Starved For Good Jazz," *Metronome*, LXI (Oct., 1945), 26, 40. (Geog)
1737. Herman, Woody. (As told to Eddie Ronan). "Herman Attacks Mathematics in 'Progressivism'," *Down Beat*, XV (May 5, 1948), 1, 3. (A & A, Bop)
1738. Herment, Georges. (Trans: Ian Munro Smyth). "La Cote du Hot," *Jazz Hot*, IV (Oct.-Nov., 1938), 7. (Crit)
1739. —— ——. "Un Grand Musicien Noir: Chick Webb," *Presence Africaine*, 3 (Mar.-Apr., 1948), 505–12. (Pers)
1740. —— ——. (Trans: Ian Munro-Smyth). "Hot—the 6th Sense," *Jazz Hot*, 9 (June, 1936), 13. (A & A, Infl)
1741. —— ——. "Perfection and Simplicity," *Jazz Hot*, IV (Apr.-May, 1938), 9. (A & A, Sw)
1742. —— ——. (Trans: Ian Munro Smyth). "Poem and Chorus," *Jazz Hot*, 29 (Jan., 1939), 9, 12. (A & A)
1743. Hershey, Burnet. "Jazz Latitude," New York *Times*, June 25, 1922, III, 8–9. (Geog)
1744. Hess, Harry. "Postgraduate Stuff," *Esquire*, XXVI (Oct., 1946), 129, 161–66. (Pers)
1745. Hess, Otto. "Otto Hess' Scrapbook," *Record Changer*, IX (May, 1950), 8–9. (Pic)
1746. Heyward, Du Bose. "Jasbo Brown," *American Mercury*, VI (Sept., 1925), 7–9. (Poet)
1747. Hibberd, Lloyd. "Jazz," *in* Willi Apel. *Harvard Dictionary of Music.* Cambridge: Harvard University Press, 1946. pp. 374–79. (A & A)

1748. Hibbs, Leonard. *21 Years of Swing Music on Brunswick Records*. London: A. White, 1937. 80 pp.
1749. Higginson, Fred. "Jack, Peck, Peewee, Snoozer, Tim," *Metronome*, LVII (Nov., 1941), 22–3, 33. (Pers)
1750. Hill, Edward Burlingame. "Copland's Jazz Concerto In Boston," *Modern Music*, IV (May-June, 1927), 35–7. (J & C)
1751. — —. "Jazz," *Harvard Graduates' Magazine*, XXXIV (Mar., 1926), 362–65. (J & C)
1752. Hinchcliffe, R. Edwin S. "Blues," *Swing Music*, 14 (Autumn, 1936), 9–10, 84–5. (Bl)
1753. — —. "Defends Jazzmen Against 'Moronic Ravings' of Foes," *Down Beat*, VIII (Sept. 15, 1941), 7. (A & A, Crit)
See: 3292.
1754. Hines, Earl. "Earl Hines Picks 'Five Greatest Jazzmen'," *Down Beat*, VIII (July 15, 1941), 7. (Pers)
1755. Hobson, Wilder. *American Jazz Music*. New York: W. W. Norton, 1939. 230 pp.
1756. — —. "Designed for Dancing," *Saturday Review of Literature*, XXXIII (Mar. 25, 1950), 64. (Disc, J & D)
1757. — —. "Duke Ellington," *in* Ralph de Toledano (Ed). *Frontiers of Jazz*. New York: Oliver Durrell, 1947. pp. 137–47. (Pers)
1758. — —. "Hits and Misses," *Saturday Review of Literature*, XXXI (Dec. 25, 1948), 46. (Disc, Pers)
1759. — —. "Jazz," *in Encyclopedia Britannica*. Chicago: Encyclopedia Britannica, 1947. Vol. 12, pp. 982–84. (A & A)
1760. — —. "Jazz and Categories," *Nation*, CLXIII (Dec. 28, 1946), 761–62. (Rev)
1761. — —. "Louis Always Has Golden Song to Offer: Hobson," *Down Beat*, XVII (July 14, 1950), 1, 19. (Pers)
1762. — —. "A Part of Hot Jazz; 'They All Played Ragtime'," *Saturday Review of Literature*, XXXIII (Nov. 25, 1950), 30. (Rev)
1763. — —. "Swing High," *Vogue*, LXXXVII (Mar. 15, 1936), 90–1, 112, 114. (A & A, Hist, Sw)
1764. Hodeir, Andre. *Introduction A La Musique de Jazz*. Paris: Libraire Larousse, 1948. 128 pp.
1765. — —. *Le Jazz Cet Inconnu*. Paris: Collection Harmoniques, 1945. 220 pp.
1766. Hodes, Art. "Everybody's In the Union," *Jazz Record*, 14 (Nov., 1943), 4–5, 11. (Hist)
1767. — —. "Jam Session," *Jazz Record*, 20 (May, 1944), 4–5. (Gen, Hist)
1768. — —. "Portrait of a Jazzman," *in* George S. Rosenthal (Ed). *Jazzways*. Cincinnati, 1946. pp. 40–1, 101. (Pers)
1769. — —. "Bessie Smith," *Jazz Record*, 58 (Sept., 1947), 8–9. (Pers)
1770. — —. "Tenor Sax," *Jazz Record*, 18 (Mar., 1944), 4–5. (Hist, Pers)
1771. Hodgkins, Barbara. "Big Bill; It Isn't Fair, It's Farrell," *Metronome*, LXVI (June, 1950), 15, 31. (Pers)
1772. — —. "Doris Day Dreams," *Metronome*, LXIV (Mar., 1948), 13, 35–6. (Pers)
1773. — —. "Desperate Desmond," *Metronome*, LXIV (May, 1948), 23–4, 28–9. (Pers)
1774. — —. "Dream Boat," *Metronome*, LXV (Oct., 1949), 17, 34–5. (Pers)
1775. — —. "The Haig," *Metronome*, LXVI (July, 1950), 17, 24. (Pers)
1776. — —. "The Incredible Crosby," *Metronome*, LXIV (June, 1948), 13. (Rev)
1777. — —. "Jolting Jo," *Metronome*, LXIV (July, 1948), 9–10, 21. (Pers)
1778. — —. "Art Lund," *Metronome*, LXIII (Aug., 1947), 11, 38. (Pers)
1779. — —. "The Monroe Doctrine," *Metronome*, LXIII (Apr., 1947), 13–14. (Pers)
1780. — —. "One Man's 'Count'... Is Another's 'Label'," *Metronome*, LXVI (Aug., 1950), 17. (Pers)

1781. Hodgkins, Barbara. "Patti Page," *Metronome*, LXIV (Apr., 1948), 48–9. (Pers)
1782. —— —. "Peggy and Dave," *Metronome*, LXVI (Oct., 1950), 14–15. (Pers)
1783. —— —. "A Real Gone Gal," *Metronome*, LXIII (Dec., 1947), 18, 38–9. (Pers)
1784. —— —. "Starr Bright," *Metronome*, LXV (Aug., 1949), 13, 31. (Pers)
1785. —— —. "We... Frankie Laine and Carl Fischer," *Metronome*, LXVI (Aug., 1950), 11–12. (Pers)
1786. Hoefer, George. "All of Bix' Okeh Records Listed," *Down Beat*, VII (Mar. 1, 1940), 12. (Disc)
1787. —— —. "Albert Ammons Left Jazz Big Legacy, Says Hoefer," *Down Beat*, XVII (Jan. 13, 1950), 11. (Pers)
1788. —— —. "Louis Armstrong Discography," *Down Beat*, XVII (July 14, 1950), 14–15; (July 28, 1950), 18; (Aug. 11, 1950), 16; (Aug. 25, 1950), 19; (Sept. 8 1950), 14. (Disc, Pers)
1789. —— —. "Lovie Austin Still Active As a Pianist in Chicago," *Down Beat*, XVII (June 16, 1950), 11. (Pers)
1790. —— —. "George Barnes Settles Perennial Problem," *Down Beat*, XVII (June 16, 1950), 13, 16. (Ork)
1791. —— —. "'Basie Led the Greatest Rythm Machine in Jazz'," *Down Beat*, XVII (Mar. 24, 1950), 11. (Ork)
1792. —— —. "Big Four Fluffs Jazz, Indies Carrying the Ball," *Down Beat* XIV (Mar. 26, 1947), 13. (Disc)
1793. —— —. "Barney Bigard," *Jazz Information*, II (Nov. 8, 1940), 7–13. (Disc, Pers)
1794. —— —. "Tony Catalano, Pioneer Riverboat Jazzman, Dies," *Down Beat*, XVII (June 2, 1950), 13. (Pers)
1795. —— —. "Chi. Group Conducts Experiment in Jazz," *Down Beat*, XIV (Nov. 5, 1947), 5, 7. (Ork)
1796. —— —. "Chicago Jazz Landmark Being Razed," *Down Beat*, XVII, (Jan. 27, 1950), 2. (Hist)
1797. —— —. "Collectors vs. Musicians," *Jazz Information*, II (July 26, 1940), 11, 32. (A & A)
1798. —— —. "Committee to Perpetuate Memory of Beiderbecke," *Down Beat*, XVII (Apr. 21, 1950), 7. (Pers)
1799. —— —. "Continental Critics Are Feudin' 'n Fitin'," *Down Beat*, XIV (Dec. 17, 1947), 11. (Crit)
1800. —— —. "Davison, Parenti Finding Current Status Palatable," *Down Beat*, XV (Apr. 7, 1948), 12. (Disc, Pers)
1801. —— —. "Death of Big Eye Louis, Stills 'Top Jazz Pioneer'," *Down Beat*, XVI (Nov. 4, 1949), 11. (Pers)
1802. —— —. "Discographies Fill Vital Role In Collectors' Work," *Down Beat*, XVII (Oct. 20, 1950), 11. (Disc)
1803. —— —. "Ellington's Annual Chicago Concert 'A Gala Evening'," *Down Beat*, XVII (Mar. 10, 1950), 7. (Crit, Ork)
1804. —— —. "Ex-King Oliver Drummer At Blue Note With Hodes," *Down Beat*, XVII (Mar. 10, 1950), 11. (Pers)
1805. —— —. "Fabulous Piano Rolls Dubbed on Records," *Down Beat*, XIV (Apr. 23, 1947), 11. (Disc)
1806. —— —. "Fans Who Misinterpreted Now Are Forgetting Bunk," *Down Beat*, XV (Dec. 15, 1948), 6. (Pers)
1807. —— —. "Few Discerys Cash In on Bechet's Popularity," *Down Beat*, XV (June 16, 1948), 12. (Disc, Pers)
1808. —— —. "'Get In B Flat' Led Joe Oliver To Throne," *Down Beat*, VIII (Sept. 15, 1941), 16. (Hist)
1809. —— —. "Hawk Discography," *Down Beat*, XVII (Oct. 20, 1950), 3. (Disc)
    See: 768; 2052.

1810. Hoefer, George. "Haymer an 'Unacclaimed Great'," *Down Beat*, XVI (June 3, 1949), 1, 13. (Pers)

1811. ——. "Here's LP, 45 RPM Jazz List," *Down Beat*, XVII (May 5, 1950), 16; (May 19, 1950), 6; (June 2, 1950), 6; (June 16, 1950), 6; (June 30, 1950), 6; (Aug. 11, 1950), 18; (Aug. 25, 1950), 16; (Sept. 22, 1950), 16; (Nov. 3, 1950), 18; (Dec. 1, 1950), 18; (Dec. 15, 1950), 18; (Dec. 29, 1950), 22. (Disc)

1812. ——. "Art Hodes Band Achieves a 'Rarely-Heard Unity'," *Down Beat*, XVII (Dec. 15, 1950), 11. (Crit, Ork)

1813. ——. "Hoefer Finds More Data on Seger Ellis Waxings," *Down Beat*, XVII (Dec. 1, 1950), 11. (Disc, Ork)

1814. ——. "The Hot Box," *Down Beat*, XII (July 1, 1945), 11. (Pers)

1815. ——. "The Hot Box," *Down Beat*, XIII (Jan. 14, 1946), 11. (Pers)

1816. ——. "Jazzmen—Past, Present—Share All-Time Honors," *Down Beat*, XVI (Mar. 11, 1949), 11. (Pers)

1817. ——. "'Jelly Roll' Rests His Case," *Down Beat*, VIII (Aug. 1, 1941), 1, 4. (Pers)

1818. ——. "Jelly Roll's Library of Congress Wax Date World's Longest Session," *Down Beat*, XIV (Sept. 24, 1947), 11. (Disc, Pers)

1819. ——. "Richard Jones Chapter Added to Jazz Legend," *Down Beat*, XIII (Jan. 14, 1946), 18. (Pers)

1820. ——. "King Louis Elected King of Zulus for Mardi Gras," *Down Beat*, XV (Dec. 29, 1948), 11. (Pers)
    See: 18; 28; 495; 1490; 2085.

1821. ——. "'Man, I Invented Jazz In—' Claimed by More Folks!" *Down Beat*, XVI (July 1, 1949), 11. (Hist)

1822. ——. "Fate Marable, 56, Riverboat Jazz King, Dies in St. Louis," *Down Beat*, XIV (Feb. 12, 1947), 2. (Pers)

1823. ——. "Mole Recalls Capone; Bullet Hole in Tram," *Down Beat*, XV (Mar. 10, 1948), 12. (Pers)

1824. ——. "Pianist Monk Getting Long Awaited Break," *Down Beat*, XV (Feb. 11, 1948), 11. (Bop, Pers)

1825. ——. "N. O. Jazz Revival Sparks Formation of Crack Crew," *Down Beat*, XVII (Nov. 3, 1950), 11. (Ork)

1826. ——. "Norvo Discography," *Down Beat*, XVII (Aug. 11, 1950), 18; (Aug. 25, 1950), 13; (Sept. 8, 1950), 16; (Sept. 22, 1950), 19. (Disc)

1827. ——. "Pops Still Going Strong After 50 Years in Jazz," *Down Beat*, XVI (May 6, 1949), 12. (Pers)

1828. ——. "Rare Morton Piano Roll Discovered in Junk Shop," *Down Beat*, XVII (Nov. 17, 1950), 7. (Disc, Pers)

1829. ——. "Re-Recording Etched of Picou 'High Society' Ride," *Down Beat*, XVII (Sept. 22, 1950), 6, 7. (Disc, Pers)

1830. ——. "Scott Experimenting With New Record Conceptions," *Down Beat*, XVI (Aug. 26, 1949), 11. (A & A, Tech)

1831. ——. "Kid Shots Dies Before Playing His New Cornet," *Down Beat*, XV (Dec. 1, 1948), 11. (Pers)

1832. ——. "Souchon Contributes to New Orleans Jazz Lore," *Down Beat*, XVII (Apr. 7, 1950), 11. (Hist, Ork)

1833. ——. "Stearns Completes Plans For a U.S. Jazz Institute," *Down Beat*, XVI (June 17, 1949), 11. (Ed)

1834. ——. "This College Jazz Group Made Up of Professors," *Down Beat*, XVI (Oct. 7, 1949), 11. (Ork)

1835. ——. "Tragedy Mars Comeback of a Former Blues Star," *Down Beat*, XVI (Dec. 16, 1949), 11. (Pers)

1836. ——. "Trombonist Laine's Life Like N. O. Book," *Down Beat*, XV (Feb. 25, 1948), 13. (Pers)

1837. Hoefer, George. "Will the Louis Sides On Cylinder Ever Turn Up?" *Down Beat*, XVII (July 14, 1950), 11. (Disc, Pers)
1838. Hoeree, Arthur. "Le Jazz," *Revue Musicale*, VIII (Oct. 1, 1927), 213–41. (A & A, Hist)
1839. ——. "Le Jazz et le Disque," *L'Edition Musicale Vivante*, IV (Dec., 1931), 7–15. (Disc)
1840. ——. "Le Jazz et la Musique d'Aujourd'hui," *Courrier Musical*, XXX (Dec. 1, 1928), 671–72. (Infl)
1841. ——. "Le Jazz et Son Influence Sur la Musique d'Aujourd'hui," *Menestrel*, XCI (Aug. 16, 1929), 361–63. (Infl)
1842. Hoffman, Dan G. "The Folk Art of Jazz," *Antioch Review*, V (Mar., 1945), 110–20. (A & A, Hist)
1843. Holiday, Billie. "I'm Cured For Good," *Ebony*, IV (July, 1949), 26–7, 28, 29, 30, 31, 32. (Gen, Pers)
1844. Holl, Karl. "Jazz im Konservatorium," *Melos*, VII (Jan., 1928), 30–2. (Ed)
1845. Hollis, Harold H. "Meet the Members of the Castle Band," *Record Changer*, VIII (Aug., 1949), 9–10. (Pers)
1846. Holloway, Jim. "Nice But Not Naughty," *Metronome*, LXIV (May, 1948), 20, 31. (Geog)
1847. ——. "Quantity But Not Quality Expanded on BBC Jazz Shows," *Metronome*, LXIII (Dec., 1947), 36–7. (Geog, Rad)
1848. Holly, Hal. "Anthony Band a Solid Hit In First West Coast Date," *Down Beat*, XVII (Nov. 17, 1950), 8. (Crit, Ork)
1849. ——. "Firehouse Chief Kimball Scorns Pollack Hassel," *Down Beat*, XVII (June 2, 1950), 9. (Ork)
See: 1851.
1850. ——. "Ina Ray Ork Looks Good on TV; Plays Well, Too," *Down Beat*, XVII (Dec. 1, 1950), 13. (Crit, Ork, Rad)
1851. ——. "Pollack Says Firehouse 5 Is 'Just a Cornball Crew'," *Down Beat*, XVII (May 5, 1950), 12. (Ork)
See: 1849
1852. ——. "Joe Sullivan Once Center of California Jazz Scene," *Down Beat*, XVII (Nov. 3, 1950), 8. (Pers)
1853. Holmes, Campbell. "The Surrealistic Aspect of Swing Music," *Jazz Hot*, III (Mar.-Apr., 1937), 13. (A & A)
1854. Holsworth, Cooper. "The Infant Terrible—Jazz," *Music News*, XXVIII (May 7, 1936), 11. (Gen, Sw)
1855. Holt, Malcolm E. "Some Still Believe in Future of Jazz," *Down Beat*, XIII (Feb. 11, 1946), 10, 16. (A & A)
1856. Hornbostel, Erich M. von. "Ethnologisches zu Jazz," *Melos*, VI (Dec., 1927), 510–12. (A & A, Hist)
1857. Houghton, John Alan. "Darius Milhaud: A Missionary of the 'Six'," *Musical America*, XXXVII (Jan. 13, 1923), 3, 42. (J & C)
1858. Houlden, D. F. "The Development of Small-Band Jazz Styles," *Jazz Journal*, II (Feb., 1949), 8, 13; (Mar., 1949), 11. (A & A, Hist, Ork)
1859. Hourwich, Rebecca. "Where the Jazz Begins," *Collier's*, LXXVII (Jan. 23, 1926), 14. (Hist)
1860. Howard, Buddy. "Ellington Celebrates 20th Year in Music," *Down Beat*, IX (Apr. 1, 1942), 4. (Pers)
1861. ——. "Noble Sissle International Star," *Down Beat*, IX (Oct. 1, 1942), 21. (Pers)
1862. Howard, John Tasker. "Jazz," *in* John Tasker Howard. *Our Contemporary Composers*. New York: Thomas Y. Crowell, 1941. pp. 286–90. (A & A)

1863. Howard, John Tasker. "'Swing' And Its Performers," *in* John Tasker Howard. *Our Contemporary Composers.* New York: Thomas Y. Crowell, 1941. pp. 290–95. (A & A, Pers)
1864. — —. "To-Day," *in* John Tasker Howard. *Our American Music.* New York: Thomas Y. Crowell, 1939. pp. 589–607. (A & A)
1865. Howe, Martin. *Blue Jazz.* Bristol: Perpetua, 1934. 33 pp.
1866. Howgate, George W. "Jazz," (lr) *Forum*, LXXX (Oct., 1928), 636–37. (A & A)
1867. Hoyle, Stanley. *Jazzing the Classics: Syncopated Transcriptions for Piano.* London: Paxton, 1938.
1868. Hubbard, W. L. "A Hopeful View of the Ragtime Roll," *Musician*, XXV (Aug., 1920), 6. (Pers, Rag)
1869. Hubner, Alma. "Of Chile and Jazz," *Jazz Record*, 14 (Nov., 1943), 6–7. (Geog)
1870. — —. "Pee Wee's Soul Is Music," *Jazz Record*, 18 (Mar., 1944), 8–10. (Pers)
1871. Hughes, Langston. "Jazzonia," *Survey*, LIII (Mar. 1, 1925), 665. (Poet)
1872. Hughes, Rupert. "A Eulogy of Ragtime," *Musical Record*, 447 (Apr., 1899), 157–59. (Rag)
1873. — —. "Music For the Man of Today," *in* James Francis Cooke. *Great Men and Famous Musicians on the Art of Music.* Philadelphia: Theo. Presser, 1925. pp. 138–40. (Gen)
1874. — —. "Will Ragtime Turn to Symphonic Poems?" *Etude*, XXXVIII (May, 1920), 305. (A & A, Rag)
1875. Hulsizer, Kenneth. "Jelly Roll Morton in Washington," *Jazz Music*, II (Feb.-Mar., 1944), 109–16. (Pers)
1876. Hunt, Ted. *Organizing and Conducting the Student Dance Orchestra.* Chicago: Rubank, 1941. 4 vols.
1877. Hurston, Zora Neale. "The Jook," *in* Nancy Cunard (Ed). *Negro.* London: Wishart, 1934. pp. 44–6. (Hist)
1878. Hutschenruyter, Wouter. "Jazz," *Caecilia en Het Muziekcollege*, LXXXV (Oct. 16, 1928), 274–77. (A & A)
1879. Huxley, Aldous. "Popular Music," *in* Aldous Huxley. *Along the Road.* London: Chatto & Windus, 1925. pp. 246–52. (Gen)
1880. — —. "Silence is Golden," *in* Aldous Huxley. *Do What You Will.* Garden City: Doubleday, Doran, 1929. pp. 55–64. (Gen)
1881. Ichaso, Francisco. "Terapeutica de Jazz," *Musicalia*, I (Sept.-Oct., 1928), 95–6. (Infl)
1882. Iger, Artur. "Die Entwicklung der Jazz-Industrie," *Zeitschrift für Instrumentenbau*, XLVI (June 15, 1926), 860–62. (A & A, Inst)
1883. — —. "Jazz-Industrie," *Auftakt*, VI (1926), 222–25. (A & A)
1884. Irving, Carter. "Jazz Brings First Dance of the City," New York *Times*, June 14, 1925, IV, 9. (J & D)
1885. Jackson, Bee. "Hey! Hey! Charleston!" *Collier's* LXXX (Dec. 10, 1927), 12, 34. (J & D)
1886. Jackson, Chubby. "Sweden Hot!" *Metronome*, LXIV (Mar., 1949), 22, 24. (Geog)
1887. Jackson, Edgar. *Parlophone Rhythm Style.* Hayes, Middx.: Parlophone, 1936. 28 pp.
1888. — —, and Leonard Hibbs. *Encyclopedia of Swing.* London: Decca, 1941. 83 pp.
1889. Jackson, Preston. "Lillian (Lil) Armstrong," *Jazz Hot*, V (Feb.-Mar., 1939), 13. (Pers)
1890. — —. "King Oliver," *in* Ralph de Toledano (Ed). *Frontiers of Jazz.* New York: Oliver Durrell, 1947. pp. 75–81. (Pers)
1891. Jacobsen, Nils. "Norwegian Jazz Interest Revived in Private Clubs," *Down Beat*, XV (July 28, 1948), 12. (Geog)

1892. Jacobson, Catherine. "Facts About Bud Hunter," *Jazz* (New York), I, no. 7 (n. d.), 20. (Pers)
1893. — —. "The Inside Story of Paul Eduard Miller's Main Currents of Jazz," *Jazz Session*, 8 (July-Aug., 1945), 14–16. (Crit)
1894. — —. "See Here, Mr. Miller," *Jazz Session*, 7 (May-June, 1945), 22–4. (Crit)
1895. — —. "Oro 'Tut' Soper," *Jazz* (New York), I (Dec., 1943), 8–9. (Pers)
1896. Jacobson, Ethel. "Air de Barrelhouse," New York *Times Magazine*, Aug. 18, 1940, 19. (Poet)
1897. James, Harry. "My Ten Favorite Trumpeters," *Music and Rhythm*, II (Dec., 1941), 16–17. (Pers)
1898. — —, and others. "Happy Birthday, Louis, From …" *Down Beat*, XVII (July 14, 1950), 2–3. (Pers)
1899. Janin, Jacques. "La Musique Americaine Devant l'Occident," *Courrier Musical*, XXXI (Feb. 15, 1929), 93–4. (A & A)
1900. Jarecki, Tadeusz. "Jazzing Up the Symphony Orchestra," *Chesterian*, VIII (July-Aug., 1927), 262–68. (Infl, Inst)
1901. — —. "Polichromizm Instrumentow Perkusyjnych," *Muzyka*, VI (Oct., 1929), 434–37; (Nov.-Dec., 1929), 508–10. (Infl, Inst, J & C)
1902. Jeanneret, Albert. "Le Negre et le Jazz," *Revue Musicale*, VIII (July, 1927), 24–7. (A & A, Hist)
1903. Jemnitz, Alexander. "Der Jazz Als Form und Inhalt," *Musikblätter des Anbruch*, VII (Apr., 1925), 188–96. (A & A)
1904. Johnson, Bunk and Frederick Ramsey, Jr. "I Am Writing You This Letter," *Jazz* (New York), I (June, 1942), 6–8. (Pers)
1905. Johnson, George. "The Wolverines and Bix," *in* Ralph de Toledano (Ed). *Frontiers of Jazz*. New York: Oliver Durrell, 1947. pp. 123–36. (Hist, Ork, Pers)
1906. — —. "Wolverine Days," *Swing Music*, 14 (Autumn, 1936), 30–2, 86–8, 93. (Hist, Pers)
1907. Johnson, Guy B. "Double Meaning in the Popular Negro Blues," *Journal of Abnormal and Social Psychology*, XXII (Apr.-June, 1927), 12–20. (Bl, Lang)
1908. Johnson, James Weldon. "Preface," *in* James Weldon Johnson (Ed). *The Book of American Negro Poetry*. New York: Harcourt, Brace, 1931. pp. 10–17. (A & A, Rag)
1909. Jones, Clifford (Ed). *Black and White, Part 1*. London: Clifford Jones, 1945. 20 pp.
1910. — —. *Black and White, Part 2*. London: Clifford Jones, 1946. 20 pp.
1911. — —. *Bob Crosby Band*. London: Clifford Jones, 1946. 27 pp. (Ork)
1912. — —. *J. C. Higginbotham*. London: Discographical Society, 1944. 24 pp. (Pers)
1913. — —. *Hot Jazz*. London: Discographical Society, 1944. 20 pp.
1914. — —. *Jazz In New York*. London: Discographical Society, 1944. 24 pp.
1915. — —. *New Orleans & Chicago Jazz*. London: Discographical Society, 1944. 24 pp.
1916. Jones, Hinton. "Insists Jazz Is No Product of Machine Age, But Negroic," New York *Times*, Mar. 20, 1927, IX, 16:6. (A & A)
1917. Jones, Isham. "American Dance Music Is Not Jazz," *Etude*, XLII (Aug., 1924), 526. (A & A)
1918. Jones, Max. *Jazz Photo Album*. London: British Yearbooks, 1947. 96 pp.
1919. — —. "Ferdinand Joseph Morton—A Biography," *Jazz Music*, II (Feb.-Mar., 1944), 86–101. (Pers)
1920. — — (Ed). *Folk: Review of People's Music, Part 1*. London: Jazz Music Books, 1945. 32 pp.
1921. — —, and Albert McCarthy (Eds). *Jazz Review*. London: Jazz Music Books, 1945. 24 pp.

1922. Jones, Max. _A Tribute to Huddie Ledbetter._ London: Jazz Music Books, 1946. 26 pp. (Pers)

1923. Jones, S. Turner. "Appreciation Through Jazz," _Educational Music Magazine,_ XX (Jan.-Feb., 1941), 53. (Infl)

1924. Judson, Arthur L. "Works of American Composers Reveal Relation of Ragtime to Art-Song," _Musical America,_ XV (Dec. 2, 1911), 29. (A & A, Rag)

1925. K. W. G. "Popular Music in the School Room," _Educational Music Magazine,_ XX (Nov.-Dec., 1940), 19. (A & A, Ed)

1926. Kahn, H. "Bebop? One Long Search For the Right Note, Says Louis Armstrong," _Melody Maker,_ XXV (Nov. 12, 1949), 3. (Bop)

1927. Kallen, Horace M. "Swing as Surrealist Music," _in_ Horace M. Kallen. _Art and Freedom._ New York: Duell, Sloan & Pearce, 1942. II, pp. 826–34. (Sw)

1928. Kamman, Leigh. "Mitch's—Nick's of the Midwest," _Down Beat,_ XVII (Apr. 7, 1950), 6. (Ork)

1929. ——. "Stan Turns Minneapolis 'Innovations' Into Music Appreciation Session," _Down Beat,_ XVII (Apr. 21, 1950), 14. (Crit)

1930. Kaplan, Charles. "Edmond Hall," _Jazz Session,_ 5 (Jan.-Feb., 1945), 2, 17. (Pers)

1931. Karberg, Paul F. "Joe Sanders and His Nighthawks," _Swing Music_ (May-June, 1936), 57–8. (Ork)

1932. Karoley, Mary E. "Sidney Bechet," _Jazz Information,_ II (Dec. 6, 1940), 8–16. (Pers)

1933. Katz, Bernard and Lola Pergament. "Why They Go For Jazz," _Parents' Magazine,_ XXXVI (Jan., 1949), 30–1, 96–7. (A & A, Infl)

1934. Kaufman, Helen L. "Blacks and Blues and Ragtime," _in_ Helen L. Kaufman. _From Jehovah to Jazz._ New York: Dodd Mead, 1937. pp. 240–54. (Bl, Rag)

1935. ——. "From Ragtime to Swing," _Scholastic,_ XXXII (Apr. 30, 1938), 29–30, 32. (Hist, Sw)

1936. ——. "Jazz and Its Composers, Our Musical Proletariat," _in_ Helen L. Kaufman. _From Jehovah to Jazz._ New York: Dodd Mead, 1937. pp. 255–71. (A & A, Pers)

1937. Kaufman, Pete. "Champion Jack Dupree," _Jazz Record,_ 58 (Sept., 1947), 24. (Pers)

1938. Kay, George W. "Ragged But Right," _Record Changer,_ IX (Mar., 1950), 5, 12. (Disc, Rag)

1939. Kay, H. B. "8 To the Bar," _Record Changer,_ VIII (May, 1949), 14, 20. (BW, Hist)

1940. Kaye, Joseph. "Says Jazz Would Galvanize American Opera," _Musical America,_ XXXVI (July 22, 1922), 23. (J & O)

1941. Keartland, Eric F. "Discography of Tommy Ladnier," _Jazz Forum,_ 3 (Jan., 1947), 17–20. (Disc)

1942. ——. "Omer Simeon Discography," _Hot Notes,_ II (Oct., 1947), 14–20. (Disc)

1943. Keepnews, Orrin. "The Big Band Period," _Record Changer,_ IX (July-Aug., 1950), 25–6. (Hist, Ork, Pers)

1944. ——. "'Changer' Editor Also Blasts Wolff," _Down Beat,_ XVI (July 15, 1949), 12. (Crit)
See: 1947; 2070; 3294; 3295.

1945. ——. "The Chestnut St. Stompers," _Record Changer,_ IX (Sept., 1950), 8. (Ork)

1946. ——. "Definition of Jazz," _Record Changer,_ VII (Dec., 1948), 9. (Lang)

1947. ——. "Downbeat Article Forces A Restatement of Policy," _Record Changer,_ VIII (Aug., 1949), 5, 17. (Crit)
See: 1944; 2070; 3294; 3295.

1948. ——. "The Evolution of Bop," _Record Changer,_ VII (Mar., 1948), 9–10, 18. (A & A, Bop, Pers)

1949. Keepnews, Orrin. "Sonny Greer, Drums," *Record Changer*, VII (July, 1948), 14, 26. (Pers)

1950. ———. "Roy King and His Komi-Kings," *Record Changer*, IX (May, 1950), 5. (Ork)

1951. ———. "Lady Day Returns," *Record Changer*, VII (June, 1948), 8–9. (Pers, Pic)

1952. ———. "Thelonius Monk's Music May Be First Sign of Bebop's Legitimacy," *Record Changer*, VII (Apr., 1948), 5, 20. (A & A, Bop, Pers)

1953. ———. "On Piano: Joe Sullivan," *Record Changer*, VIII (May, 1949), 9–10, 22. (Pers)

1954. ———. "Ory Rhythm," *Record Changer*, VIII (Jan., 1949), 13, 21. (Ork, Pers)

1955. ———. "Sweet Papa Jelly Roll," *Record Changer*, VII (Feb., 1948), 6–7. (Disc, Pers)

1956. ———. "The Tailgate Jazz Band," *Record Changer*, IX (Feb., 1950), 7, 16. (Ork)

1957. ———. "Thompson's Thumpers," *Record Changer*, IX (Mar., 1950), 7, 19. (Ork)

1958. ———. "The Webfoot Jazz Band," *Record Changer*, IX (Apr., 1950), 7, 17. (Ork)

1959. ———. "Wilber's Wildcats," *Record Changer*, VII (May, 1948), 8–9. (Ork)

1960. Kellogg, J. F. "Benny Morton's Trombone Tips," *Music and Rhythm*, I (Apr., 1941), 78–9. (Inst, Pers)

1961. Kempf, Paul, Jr. "Striking the Blue Note in Music," *Musician*, XXXIV (Aug., 1929), 29. (Bl)

1962. Kendziora, Carl. "Behind the Cobwebs," *Record Changer*, VIII (Apr., 1949), 16, 24; (May, 1949), 12, 19; (June, 1949), 9, 16; (July, 1949), 11, 15; (Aug., 1949), 8, 16; (Sept., 1949), 15, 20; (Oct., 1949), 8, 15; (Nov., 1949), 23–4; (Dec., 1949), 10, 19; IX (Jan., 1950), 10; (Feb., 1950), 8, 16; (Mar., 1950), 8; (Apr., 1950), 11; (May, 1950), 10, 18; (June, 1950), 15, 17; (Nov., 1950), 13, 18; (Dec., 1950), 6, 18. (Disc)

1963. ———. "Benny Goodman Discography," *Record Changer*, VII (Apr., 1948), 9–10, 22–4; (May, 1948), 19–21; (June, 1948), 19–21; (July, 1948), 23–5; (Aug., 1948), 16–18; (Sept., 1948), 17–18; (Oct., 1948), 17–18. (Disc)

1964. Kenton, Stan. "Sure, I Helped to Wreck the Dance Biz, Says Kenton," *Down Beat*, XVII (May 19, 1950), 1. (J & D, Pers)

1965. Kers, Robert de. "Chronique de l'Orchestration," *Hot Club Magazine*, 4 (Apr., 1946), 21; 5 (May, 1946), 21; 6 (June, 1946), 21. (Gen)

1966. Kidder, Margaret. "'Americana' in Paris," *H. R. S. Society Rag*, 4 (Jan., 1939), 16–20. (Geog)

1967. Kiefner, Walter. "Singbewegung und Jazz," *Singgemeinde*, VIII (Aug.-Sept., 1932), 162–69. (Infl)

1968. King, Alexander. "Benny Goodman," *in* George S. Rosenthal (Ed). *Jazzways*. Cincinnati, 1946. pp. 42–5, 102. (Pers)

1969. Kingsley, Walter. "Enigmatic Folksongs of the Southern Underworld," *Current Opinion*, LXVII (Sept., 1919), 165–66. (Bl, Pers)

1970. Kinnell, Bill (Ed). *Jazz Orchestras*. Chilwell, Notts.: 1946. 20 pp.

1971. Kirby, John. "My 10 Favorite Bass Players," *Music and Rhythm*, II (May, 1942), 10, 44. (Pers)

1972. Klemm, Gustav. "The Jargon of Jazz," *Etude*, LII (Aug., 1934), 455–56. (Inst, Lang)

1973. Klonsky, Milton. "Along the Midway of Mass Culture," *Partisan Review*, XVI (Apr., 1949), 362–64. (A & A)

1974. Knight, Vick. "How Many Zeds in Jazz," *Esquire*, XXVI (July, 1946), 104, 205–13. (Geog)

1975. Knowlton, Don. "The Anatomy of Jazz," *Harper's*, CLII (Apr., 1926), 578–585. Reprinted: Kendall B. Taft, and others (Eds). *Contemporary Thought*. New York: Houghton Mifflin, 1929. pp. 478–90. (A & A)

1976. Koebner, Franz Wolfgang. *Jazz und Shimmy*. Berlin: Eysler, 1921. 122 pp. (J & D)
1977. Kolisch, Mitzi. "Jazz in High Places," *Independent*, CXVI (Apr. 10, 1926), 424. (J & C, J & O)
1978. Kolodin, Irving. "The Dance Band Business," *Harper's*, CLXXXIII (June, 1941), 72–82. (Gen)
1979. ——. "Benny Goodman Isn't Hungry Anymore," *Music and Rhythm*, II (July, 1942), 11, 36, 40. (Pers)
1980. ——. "Number One Swing Man," *Harper's*, CLXXIX (Sept., 1939), 431–40. (Pers)
1981. ——. "What About Swing?" *Parents' Magazine*, XIV (Aug., 1939), 18–19. (Infl, Sw)
1982. Kool, Jaap. "The Triumph of the Jungle," *Living Age*, CCCXXIV (Feb. 7, 1925), 338–43. (A & A, Infl, Inst)
1983. Koonce, Dave. "Late Jimmy Blanton Bassdom's Greatest," *Metronome*, LXII (Aug., 1946), 48–9. (Pers)
1984. Korb, Arthur. *How To Write Songs That Sell*. New York: Greenberg, 1949. 179 pp.
1985. Kraeft, Norman. "Darnell Back to Music For Fifth Time," *Down Beat*, XV (Dec. 29, 1948), 4. (Pers)
1986. Kramer, A. Walter. "Extols Ragtime Article," (lr) *New Republic*, V (Dec. 4, 1915), 122. (Rag)
       See: 824; 1065; 2288.
1987. ——. "I Do Not Think Jazz 'Belongs'," *Singing*, I (Sept., 1926), 13–14. (A & A)
       See: 1517; 1518.
1988. Kristensen, Sven Møller. *Hvad Jazz Er*. København: E. Munksgaard, 1938. 94 pp.
1989. ——. *Jazzen Og Dens Problemer*. København: Anderson & Pedersen, 1946. 120 pp.
1990. Krupa, Gene. "Jazz Forum: Has Jazz Influenced the Symphony? No," *Esquire*, XXVII (Feb., 1947), 46, 118. (A & A, Infl, J & C)
       See: 969.
1991. ——. "Gene Krupa On Drummers," *Metronome*, LIX (Oct., 1943), 33, 67. (Pers)
1992. ——. "My Twelve Favorite Drummers," *Music and Rhythm*, II (Nov., 1941), 16. (Pers)
1993. Kyogoku, Takatoshi. "Jazz With a Classical Tint Rules Japan," *Down Beat*, XV (Dec. 1, 1948), 15. (Geog)
1994. L. "Jazz Analyzed," *Commonweal*, XXX (Apr. 28, 1939), 22–3. (Rev)
1995. L. B. "Unvarnished," *Top Notes*, I (May 10, 1930), 12. (J & C)
1996. Lachenbruch, Jerome. "Jazz and the Motion Picture," *Metronome*, XXXVIII (Apr., 1922), 94. (A & A, Infl)
1997. Lafone, Peter. "Of Tenors, They're Top," *Swing Music*, 14 (Autumn, 1936), 19–20. (Pers)
1998. Lambert, Constant. "Jazz," *Life and Letters*, I (July, 1928), 124–31. (A & A, J & C)
1999. ——. "The Spirit of Jazz," *in* Constant Lambert. *Music Ho!* London: Faber and Faber, 1934. pp. 141–52. (A & A)
2000. ——. "Symphonic Jazz," *in* Constant Lambert. *Music Ho!* London: Faber and Faber, 1934. pp. 152–62. (J & C)
2001. Land, Dick. "Carter Means Business," *Metronome*, LIX (Dec., 1943), 17. (Pers)
2002. ——. "Top Song Hits of 30 Years Are Recalled," *Down Beat*, VII (June 15, 1940), 22. (Gen)

2003. Lang, Iain. "The Background of the Blues," *in* Leonard Russell (Ed). *The Saturday Book 1941–42*. London: Hutchinson, 1941. pp. 330–57. Expanded to: *Background of the Blues*. London: Workers' Music Association, 1943. 55 pp. Expanded to: *Jazz in Perspective; the Background of the Blues*. London: Hutchinson, 1947. 148 pp. (Bl)

2004. Lange, Arthur. *Arranging For the Modern Dance Orchestra*. New York: A. Lange, 1926. 238 pp.

2005. Lapham, Claude. "China Needs American Bands," *Metronome*, LII (July, 1936), 13, 39. (Geog)

2006. — —. "If You Must Go To Japan," *Metronome*, LII (Oct., 1936), 16, 29. (Geog)

2007. — —. "Looking at Japanese Jazz," *Metronome*, LII (June, 1936), 14, 27. (Geog)

2008. Larrazet, Georges. *Le Jazz, Prescience d'un Dynamisme Nouveau*. Paris: J. Flory, 1938. 23 pp.

2009. Lastrucci, Carlo L. "The Professional Dance Musician," *Journal of Musicology*, III (Winter, 1941), 168–72. (Gen)

2010. Laubenstein, Paul Fritz. "Jazz—Debit and Credit," *Musical Quarterly*, XV (Oct., 1929), 606–24. (A & A)

2011. Lawrence, Elliot. "Dance Music, Not Bop, Is Our Bread, Butter: Elliot," *Down Beat*, XVII (May 19, 1950), 18. (J & D, Pers)

2012. Lawrence, Robert. "Fats Waller Presents Carnegie Hall Recital," New York *Herald Tribune*, Jan. 15, 1942, 14 : 3. (Crit)

2013. Leclercq, Armand. "Black Brown and Beige, Ou l'Histoire Musicale de la Race Noire," *Hot Club Magazine*, 11 (Nov., 1946), 6–7. (Disc, Ork)

2014. Lee, Amy. "Brunies Faked Magnificently!" *Metronome*, LVII (Feb., 1941), 19, 20, 26–7. (Pers)

2015. — —. "Dailey Tells Why He Hired Unknown Roy Stevens Ork," *Down Beat*, XVII (Jan. 27, 1950), 1, 13. (J & D, Ork)
   See: 2019; 2021; 2024; 2025; 2026; 2027; 2028; 3042; 3274.

2016. — —. "Figs Might Do Well to Take a Hint From Bop—Make New Dixie Sounds," *Down Beat*, XVI (May 6, 1949), 2. (A & A, Bop, NO)

2017. — —. "Jan Garber Cut Jean Goldkette's Band," *Metronome*, LVI (Aug., 1940), 20–1, 24. (Hist, Ork)

2018. — —. "Guarnieri Plays Greatest," *Down Beat*, XVI (July 1, 1949), 2. (Pers)

2019. — —. "'I'm Stunned,' Says Stevens," *Down Beat*, XVII (Feb. 24, 1950), 2. (J & D, Ork)
   See: 2015; 2021; 2024; 2025; 2026; 2027; 2028; 3042; 3274.

2020. — —. "'Jamming' With the Juniors," *Christian Science Monitor Magazine*, Aug. 17, 1946, 6. (Ork)

2021. — —. "'Lab' Band Begins Rehearsals," *Down Beat*, XVII (Jan. 13, 1950), 1, 2. (J & D, Ork)
   See: 2015; 2019; 2024; 2025; 2026; 2027; 2028; 3042; 3274.

2022. — —. "Mail Man Taught Tram to Harris," *Down Beat*, X (Oct. 1, 1943), 15. (Pers)

2023. — —. "Pingatore's Band Had 7 Girl Singers," *Metronome*, LVII (Apr., 1941), 26. (Pers)

2024. — —. "Stevens Cuts for London," *Down Beat*, XVII (Mar. 10, 1950), 4. (Disc, Ork)
   See: 2015; 2019; 2021; 2025; 2026; 2027; 2028; 3042; 3274.

2025. — —. "Roy Stevens Ork Pulls 800 First-Nighters to Dailey's Meadowbrook," *Down Beat*, XVII (Feb. 10, 1950), 1, 4. (J & D, Ork)
   See: 2015; 2019; 2021; 2024; 2026; 2027; 2028; 3042; 3274.

2026. Lee, Amy. "Stevens Reviews Own Ork," *Down Beat*, XVII (Apr. 7, 1950), 2.
(J & D, Ork)
See: 2015; 2019; 2021; 2024; 2025; 2027; 2028; 3042; 3274.
2027. ——. "Stevens Takes Stock as Dailey Date Nears End," *Down Beat*, XVII
(Mar. 24, 1950), 2, 16. (J & D, Ork)
See: 2015; 2019; 2021; 2024; 2025; 2026; 2028; 3042; 3274.
2028. ——. "A Synopsis on Stevens to Date," *Down Beat*, XVII (Apr. 21, 1950),
10. (Ork)
See: 2015; 2019; 2021; 2024; 2025; 2026; 2027; 3042; 3274.
2029. ——. "Wettling Calls Chi. Jazz 'New Orleans'," *Metronome*, LVII (May, 1941),
22–3, 30. (Chi, Pers)
2030. ——. "Wettling's Solid Tubbing Kicks With Any Size Ork," *Down Beat*, XI
(Feb. 15, 1944), 12. (Pers)
2031. ——. "Will Keep Progressing: Woody," *Down Beat*, XVII (Nov. 3, 1950),
1, 2, 3, 4. (Ork)
2032. Lee, George W. *Beale Street, Where the Blues Began*. New York: R. O. Ballou,
1934. 296 pp.
2033. ——. *River George*. New York: Macauley, 1937. 275 pp.
2034. Leonard, Herm. "Picture Gallery," *in* Barry Ulanov and George Simon (Eds).
Jazz 1950. New York: Metronome, 1950. pp. 27–42. (Pic)
2035. Leonard, Howie. "Calls Pierce Band 'Tops in the East'," *Down Beat*, XVII
(Mar. 24, 1950), 14. (Ork)
2036. Levesque, Jacques-Henry. (Trans: John Garnett). "The Heart of Jazz," *Jazz
Hot*, IV (Feb.-Mar., 1938), 7, 9, 11. (A & A)
2037. Levi, Ezio, and Gian Carlo Testoni. *Introduzione Alla Vera Musica Di Jazz*.
Milan: Edizone Magazzino Musicale, 1938. 115 pp.
2038. Levick, M. B. "Free Trade in Jazz Becomes A Mild Issue," New York *Times*,
Mar. 28, 1926, IX, 15 : 1. (Gen)
2039. Levin, Alvin. "Four-Four Time on the High C's," *Musician*, XLIV (Mar.,
1939), 46, 55. (Hist, Sw)
2040. ——. "Swing Glories in Its Humble Origin," *Musician*, XLIV (Apr., 1939),
66, 68. (Sw)
2041. ——. "Swing Marches On," *Musician*, XLIV (Dec., 1939), 219. (Rev,
Sw)
2042. Levin, Michael. "Analyzing the Poll For 10 Year Period," *Down Beat*, XIV
(Jan. 15, 1947), 1, 17. (Poll)
2043. ——. "Bad Year For Records; Says Mix," *Down Beat*, X (Jan. 1, 1943), 8.
(Disc)
2044. ——. "Beat and Readers Come of Age," *Down Beat*, X (Jan. 15, 1943), 21.
(A & A)
2045. ——. "Burns' Work Seems Nearing a Fusion," *Down Beat*, XVI (Jan. 14,
1949), 2. (A & A, J & C)
2046. ——. "Calls 'Jazz Scene' Most Remarkable Album Ever," *Down Beat*, XVII
(Jan. 13, 1950), 14–15. (Disc)
2047. ——. "Duke Fuses Classical and Jazz!" *Down Beat*, X (Feb. 15, 1943), 12–13.
(Crit)
2048. ——. "Ellington Fails to Top Himself!" *Down Beat*, XIII (Dec. 16, 1946),
2. (Crit, Ork)
2049. ——. "Ellington Pleases Concert Crowd," *Down Beat*, XV (Jan. 14, 1948), 3.
(Crit)
2050. ——. "Facts About the 1949 Band Poll," *Down Beat*, XVII (Jan. 13, 1950),
10. (Poll)
2051. ——. "Feather Does Good Job on Book, 'Inside Be-Bop'," *Down Beat*, XVI
(July 15, 1949), 8. (Rev)

2052. Levin, Michael. "'Coleman Hawkins One of Great Forces In Jazz'," *Down Beat*, XVII (Oct. 20, 1950), 2, 3, (Pers)
See: 768; 1809.
2053. — —. "Herman Herd Thrills Packed Carnegie Hall," *Down Beat*, XIII (Apr. 8, 1946), 1, 15. (Crit, Ork)
2054. — —. "Fatha Hines No Plaster-Footed Idol," *Down Beat*, XIV (Mar. 12, 1947), 18. (Pers)
2055. — —. "Jazz Is Neurotic—Stan," *Down Beat*, XV (Jan. 14, 1948), 1, 18–19. (A & A, Bop)
2056. — —. "Lawrence Ork 'Pleasant Surprise'," *Down Beat*, XVII (Feb. 10, 1950), 5. (Crit, Ork)
2057. — —. "Mix Names Best Discs of Year," *Down Beat*, XVI (Dec. 30, 1949), 3. (Disc)
2058. — —. "Most Bands Today Play Too Well—Says Scott," *Down Beat*, IX (May 1, 1942), 4. (A & A)
2059. — —. "Noone's Energy vs BG's Finesse," *Down Beat*, IX (Oct. 1, 1942), 8. (A & A, Pers)
2060. — —. "Oscar Peterson Is One of Finest Things in Years: Mix," *Down Beat*, XVII (Apr. 21, 1950), 5. (Pers)
2061. — —. "Reputation Shredded, Duke Should Disband," *Down Beat*, XVI (June 17, 1949), 1, 12. (Crit)
See: 929; 3270.
2062. — —. "Shaw's New Ork Proves 'Can't Turn Clock Back'," *Down Beat*, XVII (Apr. 21, 1950), 8. (Crit, Ork)
2063. — —. "Strings Are Dancedom's Daisy Mae!" *Down Beat*, XIII (June 17, 1946), 12–13. (Inst)
2064. — —. "Thirty Years of Dancing in U.S." *Down Beat*, XVII (May 19, 1950), 1, 20. (J & D)
2065. — —. "Torme Not All Copa-Setic," *Down Beat*, XIV (June 18, 1947), 4. (Pers)
2066. — —. "Mel Torme Sings Just Like He Writes, Refreshing and Well," *Down Beat*, XIV (Jan. 1, 1947), 4. (Pers)
2067. — —. "What Goes With Goodman?" *Down Beat*, IX (Sept. 1, 1942), 8. (A & A, Pers)
2068. — —. "Why Did Mooney Quartet Fail?" *Down Beat*, XVII (Feb. 10, 1950), 1, 19. (Ork)
2069. — —. "Alec Wilder Replies to Charges of H. E. P.," *Down Beat*, IX (Aug. 15, 1942), 19. (Pers)
2070. — —. "Wolff's Article Is Garbage," *Down Beat*, XVI (July 1, 1949), 1, 13. (Crit)
See: 1944; 1947; 3294; 3295.
2071. — —. "Woody Hits Road After NYC Bow," *Down Beat*, XVII (June 2, 1950), 16. (Crit, Ork)
2072. Levinson, Andre. "The Negro Dance Under European Eyes," *Theatre Arts Monthly*, XI (Apr., 1927), 282–93. Reprinted: Edith J. R. Isaacs (Ed). *Theatre.* Boston: Little, Brown, 1927. pp. 235–45. (J & D)
2073. Levy, Newman. "The Jazz Formula," *Modern Music*, I (June, 1924), 24–5. (A & A)
2074. — —. "Towards Defining the Jazz Formula," *Musical Digest*, VI (July 8, 1924), 6. (A & A)
2075. Lewerke, Jack. "Dave Dexter, Jr." *Record Changer*, VIII (Jan., 1949), 14. (Pers)
2076. — —. "1949 Dixieland Jubilee," *Record Changer*, VIII (Dec., 1949), 6–7. (Crit, Dix)
2077. — —, and Albert M. Otto. "How Do *You* File Your Records?" *Record Changer*, VII (Oct., 1948), 8. (Disc)

2078. Lewis, Ted. "Denies Jazz Is Low Music," (lr) New York *Times*, Feb. 14, 1926 II, 10 : 7. (A & A)
2079. Liebling, Leonard. "The Crime of Ragtime," *Musical Courier*, LXXII (1916), 21–2. (Rag)
2080. — —. "Variationettes," *Musical Courier*, LXXXIV (Mar. 30, 1922), 21. (Infl)
2081. — —. "Variationettes," *Musical Courier*, LXXXIV (May 4, 1922), 21. (Infl, Rev)
2082. Lim, Harry. "Way Down Yonder..." *Metronome*, LIX (Oct., 1943), 26, 38. (NO, Pers)
2083. Litterscheid, Richard. "Das Ende des Jazz in Deutschland," *Die Musik*, XXVIII (Dec., 1935), 236–37. (Gen)
2084. — —. "Nachruf Auf den Jazz," *Die Musik*, XXVIII (Jan., 1936), 321–27. (A & A, Gen)
2085. Liuzza, Ted. "Satchmo a Natch in N. O. Mardi Gras; B. O. at $5,000,000," *Variety*, CLXXIII (Mar. 9, 1949), 1, 63. (Pers)
    See: 18; 28; 495; 1490.
2086. Lloyd, Llewelyn C. "Jazz and the Modern Spirit," *Monthly Musical Record*, LVI (Nov., 1926), 327–28. (A & A)
2087. Loar, Lloyd. "Is 'Jazz' Constructive or Destructive?" *Melody*, VIII (June, 1924), 3–4. (A & A, Infl)
2088. Locke, Alain L. "Blues and Worksongs," *in* Alain L. Locke. *The Negro and His Music*. Washington: Associates in Negro Folk Education, 1936. pp. 28–35. (Bl)
2089. — —. "Classical Jazz and American Music," *in* Alain L. Locke. *The Negro and His Music*. Washington: Associates in Negro Folk Education, 1936. pp. 106–17. (J & C)
2090. — —. "From Jazz to Jazz Classics," *in* Alain L. Locke. *The Negro and His Music*. Washington: Associates in Negro Folk Education, 1936. pp. 93–105. (A & A)
2091. — —. "Jazz and the Jazz Age," *in* Alain L. Locke. *The Negro and His Music*. Washington: Associates in Negro Folk Education, 1936. pp. 70–92. (A & A, Hist)
2092. — —. "Ragtime and Musical Comedy," *in* Alain L. Locke. *The Negro and His Music*. Washington: Associates in Negro Folk Education, 1936. pp. 70–117. (Hist, Rag)
2093. Locke, Bob. "Jean Goldkette Band Was the Greatest—Morgan," *Down Beat* IX (Mar. 15, 1942), 8. (Ork)
2094. — —. "Men Behind the Bands: Joe Haymes," *Down Beat*, IX (May 15, 1942) 18. (Pers)
2095. — —. "Men Behind the Bands: Lowell Martin," *Down Beat*, VIII (Dec. 1, 1941), 18. (Pers)
2096. — —. "'Old-Timers Carve Soloists of Today,' Says Teagarden," *Down Beat*, VIII (Dec. 15, 1941), 4. (A & A)
2097. — —. "Sharon Pease Hits A Mean Groove Himself," *Down Beat*, IX (May 1, 1942), 16, 23. (Pers)
2098. — —. "Waxman Tells of Early Day Jazz Era," *Down Beat*, IX (May 15, 1942), 9. (Hist)
2099. Locke, Ted. "Filthy Records Are A Disgrace To the Music Business, Says Locke," *Down Beat*, VII (Mar. 1, 1940), 4. (Disc)
2100. — —. "Says Most Jazz Critics Are Not Qualified," *Down Beat*, VIII (Feb. 15, 1941), 8, 16. (Crit)
2101. Lockwood, Georgiana. "Meyer Davis Runs Sixty-Two Jazz Orchestras," *American Magazine*, XCIX (Apr., 1925), 72–3. (Pers)
2102. Lodwick, John. "Machine Jazz," *Swing Music*, 14 (Autumn, 1936), 26. (A & A, Ork)

2103. Lomakin, Nicholas. *Lomakin Pocket Fake List for Leaders, Musicians and Singers*. Pittsburg: N. Lomakin, 1944. 12 pp.

2104. Lomax, Alan. *Mister Jelly Roll*. New York: Duell, Sloan and Pearse, 1950. 318 pp. (Pers)

2105. Lomax, John A. and Alan Lomax. *Negro Folk Songs As Sung by Lead Belly*. New York: Macmillan, 1936. 242 pp.

2106. Long, Elizabeth Baker and Mary McKee. "Jazz Idiom," *in* Elizabeth Baker Long and Mary McKee. *A Bibliography of Music For the Dance*. Austin, 1936. pp. 18–19. (J & D)

2107. Lopez, Vincent. "Contemporary Music," *Collaborator*, I (Sept., 1931), 5, 28. (Gen)

2108. ——. "Vincent Lopez Comments on His Unique Experiment," *Musical Observer*, XIII (May, 1924), 30. (Gen)

2109. ——. "Lopez Speaking," *Collier's* LXXVII (Mar. 13, 1926), 12–13. (Gen)

2110. ——. (Ed: Mary Margaret McBride). "Lopez Speaking," *Ladies' Home Journal*, XLVI (Mar., 1929), 12, 163. (Gen)

2111. Lorenz, Clarice. "Jazz—the Newest Musical Phenomenon," *Melody*, VIII (July, 1924), 3–4. (A & A)

2112. Love, William C. "Louis Armstrong's Discography," *Jazz* (New York), I (Dec., 1943), 18–21. (Disc)

2113. ——. "Johnny Dodds' Discography," *Jazz* (New York), I, no. 9 (n. d.), 23–6. (Disc)

2114. ——. "Ma Rainey Discography," *Jazz Information*, II (Sept. 6, 1940), 9–14. (Disc)

2115. Lowry, Helen Bullitt. "Putting the Music Into the Jazz," New York *Times*, Feb. 19, 1922, III 8 : 1. (A & A, Pers)

2116. Lucas, John. "Dawn of Dixieland—Famous Orks, Sidemen," *Down Beat*, XIII (May 20, 1946), 12, 15; (June 17, 1946), 17, 23. Pt. II entitled: "Jazz Grows Up to BG and Woody." (Dix, Hist)

2117. ——. "Follow the Bean, Saxmen's Aim," *Down Beat*, X (Feb. 15, 1943), 21. (Pers)

2118. ——. "Great Piano Sparked Crosby Ork," *Down Beat*, X (Feb. 1, 1943), 14. (Ork)

2119. ——. "Hot Trumpets Come In Fours," *Down Beat*, IX (Oct. 15, 1942), 12. (Pers)

2120. ——. "How Louis Has Influenced Jazz," *Down Beat*, XIV (Nov. 5, 1947), 11. (A & A, NO, Pers)

2121. ——. "Jazz Clarys, Henchmen of Kings," *Down Beat*, X (Mar. 15, 1943), 19. (Pers)

2122. ——. "Lots of Traditional Jazz Albums In Last 1½ Years," *Down Beat*, XVI (Dec. 16, 1949), 3. (Disc)

2123. ——. "Lucas Hails Dixie Uprising," *Down Beat*, XVII (Nov. 3, 1950), 5. (Dix, NO)

2124. ——. "John Lucas Visits England," *Down Beat*, XVII (Sept. 8, 1950), 15. (Geog)

2125. ——. "1946–48 Era Produces 57 Significant Albums," *Down Beat*, XV (June 2, 1948), 12. (Disc)

2126. ——. "Nobody But Joe Venuti Would Think of Building Bonfire On the Stand," *Down Beat*, X (Nov. 1, 1943), 15. (Pers)

2127. ——. "Orleans Jazz Greats a Real Who's Who," *Down Beat*, XII (Dec. 15, 1945), 12; XIII (Jan. 1, 1946), 15; (Jan. 14, 1946), 14. Pt. II entitled: "Jazz Clarinet and Tram New Orleans Perfected." Pt. III entitled: "History of New Orleans Jazz Greats Concluded." (Hist, NO, Pers)

2128. ——. "Ragtime Revival," *Record Changer*, VII (Dec., 1948), 8. (Rag)

2129. Lucas, John. "Saddest Tale," *Record Changer*, VIII (July, 1949), 7. (Crit, Hist, Ork)
2130. —— ——. "Take Tailgate, Tea or Tommy?" *Down Beat*, X (Jan. 1, 1943), 22. (Pers)
2131. Lucas, Robert. "The Real Truth About Marijuana," *Ebony*, III (Sept., 1948), 46–51. (Gen)
2132. Ludwig, William. "Jazz, the Present-Day Live Issue In the Development of American Music," *Metronome*, XXXVIII (May, 1922), 78–9. (Hist, Inst)
2133. Luizzi, F. "'Jazz' e 'Anti-Jazz'," *Nuova Antologia*, CCLI (Jan. 1, 1927), 70–6. (A & A, J & C)
2134. Lunceford, Jimmie. "Is Airtime Essential? Not On My Life—Lunceford," *Metronome*, LVIII (Oct., 1942), 9, 26. (Rad)
2135. M. L. "Jazzing the Classics," (lr) New York *Times*, Feb. 2, 1934, 16 : 7. (Infl, J & C)
2136. MacKillop, Kenneth, Jr. "The Schillinger System," *Down Beat*, XVII (Sept. 22, 1950), 18; (Dec. 1, 1950), 8. (Gen)
2137. McAndrew, John. "Star Studded Shellac," *Record Changer*, IX (May, 1950), 14; (June, 1950), 11; (Oct., 1950), 10, 17; (Nov., 1950), 14, 18. (Disc) *See*: 1078.
2138. McCarthy, Albert J. "Louis Armstrong; Discography," *Record Changer*, IX (July-Aug., 1950), 37–42. (Disc)
2139. —— ——. "Collectors' Notes," *Jazz Forum*, 1 (n. d.), 25–6. (Disc)
2140. —— ——. "Discography of Big Bill Broonzy," *Jazz Forum*, 4 (Apr., 1947), 25–30. (Disc)
2141. —— ——. "Ils Cherchaient Une Ville... Notes Sur Les Styles Nouvelle-Orleans et Chicago," *Hot Club Magazine*, 3 (Mar., 1946), 6–7. (Chi, NO)
2142. —— ——. "Le Jazz et l'Age de la Machine," *Hot Club Magazine*, 7 (July, 1946), 11. (A & A)
2143. —— ——. *Jazzbook 1947*. London: Nicholson & Watson, 1948. 171 pp.
2144. —— ——. "Jelly-Roll Morton Discography," *Jazz Music*, II (Feb.-Mar., 1944), 102–06. (Disc)
2145. —— ——. "My Home Is A Southern Town," *in* Charles Harvey (Ed). *Jazz Parody*. London: Spearman, 1948. pp. 57–61. (Fict)
2146. —— ——. "Ward Pinkett; A Neglected Jazz Great," *Record Changer*, VIII (Feb., 1949), 13, 20. (Pers)
2147. —— ——. "Reflections on Leroy Carr," *Jazz Forum*, 4 (Apr., 1947), 13–14. (Pers).
2148. —— ——. "Report From Abroad," *in* George S. Rosenthal (Ed). *Jazzways*. Cincinnati, 1946. pp. 4, 6–7. (Geog)
2149. —— ——. *The Trumpet In Jazz*. London: Citizen Press, 1945. 82 pp.
2150. —— —— (Ed). *The PL Yearbook of Jazz*. London: Nicholson and Watson, 1946. 188 pp.
2151. —— ——, and Max Jones. *Jazz Folio*. London: Jazz Sociological Society, 1944. 24 pp.
2152. —— ——. *Jazz Miscellany*. London: Jazz Sociological Society, 1944. 26 pp.
2153. —— —— (Eds). *Piano Jazz, No. 1*. London: Jazz Music Books, 1945. 28 pp.
2154. —— ——. *Piano Jazz No. 2*. London: Jazz Music Books, 1945. 28 pp.
2155. McCord, Al G. "Cradle of Recorded Jazz," *Record Changer*, VIII (Mar., 1949), 6–7, 19. (Disc, Hist)
2156. McCormick, Mack. "Chubby to Settle Down in Houston," *Down Beat*, XVII (Feb. 24, 1950), 1. (Pers)
2157. McCulloch, Lyle. "Intolerance and Jazz," *Melody*, VIII (Sept., 1924), 3. (A & A)
2158. McInnes, Graham Campbell. "Jazz," *Canadian Forum*, XV (Feb., 1936), 13–14. (A & A, Hist)

2159. McMay, A. B. "A Defense of Jazz," New York *Times*, Sept. 18, 1926, 14 : 7. (A & A)
See: 15; 17; 165; 168; 233; 558; 559; 560; 2337; 3209.
2160. McKean, Gilbert. "Blues on 52nd Street," *Esquire*, XXIX (Jan., 1948), 91. (Gen)
2161. ———. "French Hot Corner," *Esquire*, XXVII (Feb., 1947), 48, 154–55. (Geog)
2162. ———. "The Jazz Beat: The Best Band In the Land," *Saturday Review of Literature*, XXXI (Apr. 24, 1948), 63. (NO, Ork)
2163. ———. "The Jazz Beat: Business in B," *Saturday Review of Literature*, XXXI (Jan. 31, 1948), 50. (Disc)
2164. ———. "The Jazz Beat: Ellington the Nonpareil," *Saturday Review of Literature*, XXX (Nov. 29, 1947), 62. (Pers)
2165. ———. "The Jazz Beat: Memo: On Bebop," *Saturday Review of Literature*, XXX (Aug. 30, 1947), sup. 18–19. (Bop, Disc)
2166. ———. "The Jazz Beat: Note on Small Bands," *Saturday Review of Literature*, XXX (Sept. 27, 1947), 52. (Ork)
2167. ———. "The Jazz Beat: The Picaresque Ledbetter," *Saturday Review of Literature*, XXX (Dec. 27, 1947), 47. (Pers).
2168. ———. "The Jazz Beat: The Progressive Movement," *Saturday Review of Literature*, XXXI (Aug. 28, 1948), 55. (Disc, Ork)
2169. ———. "The Jazz Beat: Sic Transit Something or Other," *Saturday Review of Literature*, XXXI (July 31, 1948), 52. (Gen)
2170. ———. "The Jazz Beat: Snows of Yesterday," *Saturday Review of Literature*, XXXI (Mar. 27, 1948), 53. (Gen)
2171. McKinley, Ray. "'Ooh, What You Said, Tex!'," *Metronome*, LXIII (Mar., 1947), 19, 39–41. (Crit, Sw)
See: 951.
2172. McMahon, John R. "The Jazz Path of Degredation," *Ladies' Home Journal*, XXXIX (Jan., 1922), 26, 71. (Infl, J & D)
2173. ———. "Our Jazz-Spotted Middle West," *Ladies' Home Journal*, XXXIX (Feb., 1922), 38, 181. (Infl, J & D)
2174. ———. "Unspeakable Jazz Must Go!" *Ladies' Home Journal*, XXXVIII (Dec., 1921), 34, 115–16. (Infl, J & D)
2175. McPartland, Marian. "Crowds Jam Paris Jazz Festival," *Down Beat*, XVI (July 1, 1949), 3. (Crit, Geog)
2176. McPhee, Colin. "Eight to the Bar," *Modern Music*, XX (May-June, 1943), 235–42. (A & A)
2177. ———. "Spirituals to Swing," *Modern Music*, XXIII (Jan., 1946), 224–25. (Crit)
2178. ———. "Torrid Zone," *Modern Music*, XXIII (Jan., 1946), 76–7. (Crit, Pers)
2179. Machito. "Latin Music Isn't What You Think It Is," *Metronome*, LXIII (Aug., 1947), 26. (A & A)
2180. Mackey, Henry B. "Everybody Loves Cecil," *Jazz Record*, 56 (June, 1947), 8–10. (Pers)
2181. ———. "The Phenomenal Resurgence of the Spasm Band," *Record Changer*, IX (Dec., 1950), 8, 17. (Fict)
2182. Madison, Joe. "A Discography of Tiger Rag," *Record Changer*, VIII (Apr., 1949), 21–2. (Disc)
2183. ———, and Cecile Madison. "Good and Rare: Overseas Jazz Releases," *Record Changer*, VII (Dec., 1948), 15, 19; VIII (Jan., 1949), 15; (Mar., 1949), 10, 18; (Apr., 1949), 12, 24; (May, 1949), 16; (June, 1949), 8, 15; (Aug., 1949), 12; (Sept., 1949), 16, 20; (Oct., 1949), 13–14; (Nov., 1949), 18; IX (Jan., 1950), 12; (Feb., 1950), 10, 15; (Mar., 1950), 10; (Apr., 1950), 10, 19; (May, 1950), 12; (June, 1950), 10; (Sept., 1950), 13; (Oct., 1950), 10, 17; (Nov., 1950), 14, 18; (Dec., 1950), 11, 17. (Disc)

2184. Maguire, Helena. "The Revolt Against Formalism," *Musician*, XXVII (Sept., 1922), 26. (Infl)
2185. Maier, Guy. "Battle of Boogie Woogie," *Etude*, LXI (Nov., 1943), 710. (Inst)
2186. Maine, Basil. "For My Part," *Musical Opinion*, LV (Feb., 1932), 399. (A & A)
2187. Malkiel, Henrietta. "Scheherazade in West Virginia," *Musical America*, XLII (Apr. 25, 1925), 3, 26. (J & O)
2188. Mandeville, Ernest W. "Roger Wolfe Kahn From Riches to Rags," *Outlook*, CXLIII (May 5, 1926), 34–6. (Pers)
2189. Manne, Shelly. "Track Star Manne After Own Band, Horse Farm," *Down Beat*, XV (July 28, 1948), 18. (Pers)
2190. Manone, Wingy, and Paul Vandervoort II. *Trumpet On the Wing*. Garden City: Doubleday, 1948. 256 pp.
2191. Mantler, J. Robert. "Red Beans Boston Style," *Record Changer*, VIII (May, 1949), 6–7. (Ork)
2192. Marcelli, N. "Unfortunate Trend in School Music," *School and Society*, LIX (June 17, 1944), 428. (Infl, Sw)
2193. Margulis, Max. "Record Date at Blue Note," *Jazz Record*, XX (May, 1944), 8–9. (Disc)
2194. Marine, Robert. *Robert Marine's Modern Method In Jazz Playing On the Violin*. New York: Robert Marine, 1927. 66 pp.
2195. Mario, Queena. "Confession of a Singer," New York *Times*, Mar. 31, 1927, 22 : 6. (Gen)
2196. Marshall, Kaiser. "Jimmy Harrisson," *Jazz Hot*, IV (Aug.-Sept., 1938), 3, 5. (Pers)
2197. ——. "Joe Smith," *Jazz Hot*, IV (Feb.-Mar., 1938), 12. (Pers)
2198. Martin, Donald. "The Origin of Boogie Woogie," *Etude*, LIX (July, 1941), 445, 486. (BW)
2199. Martin, John. "Inquiry Into Boogie Woogie," New York *Times Magazine*, July 16, 1944, 18, 46–7. (BW)
2200. Martin, Jose Reyes. *Heroes of the Jazz Age*. New York: The Author, 1936. 212 pp.
2201. Mascagni, Pietro. "Trucizna Jazzowa," *Muzyka*, VI (Mar. 20, 1929), 132–33. (A & A, Infl)
2202. Maserow, Henry T. "Jazz and South Africa," *Jazz Forum*, 4 (Apr., 1947), 12. (Geog)
2203. Masin, Herman L. "Jazz Lovers' Paradise," *Scholastic*, XLIV (May 1, 1944), 40, 42. (A & A, Ork)
2204. ——. "Jive in the Wax Works," *Scholastic*, XLVI (Apr. 30, 1945), 32. (Disc)
2205. Mason, Daniel Gregory. "Concerning Ragtime," *New Music Review and Church Music Review*, XVII (Mar., 1918), 112–16. (Rag)
2206. ——. "Folk Song and American Music," *Musical Quarterly*, IV (July, 1918), 323–32. (Rag)
     See: 232.
2207. ——. "Jazz For the Illiterate," *American Mercury*, LVII (Dec., 1943), 761. (A & A)
     See: 1324; 1325; 2701.
2208. ——. "The Jazz Invasion," *in* Samuel Daniel Schmalhausen. *Behold America*. New York: Farrar and Rinehart, 1931. pp. 499–513. (A & A, J & C)
2209. ——. "Stravinsky As A Symptom," *American Mercury*, IV (Apr., 1925), 465–68. (A & A, J & C)
     See: 712.
2210. Mason, Jerry. "Man With Trumpet," New York *Herald Tribune*, May 30, 1943, IX, 10 : 3–4. (Pers)

2211. Mathews, Haydn M. "Jazz—Its Origin, Effect, Future," *Flutist*, V (Feb., 1924), 32–4. (Hist, Infl)
2212. Maxwell, Elsa. "Organized Dementia Praecox," New York *Post*, May 20, 1943, 12 : 1–2. (J & D, Pers)
2213. May, Earl Chapin. "The Reign of Reeds and Rhythm," *Saturday Evening Post*, CXCVII (Jan. 10, 1925), 52, 54, 56. (A & A, Inst)
2214. ——. "Where Jazz Comes From," *Popular Mechanics*, XLV (Jan., 1926), 97–102. (A & A, Hist)
2215. Meehan, Reg. "'I'll Go Back To A Saloon If I Fail!'," *Down Beat*, X (Feb. 1, 1943), 15. (Ork)
2216. Melichar, Alois. "Walzer und Jazz," *Die Musik*, XX (Feb., 1928), 345–49. (Infl)
2217. Mellers, W. H. "Searchlight on Tin Pan Alley," *Scrutiny*, VIII (Mar., 1940), 390–405. (Gen)
2218. Mellor, Richard N. *1000 and One Best Recordings*. Auburndale, 1948. 51 pp.
2219. Mencken, H. L. "Music and Sin," *in* H. L. Mencken. *Prejudices, Fifth Series*. New York: Alfred A. Knopf, 1926. pp. 293–96. (Infl)
2220. Mendl, Robert William Sigismund. *The Appeal of Jazz*. London: P. Allan, 1927. 186 pp.
2221. Merriam, Alan. "The Dilemma of the Jazz Student Today," *Record Changer*, VIII (Nov., 1949), 8, 27. (Ed, Gen)
2222. ——. "Jazz University," *Record Changer*, IX (Mar., 1950), 11, 12. (Ed)
2223. ——. and Robert J. Benford. "Louis Armstrong; Bibliography," *Record Changer*, IX (July–Aug., 1950), 33–5. (Bibl)
2224. Merz, Charles. "Tom-Tom," *Golden Book*, IX (Jan., 1929), 58–60. (Rad)
2225. Merz, Max. "Wir und der Jazz," *Westermanns Monatsheft*, CLXIX (Sept., 1940), 3–6. (A & A)
2226. Mezzrow, Milton. "Lionel Hampton," *Jazz Hot*, V (Feb.-Mar., 1939), 11. (Pers)
2227. ——. "Really the Blues," *Jazz Record*, 56 (June, 1947), 6–7. (Bl)
2228.——, and Bernard Wolfe. *Really the Blues*. New York: Random House, 1946. 388 pp.
2229. Mila, Massimo. "Jazz Hot," *Pan*, IV (Jan., 1935), 84–96. (Ork)
2230. Milhaud, Darius. "Development of the Jazz Band, and North American Negro Music," *Metronome*, XLI (Dec. 15, 1925), 15–16. (A & A, Inst)
2231. ——. "Die Entwicklung der Jazz-band und die Nordamerikanische Negermusik," *Musikblätter des Anbruch*, VII (Apr., 1925), 200–05. (A & A, Inst)
2232. ——. "The Jazz Band and Negro Music," *Living Age*, CCCXXIII (Oct. 18, 1924), 169–73. (A & A)
2233. Millen, Gilmore. *Sweet Man*. London: Cassell, 1930. 301 pp. (Fict)
2234. Miller, Charles. "Aces Wild," *New Republic*, CXVIII (Feb. 23, 1948), 27–8. (Ork)
2235. ——. "Bebop and Old Masters," *New Republic*, CXVI (June 30, 1947), 36. (A & A, Bop)
2236. ——. "Benny Rides Again," *New Republic*, CXVI (Mar. 3, 1947), 41. (Hist, Ork)
2237. ——. "Digging For Swing," *New Republic*, CXVII (Oct. 6, 1947), 37. (Disc)
2238. ——. "Jazz; Celluloid and Wax," *New Republic*, CXVII (Dec. 29, 1947), 35. (Pers)
2239. ——. "Jazz, Pure and Simple," *New Republic*, CXVI (Apr. 14, 1947), 42. (Rad)
2240. ——. "Jazz Under the Elms," *New Republic*, CXVII (July 28, 1947), 33–4. (Ed)
2241. ——. "Jazz Without Beers," *New Republic*, CXV (Aug. 12, 1946), 174. (Crit)

2242. Miller, Charles. "New Orleans in New York," *New Republic*, CXV (Nov. 25, 1946), 694. (Bl, Ork, Pers)
2243. ———. "'Round the Bend'," *New Republic*, CXVI (June 9, 1947), 33–4. (Gen, Hist)
2244. ———. "Swing Nostalgia," *New Republic*, CXVI (May 12, 1947), 35. (Gen)
2245. ———. "Twilight of the Dance Band," *New Republic*, CXVI (Mar. 17, 1947), 40. (Gen, Hist, Ork)
2246. Miller, Fred R. "Breaking In a New Pair of Shoes," *Jazz Record*, 35 (Aug., 1945), 9, 17. (A & A, Disc)
2247. ———. "Old Bunk Opens in New York," *New Republic*, CXIII (Oct. 22, 1945), 528–29. (NO, Ork, Pers)
2248. Miller, H. M. "New American Music Drama of Redemption Utilizes Jazz," *Musical America*, XLI (Apr. 11, 1925), 3. (J & O)
2249. Miller, Paul Eduard. "Are the White Chicagoans of the '20's Overrated? Yes," *Music and Rhythm*, II (Oct., 1941), 45, 57. (Chi)
See: 3196.
2250. ———. "Classics of Jazz," A Series on Famous Jazz Classics in *Music and Rhythm*: (Disc)
"Black and Tan Fantasy," II (Sept., 1941), 34.
"Just A Mood," II (Apr., 1942), 35.
"Keep the Rhythm Going," II (June, 1941), 57.
"Mugging Lightly," II (Aug., 1941), 49.
"Radio Rhythm," II (May, 1941), 60.
"Reminiscing in Tempo," I (Feb., 1941), 36.
"Riverboat Shuffle," I (Mar., 1941), 78.
"Sugar Foot Stomp," I (Jan., 1941), 37.
"West End Blues," I (Apr., 1941), 39.
2251. ———. "Great Performances of Jazz," A Series in *Music and Rhythm*: (Disc)
"I'd Love It," II (Aug., 1941), 49.
"I'm In the Mood for Swing," II (Oct., 1941), 43.
"Lady Be Good," II (June, 1941), 69.
"Stomp Off Let's Go," II (May, 1941), 66.
2252. ———. "Ivie Joined the Duke for Four Weeks, Stays With Band for 12 Years," *Down Beat*, IX (July 15, 1942), 31. (Pers)
2253. ———. "Jazz For the Layman," *Esquire*, XXV (Feb., 1946), 60. (A & A)
2254. ———. "Judging and Appreciating the Best in Hot Music," *Music and Rhythm*, I (Nov., 1940), 78–81; (Dec., 1940), 70–2; (Jan., 1941), 68–70; (Feb., 1941), 68–70; II (May, 1941), 68–70. (A & A)
2255. ———. *Miller's Yearbook of Popular Music*. Chicago: PEM, 1943. 195 pp.
2256. ———. "'Money Invested in Swing Music Will Keep It Alive,' Says Miller," *Down Beat*, VII (Apr. 15, 1940), 6. (Sw)
2257. ———. "The Music of My Race Is Going to Live," *Music and Rhythm*, II (May, 1942), 12–13, 45. (Pers)
2258. ———. "Musical Blasphemies: Thomas (Fats) Waller," *Music and Rhythm*, I (Apr., 1941), 31. (A & A, Pers)
2259. ———. "Musicians' Ignorance Shackles Jazz to the Kindergarten of Music," *Music and Rhythm*, II (June, 1941), 22–5. (A & A)
2260. ———. "Nix Disc Packages; More Single Sales!" *Down Beat*, XV (July 28, 1948), 11. (Disc)
2261. ———. "Reminiscences on the Career of a Jazzman," *Down Beat*, XIII (Mar. 25, 1946), 10–11. (Pers)
2262. ———. "The Rhythm Section: Sidney Bechet: No Peers, Few Equals," *Esquire*, XXIV (July, 1945), 76–7. (Pers)
See: 1398; 1399; 1400; 1410; 2263; 2264; 2877.

2263. Miller, Paul Eduard. "The Rhythm Section: Richard M. Jones: Forgotten Man of Jazz," *Esquire*, XXIV (Dec., 1945), 191–96. (Pers)
See: 1398; 1399; 1400; 1410; 2262; 2264; 2877.

2264. ——. "The Rhythm Section: Max Miller: Champion of Good Jazz," *Esquire*, XXIV (Sept., 1945), 82–3. (Pers)
See: 1398; 1399; 1400; 1410; 2262; 2263; 2877.

2265. ——. "A Tribute to Bunny Berigan," *Down Beat*, IX (July 1, 1942), 14. (Pers)

2266. ——. "Where Is Small-Band Jazz Going?" *Music and Rhythm*, II (Dec., 1941), 18. (A & A)
See: 3204.

2267. ——. "White Jazzmen Today Are Superior to Negroes," *Music and Rhythm*, II (Aug., 1941), 24–5. (A & A, Pers)

2268. —— (Ed). *Downbeat's Yearbook of Swing*. Chicago: Downbeat, 1939. 183 pp.

2269. ——. *Esquire's Jazz Book*. New York: Smith & Durrell, 1944. 230 pp.

2270. ——. *Esquire's 1945 Jazz Book*. New York: A. S. Barnes, 1945. 256 pp. New York: Editions for the Armed Services, 1945. 352 pp.

2271. ——. *Esquire's 1946 Jazz Book*. New York: A. S. Barnes, 1946. 201 pp.

2272. ——, and George Hoefer. "Chicago Jazz History," *Esquire*, XXV (Feb., 1946), 51–5. (Chi, Hist)

2273. Miller, William H. "The Blues," *Jazz* (New York), I, no. 7 (n. d.), 17. (Poet)

2274. ——. "The Coming Era of Specialization," *Reprints and Reflections*, 4 (June, 1945), 2. (Disc)

2275. ——. *A Discography of the "Little" Recording Companies*. Victoria: William H. Miller, 1943. 20 pp. (Disc)

2276. ——. "Jumpin' Pete! A Short Tribute to Pete Brown," *Jazz* (New York), I, no. 7 (n. d.), 8–9. (Pers)

2277. ——. "Max Kaminsky," *Jazz Quarterly*, II (Summer, 1944), 16–18, 26–8. (Pers)

2278. ——. *The Little Discography*. Melbourne: William H. Miller, 1945. 61 pp. (Disc)

2279. —— (Ed). *Three Brass: Floyd O'Brien, Maxie Kaminsky, Shorty Sherock*. Melbourne: William H. Miller, 1945. 8 pp. (Pers)

2280. Milligan, Harold Vincent. "From Rag-Time to Classical," *Woman's Home Companion*, XLVI (Nov., 1919), 26. (J & C)

2281. Millstein, Gilbert. "For Kicks," *New Yorker*, XXII (Mar. 9, 1946), 30–4, 36, 38, 40; (Mar. 16, 1946), 34–8, 41–3. (Disc, Pers)

2282. ——. "The Twilight of a Zany Street," *New York Times*, Jan. 1, 1950, VI, 12–13, 22. (Pers)

2283. ——. "Very Good Night," *New York Times*, Oct. 15, 1950, VI, 41. (Pers)

2284. Mitchell, Bruce. "Sam Donahue Band Tasty," *Down Beat*, XV (Dec. 1, 1948), 2. (Ork)

2285. Mitchell, Charles H. "Louis Armstrong," (lr) *Disques*, I (Nov., 1930), 387. (Disc, Pers)

2286. Mitchell, Donald. "Kurt Weill's 'Dreigroschenoper' and German Cabaret-Opera in the 1920's," *Chesterian*, XXV (July, 1950), 1–6. (J & O)

2287. Mize, J. T. H. *Bing Crosby and the Bing Crosby Style*. Chicago: Who Is Who In Music, 1946. 170 pp. (Pers)

2288. Moderwell, Hiram K. "Ragtime," *New Republic*, IV (Oct. 16, 1915), 284–86. (Rag)
See: 824; 1065; 1986.

2289. ——. "Two Views of Ragtime. I. A Modest Proposal," *Seven Arts*, II (July, 1917), 368–76. (Rag)
See: 1096.

2290. Modlin, Jules. "Notes Towards a Definition of Jazz," *Needle*, I (June, 1944), 20–1. (A & A)

2291. Moerman, Ernst. "Louis Armstrong," *in* Nancy Cunard (Ed). *Negro.* London: Wishart, 1934, p. 295. (Poet)
2292. Mohr, Kurt. *Discographie du Jazz.* Geneva: Robert Vuagnat, 1945. 84 pp. (Disc)
2293. Møller, Børge J. C. *Dansk Jazz Discografi.* Copenhagen: Artum Musikforlag, 1945. 94 pp.
2294. ———. *Parlophone Bio-Discografi.* Copenhagen: A/S L. Irich's Bogtrykkeri, 1946. 64 pp.
2295. Montani, Nicola A. "Says Operatic and 'Jazz' Influence Contaminate Our Sacred Music," *Musical America*, XXXII (Aug. 21, 1920), 24. (Infl, J & O)
2296. Moon, Bucklin. "Books Noted: 'Jazz Directory'," *Record Changer*, IX (Mar., 1950), 7, 18. (Rev)
2297. ———. "Books Noted: 'They All Played Ragtime'," *Record Changer*, IX (Dec., 1950), 11. (Rev)
2298. ———. "Kenneth Lloyd Bright," *Record Changer*, VIII (Feb., 1949), 16, 20. (Pers)
2299. ———. "Frontiers of Jazz: Ralph de Toledano," *Record Changer*, VII (Feb., 1948), 8. (Rev)
2300. ———. "Good Diggin'," *Record Changer*, VII (Sept., 1948), 13. (Rev)
2301. ———. "The Horn Behind the Blues," *Record Changer*, IX (July-Aug., 1950), 14. (Bl, Disc, Pers)
2302. ———. "Index to Jazz, Orin Blackstone," *Record Changer*, VII (June, 1948), 18. (Rev)
2303. ———. "Mahalia Jackson: A Great Gospel Singer," *Record Changer*, VIII (Apr., 1949), 15–16. (Pers)
2304. ———. "Mr. Jelly Roll," *Record Changer*, IX (Sept., 1950), 5, 15. (Rev)
2305. ———. "The New Hot Discography: Charles Delaunay," *Record Changer*, VII (Nov., 1948), 15. (Rev)
2306. ———, and Kenneth Lloyd Bright. "Last of the Tubas," *Record Changer*, VII (May, 1948), 11–12, 24. (Pers)
2307. ———, and Ross Russell. "Jazz: A People's Music: Sidney Finkelstein," *Record Changer*, VII (Dec., 1948), 13, 20–1. (Rev)
2308. Moor, Paul. "In Search of a Native Muse," *Theatre Arts*, XXXIII (June, 1949), 40–1. (A & A, J & C)
2309. Moore, A. L. H. "Paul Whiteman, the Reformer of Music," *British Musician*, V (June, 1929), 165–67. (Pers)
2310. Mordkin, Mikhail. "Mordkin's Views on Jazz," *New York Times*, Dec. 3, 1924, 22 : 7. (J & D)
2311. Morgan, Tippy. "It Can Happen to Anyone," *Down Beat*, XVII (Nov. 17, 1950), 13, 19; (Dec. 1, 1950), 6. (Gen)
2312. Morgan, William J. "A Defence of Jazz and Ragtime," *Melody*, VI (Sept., 1922), 5. (Gen)
2313. Morrow, Edward and Kyle Crichton. "Dark Magic," *Collier's*, CIII (June 24, 1939), 40–1, 78–9. (BW, Hist)
2314. Morton, Jelly Roll. "I Discovered Jazz in 1902," *in* Ralph de Toledano (Ed). *Frontiers of Jazz.* New York: Oliver Durrell, 1947. pp. 104–07. (Gen)
2315. ———. (As told to Herman Rosenberg). "Buddy Petit," *Jazz Information*, II (Sept. 20, 1940), 17. (Pers)
2316. Mosher, Jack. "Drummer Boy," *Collier's*, CII (Sept. 3, 1938), 24, 56. (Pers)
2317. ———. "A Swing Band Is Born," *Collier's*, CIII (May 20, 1939), 17, 32, 34. (Ork)
2318. Motherwell, Hiram. "Hitching Jazz to a Star," *Musical America*, XLIX (Mar. 10, 1929), 13, 55. (J & C)
2319. Mougin, Stephane. "La Musique de Jazz," *Nouvelle Revue*, CXIII (May-June, 1931), 288–96. (A & A)

2320. Moynahan, James H. S. "Ragtime to Swing," *Saturday Evening Post,* CCIX (Feb. 13, 1937), 14–15, 40, 42, 44. (A & A, Ork, Sw)
2321. ———. "How to Play 'Jazz'," *Record Changer,* VII (Aug., 1948), 10, 21.
2322. ———. "Jazz—A Vanishing Art?" *Jazz Record,* 22 (July, 1944), 6–8. (A & A)
2323. Müller, E. J. "Jazz als Karikatur," *Auftakt,* VI (1926), 216–18. (A & A)
2324. Murphy, Turk and Lester Koenig. "New Orleans Has a Future," *Record Changer,* VIII (Nov., 1949), 12–13, 28–9. (NO, Pers)
2325. Murray, Ken. "Louis, Bix Had Most Influence on Der Bingle," *Down Beat,* XVII (July 14, 1950), 16. (Pers)
2326. Mylne, Dave. "V-Disc Catalogue," *Jazz Journal,* I (Aug., 1948), 10, 12; (Oct., 1948), 10; (Nov., 1948), 13; II (Jan., 1949), 13; (Feb., 1949), 13; (May, 1949), 16–17; (June, 1949), 12. (Disc)
2327. Napoleon, Phil. "Music Must Be Played Simply, Says Napoleon," *Down Beat,* XVII (May 19, 1950), 16. (J & D, Pers)
2328. Narodny, Ivan. "The Birth Processes of Ragtime," *Musical America,* XVII (Mar. 29, 1913), 27. (Rag)
2329. Neff, Wesley M. "A Biography of George Mitchell—Little Mitch—," *Jazz Information,* II (Nov., 1941), 32–6. (Pers)
2330. ———. "Discography of Jimmie Noone," *Jazz Information,* II (Nov. 8, 1940), 15–22. (Disc)
2331. ———. "Jimmie Noone," *Jazz Information,* II (Oct. 4, 1940), 6–9. (Pers)
2332. Neill, Billy and E. Gates. *Discography of the Recorded Works of Django Reinhardt and the Quintette du Hot Club de France.* London: Clifford Essex, 1944. 24 pp. (Disc)
2333. Nejedly, Gustav. "Hat die Bekämpfung der Jazzmusik für die Musikinstrumenten-Industrie Nachteile oder Vorteile?" *Zeitschrift für Instrumentenbau,* L (Aug. 1, 1930), 708. (Infl)
2334. Nelson, Stanley R. *All About Jazz.* London: Heath, Cranton, 1934. 190 pp.
2335. Nevin, Gordon Balch. "Jazz—Whither Bound?" *Etude,* XLVII (Sept., 1929), 655, 699. (A & A)
2336. Newell, George. "George Gershwin and Jazz," *Outlook,* CXLVIII (Feb. 29, 1928), 342–43, 351. (A & A, J & C, Pers)
2337. Newman, Ernest. "Summing Up Music's Case Against Jazz," New York *Times,* Mar. 6, 1927, IV, 3. (A & A)
See: 15; 17; 165; 168; 233; 558; 559; 560; 3209.
2338. Nichols, E. J. and W. L. Werner. "Hot Jazz Jargon," *Vanity Fair,* XLV (Nov., 1935), 38, 71. (Lang)
2339. Nichols, Lewis, "Tin Pan Alley Now Paved With Profits," New York *Times,* Mar. 27, 1932, V, 10, 20. (Gen)
2340. Nicholson, Roger. "The Swing to Strings," *Music and Rhythm,* II (Oct., 1941), 36, 56. (Inst, Pers)
2341. Nickel, Ed and Bill Mull. "Blues and Skiffle," *Record Changer,* VIII (Nov., 1949), 25; (Dec., 1949), 14, 19; IX (Jan., 1950), 15; (Feb., 1950), 13, 14; (Mar., 1950), 9, 19; (May, 1950), 19. (Disc)
2342. Niemoeller, A. F. *Sex Ideas in Popular Songs.* Girard: Haldeman-Julius, 1946. 32 pp.
2343. ———. *The Story of Jazz.* Girard: Haldeman-Julius, 1946. 32 pp.
2344. Niesen, Henk, Jr. "Rambling in the Past," *Swing Music,* 14 (Autumn, 1936), 6–8, 82–3. (Gen)
2345. Niles, Abbe. "Ballads, Songs and Snatches," *Bookman,* LXVII (June, 1928), 422–24. (Disc)
2346. ———. "Blue Notes," *New Republic,* XLV (Feb. 3, 1926), 292–93. Reprinted as: "The Blues," *in* Ralph de Toledano (Ed.) *Frontiers of Jazz.* New York: Oliver Durrell, 1947. pp. 32–57. Reprinted as: "The Story of the Blues," *in*

W. C. Handy (Ed). *A Treasury of the Blues*. New York: Charles Boni, 1949. pp.
1926), 9–32. (A & A, Bl, Hist)
2347. Niles, Abbe. "The Ewe Lamb of Widow Jazz," *New Republic*, XLIX (Dec. 29,
164–66. (A & A, J & C)
2348. —— —. "Jazz 1928: An Index Expurgatorius," *Bookman*, LXVIII (Jan., 1929),
570–72. (Disc)
2349. —— —. "Lady Jazz in the Vestibule," *New Republic*, XLV (Dec. 23, 1925),
138–39. (A & A, J & C)
2350. —— —. "A Note on Gershwin," *Nation*, CXXVIII (Feb. 13, 1929), 193–94.
(A & A, Pers)
2351. —— —. "Sour Notes on Sweet Songs," *New Republic*, L (Feb. 23, 1927), 19–20.
(Rev)
2352. Niles, John J. "Shout, Coon, Shout!" *Musical Quarterly*, XVI (Oct., 1930),
516–30. (Bl, Hist)
2353. Noble, Hollister. "Jazz Feels Surge of a Higher Order," New York *Times
Magazine*, Mar. 15, 1925, IV, 9. (A & A)
2354. —— —. "Sad, Raucous Blues Charm World Anew," New York *Times*, Sept. 26,
1926, IV, 2 : 1, 16. (Bl)
2355. Noble, Peter. *Transatlantic Jazz*. London: Citizen, 1945. 96 pp.
2356. —— — (Ed). *Yearbook of Jazz*. London: Citizen, 1945.
2357. Nordell, Rod. "'Danceable... Happy' Dixieland Jazz," *Christian Science
Monitor Magazine*, May 13, 1950, 16. (Dix, Pers)
2358. Norris, Frank. "Wilder Hobson," *H. R. S. Society Rag*, 3 (Jan., 1939), 1–5.
(Pers, Rev)
2359. —— —. "The Killer-Diller," *Saturday Evening Post*, CCX (May 7, 1938), 22–3,
112, 113, 114. Reprinted: Ralph de Toledano (Ed). *Frontiers of Jazz*. New York:
Oliver Durrell, 1947. pp. 148–61. (Ork, Pers)
2360. —— —. "Long Lives the King," *Life*, V (Dec. 26, 1938), 48–53. (Pers, Pic)
2361. —— —. "The Music Goes 'Round and Around," *New Republic*, LXXXV (Jan.
29, 1936), 334–35. (A & A, Sw)
See: 1420.
2362. Oakley, Helen. "Duke Ellington," *Jazz Hot*, 12 (Nov., 1936), 5–6. (Ork)
2363. —— —. "Ellington to Offer 'ToneParallel'," *Down Beat*, X (Jan. 15, 1943), 13.
(A & A)
2364. —— —. "Frank Newton a l'Onyx Club," *Jazz Hot*, III (Aug.-Sept., 1937), 11.
(Crit, Pers)
2365. Oathout, Melvin C. *Bibliography of Jazz*. Unpublished MS, Library of Congress. 21 pp. (Bibl)
2366. Obispo, Simon (Bernard Heuvelmans). "L'Histoire Mysterieuse et Passionante
du Jazz," *Europe-Amerique*, III (Nov. 20, 1947), 22–7; (Nov. 27, 1947), 20–3;
(Dec. 4, 1947), 18–22.
2367. Oehmler, Leo. "Ragtime," *Musical Observer*, XI (Sept., 1914), 14–15. (Infl,
Rag)
2368. Offbeat. "Popular Records," *New Yorker*, XXI (Nov. 24, 1945), 93–4. (Disc)
2369. O'Hara, John. "Take It!" *New Republic*, CI (Dec. 27, 1939), 287; CII (Feb. 12,
1940), 214–15. (Gen)
2370. Orem, Preston Ware. "Social Dancing and Its Music," *Etude*, LVI (July,
1938), 431–32. (J & D)
2371. Ortiz Oderigo, Nestor R. "El Arte de Harry Carney," *Ritmo y Melodia*, IV
(Sept., 1947), n. p. (Pers)
2372. —— —. "Bibliografia del Jazz," *Nosotros*, VII (Nov., 1942), 202–07. (Bibl)
2373. —— —. "Blues en el Estilo Chicago," *Ritmo y Melodia*, V (Mar.-Apr., 1949),
n. p. (Bl, Chi)
2374. —— —. "De Dixieland a Harlem," *Pauta*, I (July, 1939), 11–12, 30–1, 38. (Hist)

2375. Ortiz Oderigo Nestor R. "Duke Ellington," *El Sol*, May 26, 1940, 9. (Pers)
2376. ——. "Duke Ellington, Verdadero Rey del Jazz," *La Razon*, VI, no. 1905, n. p., Suplemento de los Sabados. (Pers)
2377. ——. "En el Mundo del Jazz," *Ritmo*, XIX (Apr., 1949), 16; (May-June, 1949), 19; (July-Aug., 1949), 19. (Gen)
2378. ——. "En el Mundo del Jazz: Kid Rena Ha Fallecido en EE. UU." *Ritmo*, XIX (Sept., 1949), 19. (Pers)
2379. ——. "Una Expression Genuina del Folklore Negro: Los Blues," *Vea y Lea*, IV (Mar. 17, 1949), 41–3, 60. (Bl)
2380. ——. "Las Grandes Orquestas Interpretes de Blues," *Ritmo y Melodia*, V (May, 1949), n. p. (Bl, Pers)
2381. ——. "El Jazz y la Cultura Negra," *Club de Ritmo*, 28 (Aug., 1948), 1–2. (A & A)
2382. ——. "El Jazz y la Musica Folklorica Afroamericana," *Ritmo y Melodia*, IV (Nov., 1947), n. p. (A & A)
2383. ——. "El Jazz Ciudadano del Mundo," *Vea y Lea*, II (Oct. 14, 1948), 42–3, 54. (Hist)
2384. ——. "El Jazz: Triunfo del Genio Musical del Negro," *Vea y Lea*, IV (Oct., 1949), 19–21, 40–1, 60. (A & A, Hist, Infl)
2385. ——. "Lonnie Johnson et la Guitare Dans le Jazz," *Hot Club Magazine*, 8 (Aug., 1946), 16–17. (Pers)
2386. ——. "Musicos Blancos Interpretes de Blues," *Ritmo y Melodia*, V (Feb., 1949), n. p. (Bl, Pers)
2387. ——. "Los Negros y el Jazz," *Nosotros*, VII (Apr., 1942), 71–5. (A & A)
2388. ——. "Origen del Boogie Woogie," *Vea y Lea*, II (Mar. 4, 1948), 28, 40. (BW)
2389. ——. "Perfil de Jack Teagarden," *Ritmo y Melodia*, IV (Apr., 1947); (May, 1947), n. p. (Pers)
2390. ——. "Al Pratt in Buenos Aires," *Playback*, II (Aug., 1949), 5–6. (Geog)
2391. ——. "A Proposito de Ed. Allen," *Ritmo y Melodia*, IV (Oct., 1947), n. p. (Pers)
2392. ——. No title. *Trayectoria*, II (Jan. 8, 1948), 16–17. (Hist)
2393. Ortmann, Otto. "Notes on Jazz," *Peabody Bulletin*, XXVIII (Dec., 1931), 11–17. (A & A)
2394. ——. "What Is Wrong With Modern Music?" *American Mercury*, XIX (Mar., 1930), 372–76. (A & A)
2395. Ory, Kid. "Louis Was Just a Little Kid In Knee Pants; Ory," *Down Beat*, XVII (July 14, 1950), 8. (Hist, Pers)
2396. —— (As told to Lester Koenig). "The Hot Five Sessions," *Record Changer*, IX (July-Aug., 1950), 17, 45. (Disc, Ork)
2397. Osgood, Henry Osborne. "The Anatomy of Jazz," *American Mercury*, VII (Apr., 1926), 385–95. (A & A, Inst)
2398. ——. "The Blooey Blues," *Musical Courier*, XCIII (Aug. 19, 1926), 7, 33. (Bl)
2399. ——. "The Blues," *Modern Music*, IV (Nov.-Dec., 1926), 25–8. (Bl)
2400. ——. "An Experiment in Music," *Musical Courier*, LXXXVIII (Feb. 21, 1924), 39. (Crit)
2401. ——. "The Jazz Bugaboo," *American Mercury*, VI (Nov., 1925), 328–30. (A & A, J & C)
2402. ——. *So This Is Jazz*. Boston: Little, Brown, 1926. 258 pp.
2403. O'Steen, Alton. "Swing In the Classroom?" *Music Educator's Journal*, XXV (Feb., 1939), 25–7. (Ed, Sw)
2404. Otto, Albert S. "Dixieland Jubilee," *Record Changer*, VIII (Jan., 1949), 6–7. (Crit)
2405. ——. "The Fabulous Collection," *Record Changer*, VIII (Apr., 1949), 13–14. (Disc)

2406. Otto, Albert S. "High Fidelity," *Record Changer*, VII (Nov., 1948), 10. (Tech)
2407. Oxtot, Dick. "Alexander's Jazz Band," *Record Changer*, VIII (Feb., 1949), 15, 20. (Ork)
2408. P. G. "Representatives of 2,000,000 Women, Meeting in Atlanta, Vote to Annihilate Jazz," *Musical Courier*, LXXXVI (May 31, 1923), 5, 29. (Infl)
2409. Page, Hot Lips. (As Told to Kay C. Thompson). "Kansas City Man," *Record Changer*, VIII (Dec., 1949), 9, 18. (KC, Pers)
2410. Page, Marian. (Marian McPartland). "British Cats Fight to Sound Their 'A'," *Down Beat*, XVII (Apr. 7, 1950), 18. (Geog)
2411. Palmer, Tom. "Fatha' Hines Thumbs His Nose at Jazz," *Music and Rhythm*, II (Nov., 1941), 10. (Pers)
2412. ——. "The Story of Count Basie and His Band," *Music and Rhythm*, II (Oct., 1941), 22–3, 57. (Ork, Pers)
2413. ——. "What's Wrong With Trombonists?" *Music and Rhythm*, I (Jan., 1941) 17–21. (Disc, Pers)
2414. Pampel, Gottfried. "German Jazz Tries to Shuck Its Zickigkeit," *Down Beat*, XV (Aug. 25, 1948), 7. (Geog)
2415. ——. "German Law Student Reveals Jazz' Status," *Down Beat*, XV (Apr. 7, 1948), 14. (Geog)
2416. Panassie, Hugues. "Alto Saxophonists," *Jazz Hot*, 13 (Dec., 1936), 3–6. (Pers)
2417. ——. "Louis Armstrong," *Presence Africaine*, 4 (1948), 687–89. (Pers)
2418. ——. "Louis Armstrong In the Past and Today," *Jazz Information*, II (Feb. 21, 1941), 11–13. (Disc, Pers)
2419. has been omitted.
2420. ——. "Aural Evidence in Record Research," *Jazzfinder*, I (June, 1948), 15–16. (Disc, Gen)
2421. ——. "Count Basie and the Blues," *Jazz Journal*, I (Nov., 1948), 2–4. (Bl, Pers)
2422. ——. (Trans: Ian Munro Smyth). "A Call to Order," *Jazz Hot*, 11 (Sept.-Oct., 1936), 5–6. (A & A)
2423. ——. *Discographie: Critique des Meilleurs Disques de Jazz.* Geneva: Ch. Grasset, 1948. 322 pp. (Disc)
2424. ——. (Trans: Nicandra McCarthy). "Johnny Dodds," *Jazz Forum*, 1 (n. d.), 24–5. (Pers)
2425. ——. *Douze Annees de Jazz (1927–1938) Souvenirs.* Paris: Correa, 1946. 281 pp.
2426. ——. (Trans: Ian Munro-Smyth). "Andre Ekyan," *Jazz Hot*, 13 (Dec., 1936), 7–8. (Pers)
2427. ——. "Teddy Hill's Orchestra," *Jazz Hot*, III (June-July, 1937), 3–4, 6. (Ork)
2428. ——. *Histoire des Disques Swing.* Geneva: Charles Grasset, 1944. 117 pp. (Disc)
2429. ——. "Hot Musicians and Author's Rights," *Jazz Hot*, 13 (Dec., 1936), 9–8. (Gen)
2430. ——. (Trans: Margaret Kidder). "Impressions of America," *Jazz Hot*, V (Feb.-Mar. 1939), 3, 5, 7, 9–10; (Apr.-May, 1939), 7–13. (Crit, Ork, Pers)
2431. ——. "Le Jazz et la Danse," *Formes et Couleurs*, 4 (1948), n. p. (J & D)
2432. ——. "El Jazz y la Musica Clasica," *Las Moradas*, I, no. 2 (n. d.), 192–98. (Hist)
2433. ——. "Jazz-Hot," *Revue Musicale*, XIV (Feb., 1933), 152–55. (Disc)
2434. ——. "Le Jazz Hot," *L'Edition Musicale Vivante*, III (Feb., 1930), 9–11. (A & A, Disc)
2435. ——. "Le Jazz 'Hot'," *Revue Musicale*, XI (June, 1930), 481–94. (A & A, Disc, Pers)
2436. ——. *Le Jazz Hot.* Paris: Correa, 1934. 432 pp. Reprinted as: *Hot Jazz, the Guide to Swing Music.* (Trans: Lyle and Eleanor Dowling). New York: M. Witmark, 1936. 363 pp.

2437. Panassie, Hugues. "Le Jazz Lukewarm," *Saturday Review of Literature*, XXX (Dec. 27, 1947), 39–40, 48. (A & A)

2438. ——. "Looking at the World's Ace Swing Clarinetists," *Metronome*, LII (Sept., 1936), 39, 45. (Rev)

2439. ——. (Trans: Ian Munro Smyth). "Jimmy Lunceford and His Orchestra," *Jazz Hot*, III (Nov.-Dec., 1937), 3–17. (Ork)

2440. ——. "Jelly Roll Morton on Records," *Jazz Information*, II (Nov., 1941), 25–8. Reprinted: Ralph de Toledano (Ed). *Frontiers of Jazz*. New York: Oliver Durrell, 1947. pp. 108–14. (Disc)

2441. ——. "Jimmie Noone," *Jazz Information*, II (Mar. 21, 1941), 10–12, 30. (Disc)

2442. ——. (Ed: John D. Reid). *144 Hot Jazz Bluebird and Victor Records*. Camden: RCA, c. 1940. 43 pp. (Disc)

2443. ——. *The Real Jazz*. (Trans: Anne Sorelle Williams, and adapted by Charles Edward Smith). New York: Smith & Durrell, 1942. 326 pp. Reprinted as: *La Veritable Musique de Jazz*. Paris: R. Laffont, 1946. 298 pp. Condensed as: *La Musique de Jazz et le Swing*. Paris: Correa, 1945. 172 pp.

2444. ——. "Recordings of Tommy Ladnier; Milton Mezzrow," *Jazz Hot*, V (July-Aug., 1939), 3–9. (Disc, Pers)

2445. ——. *Les Rois du Jazz, Notes Biographiques et Critiques Sur les Principaux Musiciens de Jazz*. Geneva: C. Grasset, 1944. 2 Pts., 252 pp.

2446. ——. "Session Don Byas," *Hot Club Magazine*, 21 (Nov., 1947), 11. (Disc, Pers)

2447. ——. "Session Tyree Glenn-Don Byas," *Hot Club Magazine*, 22 (Dec. 1, 1947), 11. (Disc, Pers)

2448. ——. (Trans: Ian Munro-Smyth). "Joe Smith Is Dead," *Jazz Hot*, IV (Feb.-Mar., 1938), 5. (Pers)

2449. ——. "Eddie South au Club des Oiseaux," *Jazz Hot*, III (Aug.-Sept., 1937), 10. (Crit, Pers)

2450. ——. "'Swinging the Blues'," *Hot Club Magazine*, 2 (Feb., 1946), 3, 5. (Bl, Ork)

2451. ——. "This Last Year's Best Recordings: 1937," *Jazz Hot*, IV (June-July, 1938), 15, 17. (Disc)

2452. ——. "Vive la Nouvelle Orleans," *Saturday Review of Literature*, XXXI (June 26, 1948), 50. (A & A)

2453. ——. "La Vraie Physionomie de la Musique de Jazz," *Revue Musicale*, XV (May, 1934), 359–71. (A & A, Sw)

2454. ——. (Trans: Ian Munro-Smyth). "Thomas 'Fats' Waller and His Rhythm," *Jazz Hot*, 8 (May, 1936), 3–5; 9 (June, 1936), 3–5. (Disc, Ork)

2455. ——. "Teddy Weatherford," *Jazz Hot*, III (June-July, 1937), 9. (Pers)

2456. ——. (Trans: Nicandra McCarthy). "Albert Wynn," *Jazz Forum*, 3 (Jan., 1947), 13–14. (Pers)

2457. ——. and Andy Gurwitch. "Postwar Jazz in France," *Saturday Review of Literature*, XXXI (Sept. 25, 1948), 51, 54. (Disc, Geog)

2458. Papo, Alfredo. "Le Jazz a Barcelone," *Hot Club Magazine*, 12 (Dec., 1946), 14. (Geog)

2459. Parker, D. C. "Its Vulgarity Lies Over the Land," *Musical News*, LXXIII (Dec. 1, 1928), 312. (A & A, J & C)

2460. ——. "The Poverty of Jazz," *Musical Standard*, XXXVI (Aug. 9, 1930), 41–2. (A & A)

2461. Pascoli, Daniel. "France Rich in Young Musicians," *in* Orin Blackstone (Ed). *Jazzfinder '49*. New Orleans: Orin Blackstone, 1949. pp. 31–6. (Geog)

2462. Patterson, Frank. "An Afternoon of Jazz," *Musical Courier*, LXXXVIII (Feb. 14, 1924), 38. (A & A, Crit)

2463. Patterson, Frank. "'Jazz'—The National Anthem," *Musical Courier*, LXXXIV (May 4, 1922), 18; (May 11, 1922), 6. (A & A, Inst, Pers)
2464. Paul, Les. "My Twelve Favorite Guitarists," *Music and Rhythm*, II (July, 1942), 14. (Pers)
2465. Pearce, Cedric. (Ed: William H. Miller). *Trumpet In the Night*. Melbourne: William H. Miller, 1945. 22 pp.
2466. Peart, Mary. "Talking About Boze," *Jazz Record*, 18 (Mar., 1944), 11. (Pers)
2467. Pease, Sharon A. "Bop Harmony a Contribution of Jimmy Jones," *Down Beat*, XVI (Apr. 8, 1949), 12. (Pers)
2468. —— —. "Bop Man Haig Serious and Well-Schooled," *Down Beat*, XVI (June 3, 1949), 12. (Pers)
2469. —— —. "Erskine Butterfield Is Jack of All Trades," *Down Beat*, VIII (Dec. 1, 1941), 16. (Pers)
2470. —— —. "Frankie Carle Actually Began His Professional Career At Age of Nine," *Down Beat*, IX (Oct. 1, 1942), 18. (Pers)
2471. —— —. "Catholic Nuns Gave Tommy Lineham His First Music Lessons," *Down Beat*, VII (Apr. 15, (1940), 16. (Pers)
2472. —— —. "Buddy Cole Is One of Busiest Recording Men," *Down Beat*, XVII (Sept. 8, 1950), 12. (Pers)
2473. —— —. "Nat Cole's Jazz Piano Wasn't Quite For Church," *Down Beat*, VIII (Oct. 1, 1941), 16–17. (Pers)
2474. —— —. "Dodo's Modern Style Is Given Pease Analysis," *Down Beat*, XIII (Dec. 16, 1946), 12. (Pers)
2475. —— —. "English Gal's 88 Sparks Jazz Unit," *Down Beat*, XIV (June 4, 1947), 12. (Pers)
2476. —— —. "Don Ewell Goes 'Back' to New Orleans Rags," *Down Beat*, XIII (Nov. 4, 1946), 12. (Pers)
2477. —— —. "Fischer One of Most Versatile of Piano Men," *Down Beat*, XVII (Feb. 24, 1950), 12. (Pers)
2478. —— —. "Froeba's First Training Was In New Orleans," *Down Beat*, XIII (Jan. 1, 1946), 14. (Pers)
2479. —— —. "Future Brightens For Danny Hurd," *Down Beat*, XIV (Mar. 26, 1947), 12. (Pers)
2480. —— —. "Erroll Garner, A Self-Trained, Creative 88er," *Down Beat*, XII (Oct. 1, 1945), 12. (Pers)
2481. —— —. "Erroll Garner Does A Repeat Piano Example," *Down Beat*, XVII (Apr. 21, 1950), 12. (Pers)
2482. —— —. "Guarnieri Uses Various Styles As Music Aids," *Down Beat*, XVI (Nov. 4, 1949), 12. (Pers)
2483. —— —. "Hamp's Pianist Reared By Band," *Down Beat*, X (Oct. 1, 1943), 14, 17. (Pers)
2484. —— —. "Health Better, Cleo Brown Set For Comeback," *Down Beat*, XII (July 1, 1945), 12. (Pers)
2485. —— —. "Horace Henderson's College Band Started Him To the Top," *Down Beat*, VII (Sept. 1, 1940), 16. (Pers)
2486. —— —. "Earl Hines the 'Dean of U.S. Dance Pianists'," *Down Beat*, XVII (Nov. 3, 1950), 12. (Pers)
2487. —— —. "Earl Hines' Piano Style," *Music and Rhythm*, II (Sept., 1941), 38. (Pers)
2488. —— —. "'Armand Hug Outstanding Contemporary'," *Down Beat*, XVII (Mar. 24, 1950), 12. (Pers)
2489. —— —. "Is Jess Stacy the Greatest White Pianist?" *Music and Rhythm*, II (June, 1941), 84–5. (Pers)
2490. —— —. "'Keep That Bass Moving,' Says Willie (the Lion) Smith," *Down Beat*, IX (Feb. 1, 1942), 16–17. (Pers)

2491. Pease, Sharon A. "Roy Kral Plays, Scores, Studies to Improve," *Down Beat*, XV (Jan. 14, 1948), 12. (Pers)
2492. — —. "Lou Levy One of Top Pianists In Bop Circles," *Down Beat*, XVI (Aug. 26, 1949), 12. (Bop, Pers)
2493. — —. "Tom Lineham's Piano Style," *Music and Rhythm*, II (Jan., 1942), 3. (Pers)
2494. — —. "Billy Maxted Studies Boogie Styles on Records," *Down Beat*, VIII (Nov. 1, 1941), 16. (Pers)
2495. — —. "Mel, 25, Vet of More Than 9 Years in Music," *Down Beat*, XVI (Jan. 14, 1949), 14. (Pers)
2496. — —. "Max Miller '88' Style, Harmonic Ideas Studied," *Down Beat*, XIII (Mar. 11, 1946), 14. (Pers)
2497. — —. "Page Got Early Hints in 1937 Pease Columns," *Down Beat*, XV (Dec. 15, 1948), 12. (Pers)
2498. — —. "Avery Parrish 'Graduated' Into Erskine Hawkins' Band," *Down Beat*, VIII (July 1, 1941), 16. (Pers)
2499. — —. "Pianist Inspired by Lombardo: Jimmy Rowles Then Turned to Teddy Wilson," *Down Beat*, X (Apr. 1, 1943), 18. (Pers)
2500. — —. "Fats Pichon A Video Star Now," *Down Beat*, XVII (Dec. 1, 1950), 12. (Pers)
2501. — —. "Mel Powell Has Fuzz On His Chin, Perfect Pitch," *Down Beat*, VIII (Sept. 1, 1941), 16. (Pers)
2502. — —. "Sammy Price Career Colorful At All Times," *Down Beat*, XIII (Apr. 22, 1946), 14. (Pers)
2503. — —. "Clarence Profit's Piano Style," *Music and Rhythm*, II (Nov., 1941), 50. (Pers)
2504. — —. "Ragtimer Ash, Busy With TV, Niteries, Radio," *Down Beat*, XVII (June 2, 1950), 18. (Pers)
2505. — —. "'Rockin' Rhythm Pays Rocco Off," *Down Beat*, IX (Nov. 1, 1942), 18. (Pers)
2506. — —. "Arnold Ross Busy With James & Wax," *Down Beat*, XIII (Oct. 7, 1946), 12. (Pers)
2507. — —. "Shearing Went Through Maze of Influence," *Down Beat*, XVII (Jan. 13, 1950), 16. (Pers)
2508. — —. "Taylor One of Creators Among Progressives," *Down Beat*, XVII (Aug. 11, 1950), 12. (Pers)
2509. — —. "This Guy Hops Around Like A Mexican Jumping Bean," *Down Beat*, VII (Mar. 1, 1940), 16. (Pers)
2510. — —. "Training On Organ Gives Buddy Cole Unique Style on Box With Alvino Rey," *Down Beat*, X (Jan. 1, 1943), 18–19. (Pers)
2511. — —. "Wilcox Nixed Farm To Play Piano," *Down Beat*, X (Feb. 1, 1943), 18. (Pers)
2512. — —. "Teddy Wilson's Piano Style Features Variety and Contrast," *Music and Rhythm*, I (Dec., 1940), 68–9. (Pers)
2513. — —. "Work in Boogie Groove Wins Fame For Pianist," *Down Beat*, IX (June 1, 1942), 16. (Pers)
2514. — —. "Wrightsman Is Unseen Pianist In Many Films," *Down Beat*, X (Nov. 1, 1943), 14. (Pers)
2515. — —. "Yancey's Been Rolling Infields With His Boogie," *Down Beat*, VIII (Aug. 1, 1941), 16. (Pers)
2516. Peck, Robert, Jr. "Milling Around With the Mills," *Record Changer*, VII (July, 1948), 15–17; (Aug., 1948), 8–9, 20; (Sept., 1948), 14–16. (Disc)
2517. Peet, Creighton. "Platter Addicts," *Pageant*, II (June, 1946), 96–7. (Disc)

2518. Pellegrini, Alfred. "Jazz-Unfug," *Rheinische Musik- und Theater-Zeitung,* XXIX (July 7, 1928), 317–18. (A & A)
2519. ———. "Musik der Jazz-Zeit," *Bayreuther Blätter,* L (1927), 25–6. (A & A)
2520. Penny, Howard E. "Feelin' Tomorrow Like I Feel Today," *Jazzfinder,* I (Jan., 1948); (Feb., 1948), 12–17; (Mar., 1948), 13–18. (Disc)
2521. Pensoneault, Kenneth and Carl M. Sarles. *Jazz Discography.* Jackson Heights: The Needle, 1944. 145 pp.
2522. Perkins, Edward C. "Referred to Mr. Dewey," (lr) New York *Times,* Apr. 19, 1938, 20 : 7. (J & C)
2523. Perkins, Francis D. "Jazz Breaks Into Society," *Independent,* CXIV (Jan. 3, 1925), 23. (Gen)
2524. Perret, Etienne-Andre. "Louis Bacon," *Hot Club Magazine,* 18 (June 15, 1947), 11–10. (Pers)
2525. Perrin, Michel. "Duke Ellington a la Salle Pleyel," *Presence Africaine,* 5 (1948), 861–62. (Crit)
2526. Perry, Don. "Up the Lazy River," *Jazzfinder,* I (Mar., 1948), 11–12. (Disc, Pers)
2527. Perry, William. "Nieuw Orleans Style," *Record Changer,* IX (Mar., 1950), 9, 18. (Ork)
2528. Pesquinne, Blaise. "Le Blues, la Musique Negre des Villes; Naissance et Avenir du Jazz," *Revue Musicale,* XV (Nov., 1934), 273–82. (Bl, Hist)
2529. ———. "De l'Improvisation Dans le Jazz," *Revue Musicale,* XV (Sept.-Oct., 1934), 177–88. (A & A)
2530. Peterson, Bill and Howard E. Penny. *Good Diggin'.* Portland: Portland Record Collectors' Club, 1948. 80 pp.
2531. Petit, Georges. "Duke Ellington et Son Orchestre," *Europe Nouvelle,* XVI (Aug. 5, 1933), 740. (Crit, Ork)
2532. Petit, Raymond. "Forecast and Review," *Modern Music,* VII (Apr.-May, 1930), 37–8. (Rev)
2533. Peyser, Ethel and Marion Bauer. "Jazz and the Dance," *Pictorial Review,* XXVI (Aug., 1925), 92. (A & A)
2534. Peyster, Herbert F. "Jazz Knocks in Vain At the Opera's Door," *Musician,* XXXIV (Mar., 1929), 12, 30. (Crit, J & O)
2535. Physter, George von. "Art a la Jazz," *Record Changer,* VII (Nov., 1948), 8–9. (Pic)
2536. Pickering, Ruth. "The Economic Interpretation of Jazz," *New Republic,* XXVI (May 11, 1921), 323–24. (Gen, J & D)
2537. Pierce, Edwin H. "The Right Way and Wrong Way to Interpret Syncopation," *Etude,* XLIX (July, 1931), 472. (A & A)
2538. Pijper, Willem. *De Quinten-Cirkel, Opstellen Over Muziek.* Amsterdam: E. Querido, 1929. 158 pp.
2539. Pimsleur, Solomon. "Jazzing the Classics," (lr) New York *Times,* Nov. 6, 1932, IX, 8 : 6. (J & C)
2540. Pinco, Joyce. "Music: Sweet Swing," (lr) New York *Times,* Feb. 19, 1939, IV, 9 : 7. (Sw)
2541. Pinkett, M. Louise. "A Note on Ward Pinkett," *Jazz Information,* II (Nov., 1941), 39, 90. (Pers)
2542. Pitts, Lella Belle. "Modern Youth and His Musical Environment," *Music Educators' National Yearbook,* XXX (1939–40), 69–73. Reprinted: *Music Educator's Journal,* XXVI (Oct., 1939), 18–19, 67–8. (A & A)
See: 840.
2543. Podolsky, Edward. "Physical Effects of Musical Vibrations," *Musician,* XLVII (May-June, 1942), 72. (Infl)
2544. Poling, James W. "Music After Midnight," *Esquire,* V (June, 1936), 92, 131, 132. (Hist, Sw)

2545. Poole, Gene. *Enciclopedia de Swing*. Buenos Aires: Academia Americana, 1939. 92 pp. (Lang)
2546. Porter, Keyes. "Jazz Is Different Today," *Metronome*, XLVII (Nov., 1931), 29, 40. (A & A)
2547. Poustochkine, C. "Le Livre de 'Mezz' Mesirow: Really the Blues," *Hot Club Magazine*, 19 (Aug. 15, 1947), 14–15; 20 (Oct. 1, 1947), 16; 21 (Nov., 1947), 13. (Pers, Rev)
2548. ———. *Het Vraagstuk der Jazzmuziek*. Den Haag: J. P. Kruseman, 1948. 16 pp.
2549. Powell, Adam Clayton. "My Life With Hazel Scott," *Ebony*, IV (Jan., 1949), 42–50. (Pers)
2550. Powers, J. F. "He Don't Plant Cotton," *in* Bucklin Moon (Ed). *Primer For White Folks*. Garden City: Doubleday, Doran, 1945. pp. 236–45. Reprinted: J. F. Powers. *Prince of Darkness and Other Stories*. Garden City: Doubleday, Doran, 1947. pp. 101–17. (Fict)
2551. Praag, Joost van. "European Jazz Musicians," *Swing Music*, 14 (Autumn, 1936), 27–8. (Pers)
2552. ———. "Bennie Goodman," *Jazz Hot*, 13 (Dec., 1936), 10–11. (Pers)
2553. ———. (Trans: Ian Munro Smyth). "Jazz and Classical Music," *Jazz Hot*, V (Jan., 1939), 5. (A & A, J & C)
2554. ———. "Hilton Jefferson," *Jazz Hot*, 9 (June, 1936), 17. (Pers)
2555. ———. "Frank Teschmaker," *Jazz Hot*, 8 (May, 1936), 9, 18. (A & A,Pers)
2556. ———. (Trans: Ian Munro Smyth). "Mary Lou Williams and Andy Kirk's Orchestra," *Jazz Hot*, IV (Apr.-May, 1938), 4–7; (June-July, 1938), 4–7. (Ork, Pers)
2557. Pragma. "In the Key of X and Why," *Melody*, X (Feb., 1926), 3–4. (A & A)
2558. Preston, Denis. *Mood Indigo*. Egham, Surrey: Citizen Press, 1946. 84 pp.
2559. Preussner, Eberhard. "Germany's New Music Literature," *Modern Music*, VII (Feb.-Mar., 1930), 38–41. (Rev)
2560. Pridgett, Thomas. "The Life of Ma Rainey," *Jazz Information*, II (Sept. 6, 1940), 8. (Pers)
2561. Priest, Dann. "The Real Jazz by Hugues Panassie," *Jazz* (New York), I, no. 7 (n. d.), 10–11. (Rev)
2562. Priestly, J. B. "On Not Hearing Whiteman's Band," *Saturday Review*, CXLI (May 1, 1926), 566–67. (A & A)
2563. Prunieres, Henry. "Chansons et Jazz," *Revue Musicale*, XIII (Jan., 1932), 78. (Gen, Pers)
2564. ———. "'Le Jazz Hot' In Paris," New York *Times*, Sept. 4, 1932, IX, 6: 1. (A & A, Geog)
2565. ———. "La Musique Par Disques," *Revue Musicale*, VII (Aug., 1926), 181–82. (Disc)
2566. Quinlisk, Robert. "Jazz Classics," *Jazz Information*, II (Aug. 23, 1940), 14, 24; (Sept. 20, 1940), 15, 29; (Oct. 4, 1940), 11, 21; (Oct. 25, 1940), 12–13; (Dec. 20, 1940), 11, 32–4; (Feb. 7, 1941), 15–18; (Feb. 21, 1941), 19–21; (Mar. 21, 1941), 26–8; (Nov., 1941), 64–6, 68–73, 75–83. (Disc)
2567. Rackett, Arthur. "Syncopatedragtimejazzdeliriumtremens," *Melody*, IX (Sept., 1925), 3–5, 28. (Crit, Rev)
2568. Radzitzky, Carlos de. "Louis Armstrong Vu par Robert Goffin et Hugues Panassie," *Hot Club Magazine*, 20 (Oct. 1, 1947), 13. (Pers)
2569. ———. "Bilan d'un Concert," *Hot Club Magazine*, 12 (Dec., 1946), 10–11. (Crit, Ork)
2570. ———. "Dixieland Jazz in Brussels, "*Hot Club Magazine*, 2 (Feb., 1946), 6–7. (Dix, Geog)
2571. ———. "Dizzy's Discussion," *Hot Club Magazine*, 17 (May, 1947), 3–5. (Bop)

2572. Radzitzky, Carlos de. "12 Annees de Jazz, un Livre de Hugues Panassie," *Hot Club Magazine*, 10 (Oct., 1946), 13. (Rev)
2573. — —. "Duke Ellington, un Livre de Jean de Trazegnies," *Hot Club Magazine*, 8 (Aug., 1946), 12. (Rev)
2574. — —. "Un Grand Clarinettiste de la Nouvelle-Orleans Albert Nicholas," *Hot Club Magazine*, 11 (Nov., 1946), 3–5. (Pers)
2575. — —. "Un Grand Musicien Disparait... Joe 'Tricky Sam' Nanton," *Hot Club Magazine*, 9 (Sept., 1946), 5. (Pers)
2576. — —. "The Gut Bucket Five," *Hot Club Magazine*, 9 (Sept., 1946), 7. (Ork)
2577. — —. "Art Hodes un Musicien Pur," *Hot Club Magazine*, 6 (June, 1946), 3, 5. (Pers)
2578.— —. "Jazz Abroad: Belgium," *Jazz Forum*, 1 (n. d.), 15–16. (Geog)
2579. — —. "Le Jazz et les Hommes d'Aujourd'hui, un Essai Sur le Jazz, de Jean David," *Hot Club Magazine*, 13 (Jan., 1947), 10–11. (Rev)
2580. — —. "Jazz Books, Revue des Livres," *Hot Club Magazine*, 1 (Jan., 1946), 14–15. (Rev)
2581. — —. "Jazz Books and Magazines," *Hot Club Magazine*, 4 (Apr., 1946), 14. (Rev)
2582. — —. "Les Livres: Jazzbook 1947, par A. McCarthy. PL Edition Poetry London," *Hot Club Magazine*, 26 (Apr., 1948), 13. (Rev)
2583. — —. "Reflexions Sur un Referendum," *Hot Club Magazine*, 11 (Nov., 1946), 10–11. (Poll)
2584. — —. "Revue des Livres: Cinq Mois a New-York par Hugues Panassie; The 'PL' Yearbook of Jazz 1946, edite sous la Direction d'Albert McCarthy," *Hot Club Magazine*, 19 (Aug. 15, 1947), 13. (Rev)
2585. — —. "Rex Stewart," *Hot Club Magazine*, 25 (Mar., 1948), 1–2. (Pers)
2586. — —, and Albert Bettonville. "Editorial," *Hot Club Magazine*, 1 (Jan., 1946), 3. (Gen)
2587. — —. "Encyclopedie du Jazz," *Jazz* (Brussels), I (Mar., 1945), 12, 13; (Apr., 1945), 12, 13; (May, 1945), 12–13; (June, 1945), 12–13; (July, 1945), 12–13; (Aug., 1945), 12–13; (Sept., 1945), 12–13; (Oct., 1945), 12–13; (Nov., 1945), 12–13; (Dec., 1945), 12–13; (Jan., 1946), 12–13; II (Mar., 1946), 13–14. *Hot Club Magazine*, I (Jan., 1946), 19; (Feb., 1946), 19; (Mar., 1946), 19; (Apr., 1946), 19; (May, 1946), 19; (June, 1946), 19; (July, 1946), 17; (Aug., 1946), 15; (Sept., 1946), 15; (Oct., 1946), 14; II (Mar., 1947), 14, 18; (June, 1947), 15–16; (Aug. 15, 1947), 15; (Nov. 1, 1947), 15, 17; (Dec. 1, 1947), 16; III (May-June, 1948), 15. (Gen)
2588. — —. "Encyclopedie du Jazz: Boogie-Woogie," *Hot Club Magazine*, 2 (Feb., 1946), 19; 3 (Mar., 1946), 19. (BW)
2589. — —. "Jam-Sessions Chez l'Ange Gabriel," *Jazz* (Brussels), I (Oct., 1945), 3, 6, 18.
2590. Raes, Jack. "Que Pensez-Vous de Be-bop?" *Hot Club Magazine*, 17 (May, 1947), 11, 13–14. (Bop)
2591. Ramsey, Frederic, Jr. *Chicago Documentary, Portrait of a Jazz Era.* London: Jazz Sociological Society, 1944. 32 pp.
2592. — —. "Contraband Jelly Roll," *Saturday Review of Literature*, XXXIII (Sept. 30, 1950), 64. (Disc)
2593. — —. "Deep Sea Rider," in Charles Harvey (Ed). *Jazz Parody.* London: Spearman, 1948. pp. 39–49. (Fict)
2594. — —. "Discollecting," in George S. Rosenthal (Ed). *Jazzways.* Cincinnati, 1946. pp. 88–92. (Disc)
2595. — —. "Going Down State Street," in George S. Rosenthal (Ed). *Jazzways.* Cincinnati, 1946. pp. 36–9, 106, 108–14, 116. (Hist)
2596. — —, and Charles Edward Smith (Eds). *Jazzmen.* New York: Harcourt Brace, 1939. 360 pp. New York: Editions for the Armed Services, 1942. 319 pp.

2597. Randolph, John. "Dewey Jackson's St. Louis Jazz," *Record Changer*, IX (Oct., 1950), 7, 16. (Ork, Pers)
2598. ——. "The St. Louis Labels: Harmograph and Herwin," *Playback*, II (Aug., 1949), 3–4, 6. (Disc)
2599. Rathaus, Karol. "Jazzdämmerung?" *Die Musik*, XIX (Feb., 1927), 333–36. (A & A)
2600. Ray, Harry. *Les Grandes Figures du Jazz*. Brussels: Les Cahiers Selection, 1945. 46 pp.
2601. Raymond, Joseph. "Jitterbug Bites Jumping Bean!" *Down Beat*, X (Apr. 1, 1943), 15. (Geog, Infl)
2602. Razaf, Andy. "Fats Waller," *Metronome*, LX (Jan., 1944), 16. (Pers)
2603. Reddick, L. D. "Dizzy Gillespie in Atlanta," *Phylon* (First Quarter, 1949), 44–9. (Bop, Crit, Pers)
2604. Redway, Jacques Wardlaw. "History of Term 'Jazz' Reviewed," *New York Times*, Oct. 21, 1934, IV, 5 : 2. (Lang)
See: 589; 2953; 3159.
2605. Reger, Muriel. "Jazz Is Music," *Jazz* (New York), I (June, 1942), 22–3. (A & A)
2606. ——. "The Negro in Relation to Jazz," *Direction*, II (Jan.-Feb., 1939), 21–2. (A & A)
2607. Reid, John D. "Discography of Sidney Bechet," *Jazz Information*, II (Nov. 22, 1940), 11–21. (Disc)
2608. Reinhardt, Ruth Sato. "Jazz Ltd. Owner Tells Tavern's Tale," *Down Beat*, XV (Apr. 21, 1948), 17. (Gen)
2609. Reinholtz, Hanns. "Jazz-Rausch...??" *Deutsche Musiker-Zeitung* LVI (July 25, 1925), 738. (A & A)
See: 1617.
2610. Renzio, Toni del. "On the Outskirts of Town," *Jazz Forum*, 1 (n. d.), 21. (Bl)
2611. Reuss, Allan. "Allan Reuss on Guitarists," *Metronome*, LIX (Oct., 1943), 30, 66. (Pers)
2612. Reynolds, Quentin. "Rhythm Man—Bop MacGimsey," *Collier's*, CIII (May 13, 1939), 22. (Bl)
2613. Reynolds, Robert R. "The Aframerican Viewpoint," *Jazz Session*, 7 (May-June, 1945), 19. (Pers)
2614. Rice, Robert. "Lena Horne," *PM Magazine*, Jan. 10, 1943, 22 : 1–4, 23 : 1–4, 24 : 1–4. (Pers)
2615. ——. "Harry James," *PM Magazine*, May 9, 1943, 21 : 1–4. (Gen)
2616. ——. "The Story of the Life of Gene Krupa," *PM Magazine*, June 20, 1943, 16–20. (Pers)
2617. Riesenfeld, Hugo. "Music As a Vocation for Americans," *Outlook*, CXXXVIII (Oct. 29, 1924), 331–32. (Gen)
2618. ——. "New Forms For Old Music," *Modern Music*, I (June, 1924), 25–6. (A & A)
2619. ——. "Hugo Riesenfeld Discusses Jazz," *Musical Courier*, LXXXV (Nov. 30, 1922), 6. (A & A)
2620. Riesenfeld, Paul. "Der Amerikanismus in der Heutigen Musik," *Rheinische Musik- und Theater-Zeitung*, XXIX (June 16, 1928), 303–05. (A & A, J & C)
2621. Rippin, John W. "Emergence of the Australian Style," *in* Orin Blackstone (Ed). *Jazzfinder '49*. New Orleans: Orin Blackstone, 1949. pp. 25–30. (Geog)
2622. Ristic. "Corrections and Additions to the Discography of the late Thomas 'Fats' Waller," *Jazz Journal*, II (Apr., 1949), 6–7. (Disc)
2623. ——. "Discography of the Late Thomas 'Fats' Waller," *Jazz Journal*, I (Aug., 1948), 12. (Disc)
2624. Rock, John. *Africa Sings and the Psychology of Jazz*. Colombo, Ceylon: General, 1946. 16 pp.

2625. Rodin, Gil. "'It's Been 5 Years of Good Kicks',—Rodin," *Down Beat*, VII (June 1, 1940), 19, 21. (Ork)
2626. Rogers, B. "Capacity House Fervently Applauds As Jazz Invades Realm of Serious Music," *Musical America*, XXXIX (Feb. 23, 1924), 32. (Crit)
2627. ——. "Enter Jazz," *Musical America*, XXXIX (Nov. 10, 1923), 9. (A & A)
2628. Rogers, B. S. "Swing Is From the Heart," *Esquire*, XI (Apr., 1939), 43, 115, 118, 120; (May, 1939), 75, 167–68. Pt. II entitled: "How Music Gets Hot." (A & A, Dix)
2629. Rogers, Charles Payne. "Delta Jazzmen," *Jazz Forum*, 1 (n. d.), 11–12. (Hist, Pers)
2630. ——. "Pioneer New Orleans Clarinetist George Baquet," *Record Changer*, VIII June, 1949), 8, 16. (Pers)
2631. ——. "Ragtime," *Jazz* (New York), I (June, 1942), 10–12. (Rag)
2632. ——. "Ragtime," *Jazz Forum*, 4 (Apr., 1947), 5–7. (Rag)
2633. ——. "Charles Thompson," *Record Changer*, IX (May, 1950), 13, 20. (Pers)
2634. Rogers, J. A. "Jazz at Home," *Survey*, LIII (Mar. 1, 1925), 665–67, 712.
2635. Rogers, M. Robert. "Jazz Influence on French Music," *Musical Quarterly*, XXI (Jan., 1935), 53–68. (Infl, J & C)
2636. Rohlf, Wayne H. "Emmet Hardy Never Taught Bix, Says Pal," *Down Beat*, IX (Jan. 15, 1942), 6. (Pers)
    See: 1725; 2637.
2637. ——. "Okay, So Bix Didn't Copy From Louis," *Down Beat*, IX (May 1, 1942), 18. (A & A, Pers)
    See: 1725; 2636.
2638. Roland, Will. "Educators: Fight Jazz Prejudices," *Metronome*, LIX (Apr., 1943), 23. (Ed)
2639. ——. "Why Don't You Do Right By Lil Green," *Metronome*, LIX (Apr., 1943), 22, 25. (Pers)
2640. Roland-Manuel. "Wiener et Doucet, ou les Plaisirs du Jazz," *Revue Pleyel*, 34 (July, 1926), 10–12. (Gen)
2641. Ronan, Eddie. "Blazing Brass Sparks James' Band," *Down Beat*, XV (Dec. 15, 1948), 2. (Ork)
2642. ——. "Concerts Keep Cats in Cakes!" *Down Beat*, XIV (Apr. 9, 1947), 1. (Gen)
2643. ——. "Dodds and Bolden Were Smiling," *Down Beat*, XV (Dec. 1, 1948), 7. (Crit)
2644. ——. "New Book·Has Good Reprints," *Down Beat*, XIV (Dec. 17, 1947), 16. (Rev)
2645. ——. "Mamie Smith Joins Immortals of Blues," *Down Beat*, XIII (Dec. 2, 1946), 9. (Pers)
2646. ——. "Square Writers Hurt Music Biz!" *Down Beat*, XIV (Mar. 26, 1947), 1, 17. (Crit)
2647. ——. "Things You Can Discover At an Ellington Concert," *Down Beat*, XIII (Dec. 26, 1946), 15. (A & A, Ork)
2648. ——. "Uncovering of New Auld Band Provides a Welcome Surprise," *Down Beat*, XVI (Feb. 25, 1949), 2. (Ork)
2649. Rootham, H. "Jazzomania and Devil Dances," *English Review*, XXXVIII (Jan., 1924), 109–11. (Infl, J & D)
2650. Rose, Billy. "The Hex of Bix," New York *Herald Tribune*, Nov. 1, 1949, 25 : 1–3. (Pers)
2651. Rosenbaum, David. "Lu Watters Won't Compromise, He Plays As He Pleases," *Metronome*, LVIII (Aug., 1942), 8. (Ork)
2652. Rosenberg, Herman and Eugene Williams. "Edmond Hall," *Jazz Information*, II (Aug. 9, 1940), 9–12, 29. (Pers)
2653. ——. "Omer Simeon," *Jazz Information*, II (July 26, 1940), 7–10. (Disc, Pers)

2654. Rosenfeld, Paul. "Jazz and Music: Music in America," *in* Paul Rosenfeld. *An Hour With American Music*. Philadelphia: J. B. Lippincott, 1929. pp. 11–27. (A & A)

2655. ———. "Musical Chronicle," *Dial*, LXXV (Nov., 1923), 518–20. (Gen)

2656. Rosenkainer, Eugen. "Jazz," *Österreische Musiker-Zeitung*, XXXV (Nov. 16, 1927), 101–02. (A & A)

2657. Rosenkrantz, Timme. *Jazz Profiler*. Copenhagen: J. A.Hansen's Forlag, 1945. 15 pp.

2658. ———. "Den Stolteste Dag I Mit Liv," *Politiken Magasinet*, Oct. 30, 1949, 3, 4. (Gen)

2659. ———. *Swing Photo Album 1939*. Copenhagen: Timme Rosenkrantz, 1939. 37 pp.

2660. Rosenthal, George S. (Ed). *Jazzways*. Cincinnati, 1946. 120 pp. Reprinted: George S. Rosenthal and Frank Zachery, in collaboration with Frederic Ramsey, Jr. and Rudi Blesh. *Jazzways*. New York: Greenberg, 1947.

2661. Rosenwald, Hans. "Speaking of Music," *Music News*, XLII (Mar., 1950), 9; (Apr., 1950), 24. (Infl)

2662. Rottweiler, Hektor. "Über Jazz," *Zeitschrift für Sozialforschung*, V (1936), 235–59. (A & A, Gen)

2663. Rowe, John. *Record Information*. London: Jazz Tempo, 1945. 24 pp.

2664. ———. *Trombone Jazz*. London: Jazz Tempo, 1945. 32 pp.

2665. ———. *Vocal Jazz*. London: Jazz Tempo, 1945. 24 pp.

2666. ———, and Ted Watson. *Junkshoppers' Discography*. London: Jazz Tempo, 1945. 36 pp.

2667. Rowland, Sam. "Debunking Swing," *Esquire*, VI (Aug., 1936), 79, 111. (A & A, Sw)

2668. Rubba, Joseph V. "Much Ado About Swinging," *Metronome*, LII (Aug., 1936), 9, 10. (A & A, Sw)

2669. Rueth, Marion U. "Can We Tame the Boogie-Woogie Bogey?" *Etude*, LXVI (Jan., 1948), 14, 50. (BW)

2670. Rundell, Wyatt. *Jazz Band*. New York: Greenberg, 1935. 246 pp.

2671. Russell, Ross. "Be-Bop Instrumentation," *Record Changer*, VII (Nov., 1948), 12–13, 22–3. (A & A, Bop, Inst)

2672. ———. "Be-Bop: Reed Instrumentation," *Record Changer*, VIII (Apr., 1949), 6–7, 20. (A & A, Bop, Inst, Pers)

2673. ———. "Bop Horn: A Discography," *Record Changer*, VIII (Feb., 1949), 10. (Disc)

2674. ———. "Bop Rhythm," *Record Changer*, VII (July, 1948), 11–13, 28. (A & A, Bop, Inst)

2675. ———. "Brass Instrumentation in Be-Bop," *Record Changer*, VIII (Jan., 1949), 9–10, 21. (A & A, Bop, Inst)

2676. ———. "Erroll Garner," *Record Changer*, VII (Oct., 1948), 9. (A & A, Pers)

2677. ———. "Grandfather of Hot Piano—James P. Johnson," *Jazz Information*, II (Nov., 1941), 20–4. Reprinted: Ralph de Toledano. (Ed). *Frontiers of Jazz*. New York: Oliver Durrell, 1947. pp. 170–76. (Pers)

2678. Russell, William. "Louis Armstrong," *in* Frederic Ramsey, Jr. and Charles Edward Smith (Eds). *Jazzmen*. New York: Harcourt, Brace, 1939. pp. 119–42. (Pers)

2679. ———. "Boogie Woogie," *Jazz Hot*, IV (June-July, 1938), 11–12; (Aug.-Sept., 1938), 11. (BW, Pers)

2680. ———. "Mutt Carey," *Record Changer*, VII (Nov., 1948), 7. (Pers)

2681. ———. "Notes on Boogie Woogie," *in* Ralph de Toledano (Ed). *Frontiers of Jazz*. New York: Oliver Durrell, 1947. pp. 58–65. (BW)

2682. Russell, William. "Play That Thing, Mr. Johnny Dodds," *Jazz Information*, II (Aug. 23, 1940), 10–11. (Pers)

2683. Rust, Brian, "The Fletcher Henderson Band," *Jazz Journal*, II (Nov., 1949), 4–5. (Ork, Pers)

2684. ——. "Ferdinand Jelly-Roll Morton: A Discography," *Jazz Journal*, II (Aug., 1949), 6; (Sept., 1949), 12; (Oct., 1949), 12, 14. (Disc)

2685. Sachs-Herbert, Hirsch. "Dangers That Lie in Ragtime," *Musical America*, XVI (Sept. 21, 1912), 8. (Gen, Rag)

2686. Saenger, Gustav. "The Ambitions of Jazz in Artistic Form," *Musical Observer*, XXV (Jan., 1926), 5. (J & C)

2687. ——. "The Musical Possibilities of Rag-Time," *Metronome*, XIX (Mar., 1903), 11; (Apr., 1903), 8. (Rag)

2688. Saerchinger, Cesar. "Business Depression Hits German Concert Life," *Musical Courier*, LXXXVI (Apr. 5, 1923), 23, 41. (J & C)

2689. ——. "Is Jazz Coming or Going?" *Metronome*, XLII (Feb. 1, 1926), 20, 26. (A & A, Hist)

2690. ——. "Jazz," *Musikblätter des Anbruch*, VII (Apr., 1925), 205–10. (Inst, Hist, J & C)

2691. Saija, Leandro. "Italy Now A Potpourri of Long-Sought Jazz Writing, Discs, Music," *Down Beat*, XV (July 28, 1948), 16. (Geog)

2692. Sales, Robert B. "Junk Pile," *Hobbies*, XLVI (Sept., 1941), 32; (Oct., 1941), 33; (Nov., 1941), 31, 32; (Dec., 1941), 22; (Jan., 1942), 19–20; (Feb., 1942), 19; XLVII (Mar., 1942), 13–14; (Apr., 1942), 14–15; (May, 1942), 14; (June, 1942), 20. (Disc, Gen)

2693. Salinger, J. D. "Blue Melody," *Cosmopolitan* CXXV (Sept., 1948), 50, 112–19. (Fict)

2694. Sanborn, Pitts. "Jazz Worship," *Independent*, CXII (May 10, 1924), 262. (Gen, Hist)

2695. Sanders, George H. "Is 'Jazz' American Music?" *Collaborator*, I (Sept., 1931), 10. (Gen)

2696. Sandor, Arpad. "American Music and Its Future," *Musical Courier*, CX (Jan. 26, 1935), 6. (A & A)

2697. Sanjek, Russell. "Bunny Berigan: He Is Either Very Good or Very Lousy," *Music and Rhythm*, I (Nov., 1940), 37–9. (Disc, Pers)

2698. ——. "Barney Bigard: Clarinet Colossus," *Needle*, I (June, 1944), 6–9, 29–30. (Pers)

2699. Sargant, Norman and Tom Sargant. "Negro-American Music Or the Origin of Jazz," *Musical Times*, LXXII (July, 1931), 653–55; (Aug., 1931), 751–52; (Sept., 1931), 847–48. (A & A, Hist)

2700. Sargeant, Winthrop. "Esquire's Jazz Book," *Musical Quarterly*, XXXI (Jan., 1945), 120–22. (Rev)

2701. ——. "Is Jazz Music?" *American Mercury*, LVII (Oct., 1943), 403–09. Reprinted: *Needle*, I (July, 1944), 12–18. (A & A)
See: 1324; 1325; 2207.

2702. ——. "Jazz," *in* Nicolas Slonimsky (Ed). *International Cyclopedia of Music and Musicians*. New York: Dodd, Mead, 4th Ed., 1946. pp. 896–900. (A & A)

2703. ——. *Jazz, Hot and Hybrid*. New York: Arrow, 1938. 234 pp. Revised Edition: New York: E. P. Dutton, 1946. 287 pp.

2704. ——. "Jazz, Hot and Hybrid," *in* Elie Siegmeister (Ed). *The Music Lover's Handbook*. New York: William Morrow, 1943. pp. 692–711. (Extract from book of the same title).

2705. Sartre, Jean-Paul. (Trans: Ralph de Toledano). "I Discovered Jazz In America," *Saturday Review of Literature*, XXX (Nov. 29, 1947), 48–9. (Gen, Infl)

2706. Saunders, R. Crombie. "Jazz and the Future," *Swing Music*, 14 (Autumn, 1936), 11–12. (A & A)

2707. Savage. "Tower Ticker," Chicago Daily *Tribune*, May 5, 1949, 27 : 2–3. (A & A, Bop, Lang)

2708. — —. "Tower Ticker," Chicago Daily *Tribune*, May 12, 1949, 12. (A & A, Chi, Hist, NO)

2709. Savitt, Jan. "Music: Blues Banned," (lr) New York *Times*, Sept. 24, 1939, IV, 9 : 7. (Infl)

2710. Scarborough, Dorothy. "Blues," *in* Dorothy Scarborough. *On the Trail of Negro Folk Songs*. Cambridge: Harvard University Press, 1925. pp. 264–80. (Bl)

2711. — —. "The Blues As Folksongs," *Publications of the Texas Folklore Society*, no. 2 (1923), 52–66. Reprinted: *Coffee in the Gourd*. Dallas: Texas Folk-Lore Society, 1935. pp. 52–66. (Bl)

2712. Schaaf, Edward. "Jazz and the Picture House," *Musical Advance*, XVI (May, 1929), 3. (A & A, Infl)

2713. Schaap, Walter. "Claude Luter et Son Orchestre," *Record Changer*, VII (Sept., 1948), 6–7, 19. (Ork, Pers)

2714. Schaeffner, Andre. "Jack Hylton et Son Jazz," *Revue Musicale*, IX (Feb., 1928), 67–8. (A & A, Ork)

2715. — —. "Le Jazz," *Revue Musicale*, IX (Nov. 1, 1927), 72–6. (A & A)

2716. — —. "Romantisme du Jazz," *Revue Musicale*, VII (Oct. 1, 1926), 221–24. (A & A)

2717. — —, and Andre Coeuroy. "Die Romantik des Jazz," *Auftakt*, VI (1926), 218–21. (A & A)

2718. Schafer, Karl. "Etwas von Komponieren im Allgemeinen und vom Jazz im Besonderen," *Deutsche Musiker-Zeitung*, LVII (Mar. 20, 1926), 269. (A & A)

2719. Schauffler, Robert Haven. "Jazz May Be Lowbrow, But ..." *Collier's*, LXXII (Aug. 25, 1923), 10, 20. (Inst)

2720. — —. "Jazz May Be Lowbrow, But ..." *Melody*, VII (Oct.-Nov., 1923), 5, 7–8. (Inst)
See: 404.

2721. — —. "Where Have I Heard That Tune Before ?" *Collier's*, LXXVIII (July 3, 1926), 16–17. (Infl, J & C)

2722. — —. "Who Invented Jazz ?" *Collier's*, LXXV (Jan. 3, 1925), 38. (Gen, J & C, Hist)

2723. Schawlow, Arthur and Clyde H. Clark. "Jazz In Canada," *Jazz Forum*, 3 (Jan., 1947), 11–12. (Geog)

2724. Schenck, John T. "The Colorful Saga of Darnell Howard," *Jazz Session*, 6 (Mar.-Apr., 1945), 2–3, 8–9, 16–17. (Pers)

2725. — —. "Lament for Snags," *Jazz Record*, 55 (May, 1947), 18, 34. (Pers)

2726. — —. "Life History of Voltaire de Faut," *Jazz Session*, 8 (July-Aug., 1945), 2–3, 13. (Pers)

2727. Schenke, Jean-Gustave. "Reflexions Sur le Rhythme du Plain-Chant et du Jazz-Band," *Courrier Musical*, XXVI (Nov. 1, 1924), 516–17. (A & A)

2728. Schiedt, Duncan. "Fats in Retrospect," *Record Changer*, IX (Dec., 1950), 7, 16. (Pers)

2729. — —. "Fats Waller," *Record Changer*, IX (Sept., 1950), 7, 12. (Pers)

2730. Schildberger, Hermann. "Jazz-Musik," *Die Musik*, XVII (Sept., 1925), 914–23. (A & A)

2731. Schillinger, Joseph. "At Long Last—Here It Is—An Explanation of 'Swing'," *Metronome*, LVIII (July, 1942), 19, 23. (A & A, Sw)

2732. Schillinger, Mort. "Dizzy Gillespie's Style, Its Meaning Analyzed," *Down Beat*, XIII (Feb. 11, 1946), 14–15. (A & A, Bop, Pers)

2733. Schleman, Hilton R. *Rhythm On Record.* London: Melody Maker, 1936. 333 pp. (Disc)

2734. Schloezer, Boris de. "Musique Negre," *Revue Pleyel,* 41 (Feb., 1927), 159–61. (Rev)

2735. Schmitz, E. Robert. "Jazz," *Franco-American Musical Society Bulletin,* III (Mar., 1924), 20–2. (A & A)

2736. Schneider, Hans. "Eine Lanze für die Jazzmusik," *Österreichische Musiker-Zeitung,* XXXV (June 16, 1927), 65–6. (A & A)

2737. Schoen, Ernst. "Jazz und Kunstmusik," *Melos,* VI (Dec., 1927), 512–19. (A & A, J & C)

2738. Scholes, Percy A. "Jazz, the B.B.C., and Popular Taste," *Musical Times,* LXXVII (Sept., 1936), 831–32. (Gen)

2739. — —. "Ragtime and Jazz," *in* Percy A. Scholes. *The Oxford Companion to Music.* London: Oxford University Press, 1947. pp. 775–79. (A & A)

2740. Scholl, Warren W. "The Complete Discography of Bix Beiderbecke," *American Music Lover,* III (Oct., 1937), 207–10; (Nov., 1937), 251–53, 276. (Disc)

2741. Schontag, Werner. "Lebendige Musik," *Melos,* IX (Jan., 1930), 12–13. (A & A)

2742. Schuck, Karl. "Jazz in America," *Melos,* VIII (Sept.-Aug., 1929), 391–93. (A & A, Geog)

2743. Schuloff, Erwin. "Eine Jazz-Affaire," *Auftakt,* V (1925), 220–22. (A & A)

2744. — —. "Der Mondane Tanz," *Auftakt,* IV (1924), 73–7. (J & D)

2745. — —. "Saxophon und Jazzband," *Auftakt,* V (1925), 179–83. (Inst)

2746. Schultz, William J. "Jazz," *Nation,* CXV (Oct. 25, 1922), 438–39. (A & A)

2747. Schulz, Dietrich. "Swing Fever in Germany," *Swing Music,* 14 (Autumn, 1936), 23, 94. (Geog)

2748. Schumach, Murray. "'Revolution' in Tin Pan Alley," New York *Times Magazine,* Oct. 19, 1947, 20, 69–71. (Gen)

2749. Schwaninger, A. and A. Gurwitch. *Swing Discographie.* Geneva: Ch. Grasset, 1945. 200 pp. (Sw, Disc)

2750. Schwerke, Irving. "Le Jazz est Mort! Vive le Jazz," *Guide du Concert,* XII (Mar. 12, 1926), 647–49; (Mar. 19, 1926), 679–82. Reprinted: Irving Schwerke. *Kings Jazz and David.* Paris: Les Presses Modernes, 1927. pp 15–30; 33–48. (A & A)

2751. Schwers, Paul. "Die Frankfurter Jazz-Akademie im Spiegel der Kritik," *Allgemeine Musikzeitung,* LIV (Dec. 2, 1927), 1246–48. (Ed)

2752. — —. "Jazz Als Akademisches Lehrfach!" *Allgemeine Musikzeitung,* LIV (Nov. 18, 1927), 1194–95. (Ed, Infl)

2753. Scoggins, Charles H. "The Ragtime Menace," *Musical Progress,* II (Apr., 1913), 3–4. (Infl, Rag)

2754. Scott, Cyril. "Jazz," *in* Cyril Scott. *The Influence of Music on History and Morals.* London: Theosophical Publishing House, 1928. pp. 151–53. (Infl)

2755. Scott, Raymond (Ed: David Ewen). "Artistic Possibilities of Good Jazz," *Etude,* LXI (July, 1943), 431–32. (A & A)

2756. — —. "Jazz Is A Deep Rich Thing," *Music and Rhythm,* I (Nov., 1940), 10–13. (A & A)

2757. — —. "Many People Think I'm 'Whacky'," *Music and Rhythm,* II (Sept., 1941), 11. (Pers)

2758. Sebastian, John. "From Spirituals to Swing," *New Masses,* XXX (Jan. 3, 1939), 28. (Hist, Pers)

2759. Scruggs, Anderson M. "Meditation on Swing," *Hygeia,* XIX (Mar., 1941), 195. (Poet)

2760. Secor, Ethan A. "Just What Really Is Swing Music?" *Etude,* LVIII (Apr., 1940), 240. (A & A, Sw)

2761. Seiber, Matyas. "Jazz als Erziehungsmittel," *Melos*, VII (June, 1928), 281–86. (A & A, Ed)

2762. — —. "Jazz-Instrumente, Jazz-Klang und Neue Musik," *Melos*, IX (Mar., 1930), 122–26. (Inst)

2763. Seldes, Gilbert. "The Incomparable Bing," *Esquire*, XXI (Feb., 1944), 38. (Pers)

2764. — —. "Jazz and Ballad," *New Republic*, XLIII (Aug. 5, 1925), 293–94. (A & A, Pers)

2765. — —. "Jazz Music Not Such an 'Enfant Terrible' After All But Clever Adaptation in Current Style, Says Seldes," *Musical America*, XL (July 19, 1924), 13. (A & A)

2766. — —. "Jazz Opera or Ballet ?" *Modern Music*, III (Jan.-Feb., 1926), 10–16. (Crit, J & O)

2767. — —. "No More Swing ?" *Scribner's*, C (Nov., 1936), 70–1. (A & A, Hist, Sw)

2768. — —. "Position of Jazz in American Musical Development," *Arts and Decoration*, XX (Apr., 1924), 21. Reprinted as: "A Jazz 'Characterization'," *Etude*, XLII (Sept., 1924), 596. (A & A, J & C)

2769. — —. "Shake Your Feet, the Charleston," *New Republic*, XLIV (Nov. 4, 1925), 283, 284. (J & D)

2770. — —. "Torch Songs," *New Republic*, LXV (Nov. 19, 1930), 19–20. (A & A)

2771. — —. "Toujours Jazz," *Dial*, LXXV (Aug., 1923), 151–66. (A & A, Ork, Pers)

2772. — —. "What Happened to Jazz ?" *Saturday Evening Post*, CXCIX (Jan. 22, 1927), 25, 102, 107. (A & A, Gen)

2773. Sem. "La Jazz-Band," *Monde Musical*, XXXIV (Aug., 1923), 259–60. (Gen)

2774. Seton, Grace Thompson. "The Jazzing Japanese," *Metronome*, XXXIX (July, 1923), 52–4. (Geog, Infl)

2775. Sexton, Susie. "Paul Whiteman Made Jazz Contagious," *American Magazine*, XCVII (June, 1924), 74–5. (Ork)

2776. Shain, Cy. "The Frisco Jazz Band," *Jazz Record*, 55 (May, 1947), 17. (Ork)

2777. Shane, Ted. "Song of the Cuckoo," *Collier's* CXVIII (Oct. 5, 1946), 21, 94, 96. (Lang)

2778. Shaw, Artie. "String Music Helps ... Keep Our Sanity!" *Music and Rhythm*, II (Dec., 1941), 12. (A & A, Pers)

2779. — —, and Bob Maxwell. "Music Is A Business," *Saturday Evening Post*, CCXII (Dec. 2, 1939), 14–15, 66–8. (Gen)

2780. Shaw, Billy. "Satchmo Knows the Secret of Grosses, Says Booker Shaw," *Down Beat*, XVII (July 14, 1950), 16. (Pers)

2781. Shelly, Low (Ed). *Hepcats Jive Talk Dictionary*. Derby: T. W. O. Charles, 1945. 50 pp. (Lang)

2782. Sherlock, Charles Reginald. "From Breakdown to Rag-Time," *Cosmopolitan*, XXXI (Oct., 1901), 631–39 (Rag)

2783. Shirley, Peter. "Drink and Be Merry," *in* Charles Harvey (Ed). *Jazz Parody*. London: Spearman, 1948. pp. 32–8. (Fict)

2784. — —. "Sweet and Hot," *in* Charles Harvey (Ed). *Jazz Parody*. London: Spearman, 1948. pp. 92–8. (Fict)

2785. Shore, Dinah. "My Ten Favorite Vocalists," *Music and Rhythm*, II (Apr., 1942), 11, 48. (Pers)

2786. Shubarsky, Zachariah. "Jazz In the Schools," (lr) New York *Times*, May 22, 1937, 14 : 6. (Ed)
See: 290.

2787. Shultz, William J. "Jazz," *Nation*, CXV (Oct. 25, 1922), 438–39. (A & A)

2788. Sidran, Louis. "Esquire's All-American Jazz Band, 1947," *Esquire*, XXVII (Feb., 1947), 45, 124. (Poll)

2789. Siegmeister, Elie. "What Is Jazz?" *in* Elie Siegmeister (Ed). *The Music Lover's Handbook*. New York: William Morrow, 1943. pp. 691–92. (A & A)

2790. Silverman, Herbert. *Units in the Study of Modern Jazz Music*. Boston, 1946. 54 pp.

2791. Simon, Alicja. "Jazz," *Auftakt*, VI (1926), 211–13. (Gen)

2792. Simon, George T. "Armstrong, Commercialism and Music," *Metronome*, LXV (Oct., 1949), 38. (A & A, Crit)

2793. ———. "Bebop's the Easy Out, Claims Louis," *Metronome*, LXIV (Mar., 1948), 14–15. (Bop)

2794. ———. "Bop Confuses Benny," *Metronome*, LXV (Oct., 1949), 15, 35. (Bop, Pers)

2795. ———. "Bop's Dixie to Monk," *Metronome*, LXIV (Apr., 1948), 20, 34–5. (Bop, Pers)

2796. ———. ". . . But the Horn Is Weak!" *Metronome*, LXVI (Oct., 1950), 18, 20. (Ork)

2797. ———. "Chant of the Weed," *Metronome*, LXII (July, 1946), 22–3. (Pers)

2798. ———. "Buddy Clark, 1911–1949," *Metronome*, LXV (Nov., 1949), 12. (Pers)

2799. ———. "A Concert to End All Concerts," *Metronome*, LXIV (Apr., 1948), 13–14, 42. (Crit)

2800. ———. "Crosby Band Had Many Ups and Downs," *Metronome* ,LVII (Dec., 1941), 16–18, 37. (Ork)

2801. ———. "The Decline of the Big Band," *in* Barry Ulanov and George Simon (Eds). *Jazz 1950*. New York: Metronome, 1950. pp. 56–9, 60, 62, 64. (Hist)

2802. ———. "Dixie 1950," *Metronome*, LXVI (May, 1950), 24, 28. (Dix)

2803. ———. "The Fabulous Dorseys," *Metronome*, LXIII (Mar., 1947), 15–16, 32–3. (Pers)

2804. ———. "Farnesio Dutra e Silva," *Metronome*, LXIII (Oct., 1947), 20, 36–7. (Geog, Pers)

2805. ———. "The Future of the Record," *in* Barry Ulanov and George Simon (Eds). *Jazz 1950*. New York: Metronome, 1950. pp. 74, 76, 78, 80, 82. (Disc)

2806. ———. "Jerry Gray Strikes Back," *Metronome*, LXVI (June, 1950), 17, 33. (Ork)

2807. ———. "He Has Great Pride As He Follows the Miller Style But . . . He's Not Following Glenn At All," *Metronome*, LXIV (May, 1948), 15–16. (Pers)

2808. ———. "History of the Year," *in* Barry Ulanov and George Simon (Eds). *Jazz 1950*. New York: Metronome, 1950. pp. 4–9. (Hist)

2809. ———. "If Red McKenzie Had Only Been Younger," *Metronome*, LXIV (Mar., 1948), 50. (Pers)

2810. ———. "I'm Not Crazy! Says Scott," *Metronome*, LXIV (Mar., 1948), 18, 33–5. (Ork, Pers)

2811. ———. "Harry James Rides Again," *Metronome*, LXIII (Aug., 1947), 9–10, 49. (Ork)

2812. ———. "Jazz Cavalcade," *Metronome*, LXIII (Jan., 1947), 52. (Rev)

2813. ———. "Jazz in the Southwest," *Metronome*, LXIV (June, 1948), 19–22. (Geog)

2814. ———. "Jazz Is What It Is and You Shouldn't Criticise It, Insists Harry James," *Metronome*, LXIV (July, 1948), 12, 17. (A & A, Ork, Pers)

2815. ———. "Stan Kenton," *Metronome*, LVII (Nov., 1941), 14, 46. (Ork)

2816. ———. "L", *Metronome*, LXVI (July, 1950), 15. (Pers)

2817. ———. "The Last Time I Heard Paris," *Metronome*, LXIV (May, 1948), 21, 31. (Ork)

2818. ———. "Elliot Lawrence Wants To Jump!" *Metronome*, LXIII (Oct., 1947), 18, 44–6. (Ork, Pers)

2819. ———. "Glenn Miller Precise," *Metronome*, LVIII (Jan., 1942), 10, 25. (Ork)

2820. Simon, George T. "Fats Navarro," *Metronome*, LXVI (Oct., 1950), 13. (Pers)
2821. ——. "No Hits, One Error," *Metronome*, LXVI (Aug., 1950), 34. (Gen)
2822. ——. "A Pictorial History of Jazz," *Metronome*, LXV (Nov., 1949), 17–27, 30–6, 40–3. (Hist, Pic)
2823. ——. "Pollack's Band Broke Up Slowly," *Metronome*, LVII (Nov., 1941), 18–19. (Hist, Ork)
2824. ——. "Poor Piano, Sound and Management," *Metronome*, LXVI (May, 1950), 50. (Gen)
     See: 2831.
2825. ——. "Simon Says," *Metronome*, LIX (Oct., 1943), 14, 60–2. (Hist)
2826. ——. "George Simon Says Back..." *Metronome*, LX (Jan., 1944), 49. (Crit)
     See: 1382.
2827. ——. "Mugsy Spanier," *Metronome*, LVII (Nov., 1941), 14, 47. (Ork)
2828. ——. "Summer Night's Dream," *Metronome*, LXVI (Oct., 1950), 34. (Rad)
2829. ——. "Swing in Philadelphia," *Metronome*, LXII (July, 1946), 16–17, 28–9. (Geog)
2830. ——. "The Thornhill Mystery," *Metronome*, LXV (Aug., 1949), 11–12, 24. (Ork)
2831. ——. "Those Bad Sounds," *Metronome*, LXVI (July, 1950), 34. (Gen)
     See: 2824.
2832. ——. "A Tip From Tommy," *Metronome*, LXIV (Nov., 1948), 13–14, 29, 31. (Ork, Pers)
2833. ——. "Mel Torme," *Metronome*, LXIII (Feb., 1947), 23, 40. (Pers)
2834. ——. "Up For the Count," *Metronome*, LXIV (Nov., 1948), 18, 23. (Ork, Pers)
2835. ——. "Video's Schmoes," *Metronome*, LXVI (June, 1950), 34. (Rad)
2836. ——. "Who Played What and When With Herman," *Metronome*, LXI (Dec., 1945), 36, 54. (Ork, Pers)
2837. ——. "Woody Returns!" *Metronome*, LXIII (Dec., 1947), 13–15, 27. (Ork)
2838. Simon, Henry W. "Benny Goodman Grows Long Hair," *PM*, Dec. 13, 1940, 13 : 1–2. (Pers)
2839. Sinatra, Frank. "Frank Sinatra On Singers," *Metronome*, LIX (Oct., 1943), 34, 72. (Pers)
2840. ——. "Sinatra on Ulanov on Crosby," *Metronome*, LXIV (June, 1948), 14. (Rev)
2841. Singleton, Zutty. "I Remember the Queen," *Jazz Record*, 58 (Sept., 1947), 10–11. (Pers)
2842. ——. "Zutty First Saw Louis in Amateur Tent Show," *Down Beat*, XVII (July 14, 1950), 6. (Hist, Pers)
2843. Sisson, Kenn. "Modern Masters of Music; The Arrangers," *Metronome*, LII (Feb., 1936), 36; (Mar., 1936), 37; (Apr., 1936), 34; (May, 1936), 31–2; (June, 1936), 27; (Aug. 1936), 22; (Sept., 1936), 47–8; (Oct., 1936), 24. (Pers)
2844. Skaarup, Victor and Martin Goldstein. *Jazz*. Copenhagen: E. Pedersen's Forlag, 1934. 128 pp.
2845. Skerret, Frank. "A Guy Called Joe," *Jazz Journal*, I (Oct., 1948), 10–11. (Pers)
2846. Skinner, Frank. *Frank Skinner's New Methods for Orchestra Scoring*. New York: Robbins, 1935. 171 pp.
2847. Skinner, Jane. "When Chubby Runs Wit, Wisdom and Great Musical Accomplishment Run With Him," *Metronome*, LXI (Dec., 1945), 28. (Pers)
2848. Skinrood, C. O. "Eva Gauthier Silences Hissing of Jazz Songs in Milwaukee Recital," *Musical America*, XXXIX (Feb. 23, 1924), 13. (Crit)
2849. Sklar, George. *The Two Worlds of Johnny Truro*. Boston: Little, Brown, 1947. 372 pp. (Fict)
2850. Slate, Lane. "It Smacks of Showmanship — With Reference to Sidney Catlett," *Jazz Session*, 5 (Jan.-Feb., 1945), 14–15. (Crit, Pers)

2851. Slawe, Jan. *Einführung in die Jazzmusik.* Basel: National-Zeitung, 1948. 135 pp.

2852. Slonimsky, Nicholas. "Jazz, Swing, and Boogie Woogie," *Christian Science Monitor Magazine,* May 20, 1944, 5. (A & A, BW)

2853. ——. "Our Jazzing, Their Jazzing, Reasons Why," Boston *Evening Transcript,* Apr. 21, 1929, III, 12 : 1–6; 15 : 2–3. (Geog)

2854. Slotkin, J. S. "Jazz and Its Forerunners As An Example of Acculturation," *American Sociological Review,* VIII (Oct., 1943), 570–75. (A & A, Hist)

2855. Smith, Carleton. "Artie Shaw," *Esquire,* XII (Oct., 1939), 94, 155–57. (Pers)

2856. Smith, Charles Edward. "Backdrop For Jazz Composers," *Esquire,* XXV (May, 1946), 112–13. (A & A)

2857. ——. "El Baile del Jazz," *Ultra,* I (Aug., 1936), 101–03. (A & A)

2858. ——. "BG: Benny Goodman," *Christian Science Monitor Magazine,* Aug. 30, 1941, 4 : 1–4; 15 : 1–3. (Pers)

2859. ——. "Blues Stanzas," *New Republic,* XCVI (Sept. 21, 1938), 184. (Poet)

2860. ——. "The Chicken and the Egg," *Record Changer,* VIII (Aug., 1949), 7, 17; (Sept., 1949), 13–14, 19. Pt. II entitled "From Jelly Roll to Bop." (A & A, Hist, Rag)
See: 3002.

2861. ——. "Collecting Hot," *Esquire,* I (Feb., 1934), 79. (A & A, Disc)

2862. ——. "Collecting Hot: 1944," *Esquire,* XXI (Feb., 1944), 27, 98–100. (A & A, Disc)

2863. ——. "Cultural Anthropology and the Reformed Tramp," *Record Changer,* VII (June, 1948), 11–12, 24. (A & A)

2864. ——. "Esquire's Jazz Bookshelf," *Esquire,* XXIII (Feb., 1945), 73, 138–43. (Rev)

2865. ——. "Folk Music, the Roots of Jazz," *Saturday Review of Literature,* XXXIII (July 29, 1950), 35–6, 48. (Disc)

2866. ——. "Hard Liquor and Hot Jazz," *Stage,* XIII (Mar., 1936), 58–9. (Gen)

2867. ——. "Heat Wave," *Stage,* XII (Sept., 1935), 45–6. (Hist, Ork)

2868. ——. "'Hitch-Hiking' Has Hurt Hot Music," *Down Beat,* VII (June 1, 1940), 5; (June 15, 1940), 8. Pt. II entitled "Is There Really a 'New Orleans' Formula?" (A & A, NO)

2869. ——. "Jazz; Some Little Known Aspects," *Symposium,* I (Oct., 1930), 502–17). (A & A)

2870. ——. "Key Men in Harlem Piano," *Esquire,* XXIV (Aug., 1945), 56–7, 120, 122, 124. (Pers)

2871. ——. "The Making of a King," *Record Changer,* IX (July-Aug., 1950), 19–21, 45, 46. (Hist, Pers)

2872. ——. *Jelly Roll Morton's New Orleans Memories.* New York: Consolidated Records, n. d. 16 pp. (Pers, Disc)

2873. ——. "New Orleans Comes to New York," *Esquire,* XXV (Mar., 1946), 93–4, 114. (NO, Pers)

2874. ——. "Oh, Mr. Jelly," *Jazz Record,* 17 (Feb., 1944), 8–10. (Pers)

2875. ——. "Over My Shoulder," *Record Changer,* VII (Oct., 1948), 13–14. (Gen, Pers)

2876. ——. "The Rag Time," *New York Times Book Review,* Oct. 15, 1950, VII, 7. (Rev)

2877. ——. "The Rhythm Section," *Esquire,* XXV (Jan., 1946), 123–24, 126. (Gen)
See: 1398; 1399; 1400; 1410; 2262; 2263; 2264.

2878. ——. "Some Like It Hot," *Esquire,* V (Apr., 1936), 42, 186, 188. (Disc, Hist, Pers)

2879. ——. "Swing," *New Republic,* XCIV (Feb. 16, 1938), 39–41. (Hist, Sw)

2880. Smith, Charles Edward. "Time Out of Hand," *Record Changer*, IX (Jan., 1950), 11. (Pers)

2881. ——. "Two Ways of Improvising on a Tune," *Down Beat*, V (May, 1938), 5, 27. (Pers)

2882. ——. "Clarence Williams," *Record Changer*, VII (Apr., 1948), 6–7. (Pers)

2883. ——, with Frederic Ramsey, Jr., Charles Payne Rogers and William Russell. *The Jazz Record Book*. New York: Smith & Durrell, 1942. 515 pp.

2884. Smith, David Stanley. "The Other Side of Jazz," New York *Herald Tribune*, June 1, 1924, VII–VIII, 20: 1–2. (A & A)

2885. Smith, Dick. "Who Said Jazz Ended in King Oliver's Time ?" *Down Beat*, IX (Feb. 15, 1942), 8. (A & A)

2886. Smith, S. Stephenson. "The Gayer Arts," *in* S. Stephenson Smith. *The Craft of the Critic*. New York: Thomas Y. Crowell, 1931. pp. 279–96. (A & A, Bl, J & C)

2887. ——. "Benny Goodman — 1949," *International Musician*, XLVIII (Oct., 1949), 15–16. (Crit, Pers)

2888. ——. "The Grand Duke of Jazz," *International Musician*, XLVIII (Dec., 1949), 14, 34. (Pers)

2889. ——. "The Saga of Tommy Dorsey," *International Musician*, XLVIII (Nov., 1949), 16. (Pers)

2890. Soby, Olaf. *Jazz Kontra Europaeisk Musikkultur*. Copenhagen: Levin & Munksgaard, 1935. 96 pp.

2891. Sommer, Reinhold. "Gesellschaftstanz und Tanzmusik," *Die Musik*, XXVIII (May, 1936), 588–90. (J & D)

2892. Sonner, Rudolf. "Großstädtische Volksmusik," *Deutsche Musikkultur*, I (June-July, 1936), 84–90. (Gen)

2893. ——. "Jazz" *Schweizerische Musikzeitung*, LXIX (Oct., 1929), 633–39. (A & A)

2894. ——. *Musik und Tanz; Vom Kulttanz zum Jazz*. Leipzig: Quelle & Meyer, 1930. 124 pp.

2895. Soria, Massimo. "Prolegomeni del Jazz," *Rivista Musicale Italiana*, XL (1936), 126–30. (A & A, Sw)

2896. Spaeth, Sigmund. "Dixie, Harlem, and Tin Pan Alley," *Scribner's*, XCIX (Jan., 1936), 23–6. (Pers)

2897. ——. "Jazz Is Not Music," *Forum*, LXXX (Aug., 1928), 267–71. (A & A, J & C)
See: 331; 807; 843; 845.

2898. ——. "Jazzmania," *North American Review*, CCXXV (May, 1928), 539–44. (A & A, Gen, J & C)

2899. ——. "Ragtime to Jazz," *in* Sigmund Spaeth. *A History of Popular Music in America*. New York: Random House, 1948. pp. 369–424. (Hist)

2900. Spalding, L. "The Jazzing of Masterpieces," (lr) *Musical News and Herald*, LXV (Nov. 24, 1923), 462. (J & C)

2901. Spanier, Muggsy. "Louis My Idol and Inspiration: Spanier," *Down Beat*, XVII (July 14, 1950), 4. (Hist, Pers)

2902. ——. "Why I Left the Bob Crosby Band," *Music and Rhythm*, I (Apr., 1941), 12–13. (Pers)

2903. Sparling, Earl. "Debutante's Delight," *American Magazine*, CXXVII (Mar., 1939), 36–7, 109–12. (Ork, Pers)

2904. ——. "Ghost Writer of Jazz," *Scribner's*, XC (Dec., 1931), 594–600. (Inst, Pers)

2905. Specht, Paul. "American Popular Music and Its Progress," *Melody*, VIII (July, 1924), 7. (Gen)

2906. ——. "Good Jazz and Bad," (lr) New York *Times*, Jan. 29, 1925, 20: 8 (A & A)

2907. Specht, Paul. *How They Became Name Bands.* New York: Fine Arts, 1941. 175 pp.
2908. —— ——. "Yankee Jazz Abroad," *Jacobs' Orchestra Monthly,* XVIII (Oct., 1927), 9–10. (Geog)
2909. Spelberg, E. D. "Jazz," *De Smidse,* II (Sept., 1927), 264–72. (Gen)
2910. Spencer, Onah. "First Blues Disc Was Made by Mamie Smith," *Down Beat,* VIII (June 15, 1941), 8. (Bl, Pers)
2911. —— ——. "'Hog Mouth Was So Powerful He Could Play Your Name'," *Down Beat,* VII (July 1, 1940), 5. (Hist)
2912. —— ——. "Preston Jackson Recalls First Gig — and Satchmo's Box Coat and Tan Shoes," *Down Beat,* IX (Nov. 1, 1942), 23. (Hist, Pers)
2913. —— ——. "'Jelly Would Flash that G-Note, Laugh In Your Face'," *Down Beat,* VIII (Aug. 1, 1941), 4. (Pers)
2914. —— ——. "Mamie Smith First Girl to Record Blues," *Down Beat,* VII (May 15, 1940), 13. (Bl)
2915. —— ——. "Trumpeter Freddie Keppard Walked Out On Al Capone!" *Music and Rythm,* II (June, 1941), 13–17. (Pers)
2916. Sperling, Grace Dickenson. "Jazz — Our Race Emotion," *Musical Observer,* XXV (July, 1926), 15, 30–1. (A & A)
2917. Spivak, Charlie. "The Jazz of the Future Is Going To Be Sweet," *Music and Rhythm,* II (Nov., 1941), 28. (A & A)
2918. Spry, Walter. "What Effect Has Jazz Upon Present Day Music and Composers?" *Etude,* XLV (June, 1927), 420. (A & A, Infl)
2919. Squire, W. H. Haddon. "Jazz Dressed-Up and Uneasy," *Christian Science Monitor,* Jan. 8, 1927, 10. (A & A)
2920. —— ——. "Of Symphonized Syncopation," *Christian Science Monitor,* Feb. 28, 1925, 8. (A & A)
2921. Stacy, Frank. *Harry James' Pin-Up Life Story.* New York: Arco, 1944. 32 pp. (Pers)
2922. —— ——. "Popsie, Benny's Bandboy Belongs to Unsung Craft," *Down Beat,* IX (Nov. 15, 1942), 13. (Pers)
2923. —— ——. "Raeburn's Jazz Too Hip for Success?" *Down Beat,* XII (July 1, 1945), 2. (Ork)
2924. —— ——. "Swing," *in* George S. Rosenthal (Ed). *Jazzways.* Cincinnati, 1946. pp. 49–51, 104–05. (A & A, Sw)
2925. —— ——. "Timme Talks About European Jazz," *Down Beat,* XVI (June 3, 1949), 18. (Disc)
2926. —— ——, and Mike Levin. "Says Hot Jazz Is Commercial," *Down Beat,* IX (Aug. 15, 1942), 18–19. (A & A, Geog)
See: 1510.
2927. Staley, S. James. "Is It True What They Say About China?" *Metronome,* LII (Dec., 1936), 17, 47–8. (Geog)
2928. Stannard, Douglas. "The Negro and Tin Pan Alley," *New Statesman and Nation,* XXI (Jan. 25, 1941), 82–3. (A & A, Hist)
2929. Stearns, Marshall (Pseud: Guy Sykes). "Almost Fair Enough," *H. R. S. Society Rag,* 3 (Jan., 1939), 6–7. (Crit, Pers)
2930. —— ——. "Critic Rapped; Crowds Pleased," *Down Beat,* XV (Feb. 25, 1948), 16. (Crit, Pers)
2931. —— ——. "Rebop, Bebop, and Bop," *Harper's,* CC (Apr., 1950), 89–96. Discussion: *Harper's,* CC (June, 1950), 21, 22, 24. (A & A, Bop, Hist)
2932. Stege, Fritz. "Gibt es eine 'Deutsche Jazzkapelle'?" *Zeitschrift für Instrumentenbau,* LVI (May 1, 1936), 251–53. (Gen)
2933. —— ——. "Der Yazz in Äußerungen unserer Zeitgenossen," *Zeitschrift für Musik,* XCVI (July, 1929), 410–11. (A & A)

2934. Steig, Arthur. "Jazz, Clock and Song of Our Anxiety," *Jazz Forum*, 1 (n. d.), 5–6. (A &A)
2935. Steig, Henry Anton. "Alligators' Idol," *New Yorker*, XIII (Apr. 17, 1937), 27–30, 32, 34. (Gen, Pers, Sw)
2936. ——. "Gertie and the Pied Piper," *Esquire*, XXIII (Feb., 1945), 44–5, 123–25. (Fict)
2937. ——. *Send Me Down*. New York: Alfred A. Knopf, 1941. 461 pp. London: Jarrolds, 1943. (Fict)
2938. Stein, Ruth. "Buddy Stewart—From Ballads to Scat Singing," *Down Beat*, XIV (Nov. 5, 1947), 4–5. (Pers)
2939. Steiner, John. "Kansas City Frank," *Jazz* (New York), I, no. 8 (n. d.), 5–8. (Pers)
2940. Steinhard, Erich. "Whitemans Jazzorchester in Paris," *Auftakt*, VI (1926), 221–22. (Crit)
2941. Stevens, Paul. "Back Bay Boogie," *American Magazine*, CXXXVIII (Dec., 1944), 46–7. (Ork)
2942. Steward, Ollie. "What Price Jazz!" *Southern Workman*, LXIV (Mar., 1935), 78–81. (A & A, Infl)
2943. Stewart-Baxter, Derrick. "Lovie Austin Discography," *Playback*, II (Aug., 1949), 14–18. (Disc)
2944. ——. "The Australian Jazz Band, Graeme Bell," *Record Changer*, VII (July, 1948), 8–9, 29. (Ork)
2945. ——. "Buddy Bolden," *Hot Club Magazine*, 14 (Feb., 1947), 3–4. (Pers)
2946. ——. "Bunk Johnson: An Appreciation," *Jazz Journal*, II (Sept., 1949), 2–3. (Pers)
2947. ——. "Humphrey Lyttleton and His Band," *Record Changer*, VIII (Mar., 1949), 8–9. (Geog, Ork, Pers)
2948. ——. "Un Portrait Garland Wilson," *Hot Club Magazine*, 18 (June 15, 1947), 13–14. (Pers)
2949. ——. "Words on Vocal-Blues," *Jazz Journal*, II (Jan., 1949), 2–3. (Bl)
2950. Stilwell, Arnold. "Oh Didn't He Ramble," *Record Changer*, VII (Nov., 1948), 11. (Gen)
2951. ——. *Record Dating Chart, Part I*. New York: Record Changer, 1948. (Disc)
2952. Stine, Jack. "American Jazz, 1949," *Jazz Journal*, II (Oct., 1949), 4–5. (A & A, Bop, Geog)
2953. Stjernberg, Lydia Nilsson. "Finding Merit In Jazz," (lr) New York *Times*, Oct. 20, 1934, 14 : 7. (Gen)
See: 589; 2604; 3159.
2954. Stoddard, Hope. "Don't Look Now—But You're Improvising!" *International Musician*, XLVIII (Dec., 1949), 15–16, 34. (A & A, Pers)
2955. Stolz, Ernst. "Jazzkultur," *Allgemeine Musik-Zeitung*, LIII (Mar. 19, 1926), 225–26. (A & A, Crit)
2956. Stone, Richard. "Basie and Bop," *Record Changer*, VII (Dec., 1948), 10. (Bop, Ork)
2957. Stout, Clarence. "Red-Light Piano Men," *Music and Rhythm*, I (Dec., 1940), 17–18. (Hist, Pers)
2958. Straight, Charley. "Straight Fired Bix In a Hurry!" *Down Beat*, VII (Oct. 15, 1940), 24. (Pers)
2959. Strate, Marvin W. "Swing—What Is It?" *Musical America*, LVI (May 25, 1936), 6–7. (A & A, Sw)
2960. Straus, Henrietta. "Jazz and 'The Rhapsody In Blue'," *Nation*, CXVIII (Mar. 5, 1924), 263. (A & A, Hist)
2961. ——. "Marking the Miles," *Nation*, CXIV (Mar. 8, 1922), 292, 294. (J & C)
2962. Strayhorn, Billy. "Billy Strayhorn On Pianists," *Metronome*, LIX (Oct., 1943), 29, 66. (Pers)

2963. Stringham, Edwin J. "'Jazz'—An Educational Problem," *Musical Quarterly*, XII (Apr., 1926), 190–95. (A & A, Infl)
2964. Strunsky, Simeon. "In the Matter of Jazz," New York *Times*, Feb. 8, 1925, III, 4. (A & A)
2965. Stuart, Dave. "Kid Ory," *Jazz Information*, II (Nov. 22, 1940), 5–8. (Pers)
2966. Stubbs, G. Edward (Ed). "Ecclesiastical Music," *New Music Review*, XXI (Mar., 1922), 127–28. (Infl)
2967. Stuckenschmidt, H. H. "Hellenic Jazz," *Modern Music*, VII (Apr.-May, 1930), 22–4. (J & O)
2968. Studebaker, J. W. "The Age of Jazz," *Journal of Education*, CIX (Jan. 21, 1929), 68. (A & A)
2969. Swift, Vincent. "A Word In Favour of Jazz," *Musical Standard*, XXX (July 30, 1927), 43–4. (A & A)
2970. Sylvester, Robert. "Barefoot Boy and His Band," *Saturday Evening Post*, CCXVIII (May 18, 1946), 16–17, 52, 54, 56. (Ork, Pers)
2971. — —. "Music Union Contends 15,000 Jazzmen Can't All Be Wrong," New York *Daily News*, Dec. 15, 1949, 81 : 1–2. (Gen)
2972. — —. "Ol' Satch and Horn in Best Jazz Concert of Town Hall Series," New York *Daily News*, May 19, 1947, 31 : 1–2. (Crit)
2973. — —. "Some Showmanship Gives Hampton Band A Terrific Lift," New York *Daily News*, Dec. 13, 1949, 85 : 1–2. (Crit)
2974. Talmadge, I. D. W. "Communism and Jazz," *Music and Rhythm*, I (Nov., 1940), 27–8. (Geog)
2975. Tanner, Peter. "American Impressions No. 1," *Hot Club Magazine*, 21 (Nov. 1, 1947), 7–6. (Gen)
2976. — —. "American Impressions No. 2," *Hot Club Magazine*, 22 (Dec. 1, 1947), 12. (Gen)
2977. — —. (Trans: A. Bettonville). "'Big Jim', L'Histoire de Jimmy Harrisson," *Hot Club Magazine*, 14 (Feb., 1947), 10. (Pers)
2978. — —. "The British Scene," *Record Changer*, VII (Apr., 1948), 8–9. (Geog)
2979. — —. "It's Tough to Write About Jazz in Britain Today," *Down Beat*, XIV (Sept. 24, 1947), 15. (Geog)
2980. — —. (Trans: E. Colomer Brossa). "Illinois Jacquet," *Club de Ritmo*, 41 (Sept., 1949), 1–2. (Pers)
2981. — —. "Real Gone Gal—The History of Nellie Lutcher," *Jazz Journal*, I (Aug., 1948), 2–3. (Disc, Pers)
2982. — —. "Revue des Livres: Jazz Cavalcade par Dave Dexter, Jr.," *Hot Club Magazine*, 15 (Mar., 1947), 5. (Rev)
2983. Tao. "Jazzkonfetti," *Det ny Radio Blad*, 46 (Nov. 11, 1949), 7. (Bop)
2984. Taubman, Howard. "An Album With Music, Pictures and Text, Devoted to Current Scene," New York *Times*, Jan. 15, 1950, II, 4 : 1–2. (Disc)
2985. — —. "'Duke' Invades Carnegie Hall," *New York Times Magazine*, Jan. 17, 1943, 10, 30. (Ork, Pers)
2986. — —. "Jam Session With No Holds Barred," *New York Times Magazine*, Dec. 5, 1943, VI, 13, 48–9. (Ork, Pers)
2987. — —. "Swing and Mozart, Too," New York *Times*, Dec. 29, 1940, VII, 7. (Pers)
2988. Taylor, G. R. Stirling. "Political Music," *Outlook*, LVII (June 12, 1926), 420. (Infl)
2989. Taylor, Peter and Geoffrey Helliwell. "A Discography of Johnny Dodds," *Jazz Journal*, II (May, 1949), 8; (June, 1949), 15; (Nov., 1949), 8. (Disc)
2990. Teagarden, Jack. "The Ten Greatest Trombone Players," *Music and Rhythm*, II (June, 1942), 14. (Pers)
2991. Terry, Margo. "Jazz Moods on Canvas," *Record Changer*, IX (Jan., 1950), 8–9, 16. (Gen)

2992. Terry, Sir Richard. "Voodooism in Music," *in* Sir Richard Terry. *Voodooism in Music and Other Essays.* London: Burns Oates & Washbourne, 1934. pp. 1–17. (A & A, Infl)

2993. Thiele, Bob. "The Case of Jazz Music," *Jazz* (New York), I, no. 9 (n. d.) 19–20. (A & A, Pers)

2994. ——. "Rod Cless," *Jazz* (New York), I, no. 8 (n. d.), 10–11. (Pers)

2995. Thomas, Lagniappe. "Jazz and G-String Keep New Orleans' Vieux Carre From Being Old in Anything But Name," *Holiday,* VII (May, 1950), 6, 8–9, 10, 11. (Gen)

2996. Thompson, Bob. "Jazz! Chicago! Muggsy!" *Record Changer,* VII (Oct., 1948), 11, 19. (Chi, Pers)

2997. Thompson, Kay C. "Improvisation: The Fact and the Fable," *Record Changer,* VIII (June, 1949), 5, 15. (A & A)

2998. ——. "An Interview With Sidney Bechet," *Record Changer,* VIII (July 1949), 9–10. (Pers)

2999. ——. "Lottie Joplin," *Record Changer,* IX (Oct., 1950), 8, 18. (Pers)

3000. ——. "Louis and the Waif's Home," *Record Changer,* IX (July-Aug., 1950), 8, 43. (Hist, Pers)

3001. ——. "More on Ragtime," *Record Changer,* VIII (Oct., 1949), 9–10, 14. (Rag)

3002. ——. "Rag-Time and Jelly Roll," *Record Changer,* VIII (Apr., 1949), 8, 23. (A & A, Pers, Rag)
   See: 2860.

3003. ——. "The Western Heritage of Jazz," *Record Changer,* IX (Apr., 1950), 8, 17. (A & A, Hist)

3004. Thompson, Oscar. "Jazz, As Art Music, Piles Failure on Failure," *Musical America,* XLIII (Feb. 13, 1926), 3, 23. (A & A, J & C)

3005. ——. "Jazz As a Diversion and the Subsidence of Hopes That It Might Mean a New Musical Force," New York *Evening Post,* Dec. 21, 1929, III, 11 : 1. (J & C)

3006. ——. "Much-Bruited Jazz Concerto Causes Stir When Given Orchestral Baptism," *Musical America,* XLIII (Dec. 12, 1925), 4. (Crit, J & C)

3007. ——. "Twilight Descends on the Gods of Tin Pan Alley," *Musical America,* XL (Aug. 16, 1924), 5. (A & A)

3008. Thompson, Robert. "The Dixieland Ohio Rhythm Kings," *Record Changer,* IX (Apr., 1950), 9, 18. (Ork)

3009. Thomson, Virgil. "The Cult of Jazz," *Vanity Fair,* XXIV (June, 1925), 54, 118. (J & C)

3010. ——. "I Say Its Jazz—Hot," *Vogue,* CI (Feb. 15, 1943), 32, 72. (A & A)

3011. ——. "Jazz," *American Mercury,* II (Aug., 1924), 465–67. (A & A, Inst, J & D)

3012. ——. "Swing Again", *Modern Music,* XV (Mar.-Apr., 1938), 160–66. (A & A, Sw)

3013. ——. "Swing Music," *Modern Music,* XIII (May-June, 1936), 12–17. (A & A, Sw)

3014. Thoorens, Leon. *Essai Sur le Jazz.* Liege: L'Horizon Nouveau, 1942. 36 pp.

3015. Thornes, Vernon M. *Swing Music Art.* Dewsbury, Yorks.: 1943. 24 pp.

3016. Tilford, William Roberts. "Swing, Swing, Swing!" *Etude,* LV (Dec., 1937), 777–78, 835. (Lang, Sw)

3017. Tillotson, Frederic. "The Place of Jazz," (lr) *Musical America,* XXXIX (Apr. 5, 1924), 10–11. (Gen)

3018. Toledano, Ralph de. "Autobiography in Tone," *Saturday Review of Literature,* XXXI (Jan. 31, 1948), 47. (Disc, Pers)

3019. ——. "Directions of Jazz," *in* Ralph de Toledano (Ed). *Frontiers of Jazz.* New York: Oliver Durrell, 1947. pp. 66–71. (A & A)

3020. ——. "Eugene Williams," *Record Changer,* VII (July, 1948), 18. (Pers)

3021. Toledano, Ralph de (Ed). *Frontiers of Jazz*. New York: Oliver Durrell, 1947. 178 pp.
3022. Toll, Ted. "Ellington Lauded As All Time Greatest," *Down Beat*, VII (Sept. 1, 1940), 3. (Ork)
3023. ——. "Men Behind the Bands: Ben Homer," *Down Beat*, VIII (June 15, 1941), 20. (Pers)
3024. Tonks, Eric S. "Discography of the Original Dixieland Jazz Band," *Jazz Forum*, I (n. d.), 28–9. (Disc)
3025. ——. "The Luis Russell Orchestra," *Jazz Journal*, II (Jan., 1949), 6. (Ork)
3026. Torme, Mel. "Of Singing and Singers," *Metronome*, LXVI (May, 1950), 21–2, 30–1, 32. (Inst)
3027. ——. (As Told to Ted Hallock). "Torme Raps None, Advises All," *Down Beat*, XV (Apr. 21, 1948), 2, 16, 23. (A & A, Pers)
3028. Toscana Pouchan, Mario A. "Glimpse of Argentina," *in* Orin Blackstone (Ed). *Jazzfinder '49*. New Orleans: Orin Blackstone, 1949. pp. 45–8. (Geog)
3029. Toye, Francis. "Ragtime: The New Tarantism," *English Review*, XIII (Mar., 1913), 654–58. (Infl, Rag)
3030. Tracy, Jack. "Alvin Adds to Dixie Revival," *Down Beat*, XVII (June 2, 1950), 2. (Dix, Ork)
3031. ——. "Basie Best of What's Left?" *Down Beat*, XVII (Jan. 13, 1950), 21. (Crit, Ork)
3032. ——. "Gillespie's Crew Great Again, But May Break Up," *Down Beat*, XVII (June 16, 1950), 1. (Crit, Ork)
3033. ——. "Guitarist Farlow 'One of Jazz Greats'," *Down Beat*, XVII (Dec. 29, 1950), 2. (Pers)
3034. ——. "Herman Discography," *Down Beat*, XVII (Nov. 3, 1950), 19. (Disc)
3035. ——. "Jazz Being Plagued By a Cult: Chubby Jackson," *Down Beat*, XVII (Oct. 20, 1950), 1, 19. (Gen, Pers)
3036. ——. "Make Jazz Respectable, Asks Rodney," *Down Beat*, XVII (June 2, 1950), 3. (Pers)
3037. ——. "Mendez, At Age 6, Faced Firing Squad," *Down Beat*, XVII (Apr. 21, 1950), 3. (Pers)
3038. ——. "Must Raise Standards of Jazz, Insists Miller," *Down Beat*, XVII (Nov. 3, 1950), 13. (A & A, Pers)
3039. ——. "New Jazz Stars 'A Swinging Group'," *Down Beat*, XVII (Feb. 10, 1950), 3. (Crit, Ork)
3040. ——. "Red Norvo Trio 'Astounding, Impeccable'," *Down Beat*, XVII (Nov. 17, 1950), 4. (Crit, Ork)
3041. ——. "Please Note: Terry Gibbs Is No Girl," *Down Beat*, XVII (Mar. 10, 1950), 19. (Pers)
3042. ——. "Stevens Well On Way to Hitting the Top Echelon," *Down Beat*, XVII (Sept. 22, 1950), 3. (J & D, Ork)
        See: 2015; 2019; 2021; 2024; 2025; 2026; 2027; 2028; 3274.
3043. ——. "'Ventura Could Climb Right to Top'," *Down Beat*, XVII (May 19, 1950), 23. (Crit, Ork)
3044. Traill, Sinclair. "Armstrong Completes His Half-Century of European Concerts," *Melody Maker*, XXV (Nov. 12, 1949), 2. (Crit)
3045. ——. "Britain Bounces," *in* Orin Blackstone (Ed). *Jazzfinder '49*. New Orleans: Orin Blackstone, 1949. pp. 37–9. (Geog)
3046. ——. "Bennie Moten; Histoire et Discographie du Celebre Orchestre de Kansas City," *Hot Club Magazine*, 25 (Mar., 1948), 8–9; 26 (Apr., 1948), 10–11. (Disc, Ork, Pers)
3047. ——. *Way Down Yonder*. London: Parade, 1949. 256 pp. (Fict)
3048. ——. "When Buddha Smiled," *Record Changer*, VIII (Aug., 1949), 6, 15. (Disc)

3049. Trazegnies, Jean de. "Tommy Dorsey," *Hot Club Magazine*, 5 (May, 1946), 10. (Ork)
3050. ——. *Duke Ellington: Harlem Aristocrat of Jazz*. Brussels: Hot Club de Belgique, 1946. 63 pp. (Pers)
3051. ——. "Un Grand Sax-Alto Noir, Hilton Jefferson," *Hot Club Magazine*, 7 (July, 1946), 9. (Pers)
3052. ——. "Harry Hayes, le Benny Carter Anglais," *Hot Club Magazine*, 6 (June, 1946), 11. (Pers)
3053. ——. "Spike Hughes," *Hot Club Magazine*, 14 (Feb., 1947), 16–17. (Pers)
3054. ——. "Un Theme ... Deux Styles," *Hot Club Magazine*, 10 (Oct., 1946), 15. (Disc)
3055. Treadwell, Bill. *Big Book of Swing*. New York: Cambridge House, 1946. 130 pp.
3056. Trebor, Haynes. "Ethnography of Jazz," (lr) New York *Times*, Apr. 17, 1927, VII, 6 : 5. (A & A)
3057. Trienes, Walter. *Musik in Gefahr*. Regensburg: G. Bosse, 1940. 150 pp.
3058. Tristano, Lennie. "What's Right With the Beboppers," *Metronome*, LXIII (July, 1947), 14, 31. (A & A, Bop)
3059. Trumbauer, Frankie. "Frankie Trumbauer Recalls the Good Old Days," *Down Beat*, IX (Apr. 15, 1942), 6. (Hist)
3060. Trussell, Jake, Jr. "Ellington Hits the Top, and the Bottom," *Jazz* (New York), I, no. 8 (n. d.), 16, 20. (Ork)
3061. ——. "In Defense of Hammond," *Jazz* (New York), I, no. 9 (n. d.), 22. (Crit, Pers)
See: 1384; 1670.
3062. Tschudi, Ernst Felix. "The Immortals Object," *Living Age*, CCCXXI (Apr. 5, 1924), 653–55. Reprinted: *Etude*, XLII (Oct., 1924), 670. (A & A, J & C)
3063. Turnbull, Stanley. *How to Run A Small Dance Band For Profit*. London: Nelson & Sons, 1937. 86 pp.
3064. Turner, Chittenden. "Dance, the Foe of American Song," *Arts and Decoration*, XX (Nov., 1923), 21, 75–7. (J & D)
3065. Turner, Melani. "Jazzing the Classics," (lr) New York *Times*, July 3, 1932, II, 2 : 5. (J & C)
3066. Turner, W. J. "Jazz Music," *New Statesman*, XVI (Feb. 5, 1921), 532. (A & A, J & C)
3067. ——. "Jazz Music," *in* W. J. Turner. *Music and Life*. London: Methuen, 1921. pp. 193–97. (Gen)
3068. ——. "Syncopated–Jazz–Ragtime," *New Statesman*, XXII (Oct. 13, 1923), 14–15. Reprinted: W. J. Turner. *Variations on the Theme of Music*. London: William Heinemann, 1924. pp. 99–105. (A & A, J & C)
3069. ——. "Vitamins in Music," *New Statesman*, XXIV (Jan. 10, 1925), 390–91. (A & A, J & C)
3070. ——. "Waltz-Kings and Jazz-Kings," *New Statesman*, XXVII (Apr. 17, 1926), 13–14. Reprinted: W. J. Turner. *Musical Meanderings*. London: Methuen, 1928. pp. 59–64. (A & A, J & C)
3071. Tyler, Marian. "Jazz Leaves Home," *Nation*, CXXII (Jan. 20, 1926), 68. (J & D, J & O)
3072. Uenoda, Setsuo. "Jazz Songs of Japan," *Trans-Pacific*, XVII (Sept. 26, 1929), 6. (Geog)
3073. Ugge, Emanuel. *Don Redman*. Praha: Gramoklub, 1947. 12 pp. (Pers)
3074. Ulanov, Barry. "Another Month, Another Boom," *Metronome*, LXVI (June, 1950), 34. (Dix)
3075. ——. "Aux Derrieres du Jazz," *Metronome*, LXIV (May, 1948), 36, 42. (Rev)
3076. ——. "Sonny Berman," *Metronome*, LXIII (Mar., 1947), 21. (Pers)

3077. Ulanov, Barry. "The Blues For the Times," *Esquire*, XXIII (Feb., 1945), 27, 93. (Bl)
3078. ——. "Bud Is A Free Man," *Metronome*, LXIII (Oct., 1947), 17, 40. (Pers)
3079. ——. "A Call to Arms—and Horns," *Metronome*, LXIII (Apr., 1947), 15, 44. (A & A)
3080. ——. "The Clarinet Comes Back," *Metronome*, LXIII (Dec., 1947), 17, 41. (Pers)
3081. ——. "Critics and Criticism," *Metronome*, LXIII (Dec., 1947), 19, 32–5. (Crit)
    See: 1058.
3082. ——. "Tad Dameron," *Metronome*, LXIII (Aug., 1947), 24, 35. (Pers)
3083. ——. "Don't Fluff Benny Carter's Stuff," *Metronome*, LXII (Aug., 1946), 22. (Ork)
3084. ——. *Duke Ellington*. New York: Creative Age, 1946. 322 pp. Buenos Aires: Editorial Estuardo, 1946. 400 pp. (Pers)
3085. ——. "An Evening in Philadelphia," *Metronome*, LXVI (Aug., 1950), 34. (Ork)
3086. ——. "File for the Future: the Page Cavanaugh Trio," *Metronome*, LXIII (Feb., 1947), 24. (Ork)
3087. ——. "Flying Hampton," *Metronome*, LIX (Dec., 1943), 14–15. (Ork)
3088. ——. "The Four Men Who Made Modern Jazz," *in* Barry Ulanov and George Simon (Eds). *Jazz 1950*. New York: Metronome, 1950. pp. 19–22. (Pers)
3089. ——. "The Function of the Critic in Jazz," *Metronome*, LXV (Aug., 1949), 16–17. (Crit)
3090. ——. "The Function of the Musician," *Metronome*, LXV (Oct., 1949), 16, 26. (A & A)
3091. ——. "Goffin: His Book on Jazz is Bumptiously Self-Righteous, Pits Jazz vs. Swing, Though They're Both the Same Thing," *Metronome*, LX (Feb., 1944), 19, 32. (Rev)
3092. ——. "Goffin's Horn Fluffs A-Plenty," *Metronome*, LXIII (July, 1947), 38. (Rev)
3093. ——. "A History of Jazz," *Metronome*, LXVI (July, 1950), 18–19; (Aug., 1950), 14–15, 20. (Hist)
3094. ——. "The Hot War," *Metronome*, LXIV (May, 1948), 17, 30–1. (Crit)
3095. ——. "The Human Sarah," *Metronome*, LXV (Oct., 1949), 11–12. (Pers)
3096. ——. "In the Mud," *Metronome*, LXVI (May, 1950), 50. (Gen)
3097. ——. *The Incredible Crosby*. New York: McGraw-Hill, 1948. 336 pp.
3098. ——. "It's Not the Book, It's the Attitude!" *Metronome*, LVIII (Mar., 1942), 11. (Rev)
3099. ——. "Jazz in Chicago," *Metronome*, LXVI (May, 1950), 26–7. (Ork)
3100. ——. "Jazz in Los Angeles," *Metronome*, LXII (Aug., 1946), 19–21. (Geog, Pers)
3101. ——. "Jazz in San Francisco," *Metronome*, LXIII (Feb., 1947), 26, 46. (Geog)
3102. ——. "The Jukes Take Over Swing," *American Mercury*, LI (Oct., 1940), 172–77. (A & A, Disc, Sw)
3103. ——. "Dave Lambert," *Metronome*, LXIII (July, 1947), 12, 48. (Pers)
3104. ——. "LP," *in* Barry Ulanov and George Simon (Eds). *Jazz 1950*. New York: Metronome, 1950. pp. 66, 68. (Tech)
3105. ——. "Manhattan Serenade," *Metronome*, LIX (Oct., 1943), 40–3. (Hist)
3106. ——. "Master in the Making," *Metronome*, LXV (Aug., 1949), 14–15, 32–3. (Pers)
3107. ——. "Miles and Leo," *Metronome*, LXIII (July, 1947), 19. (Pers)
3108. ——. "Mr. B.," *Metronome*, LXVI (July, 1950), 13–14. (Pers)
3109. ——. "Mitch the Goose Man," *Metronome*, LXVI (July, 1950), 34. (Pers)

3110. Ulanow, Barry. "Musicians Are Not Dope Fiends," *Metronome*, LXIII (Aug., 1947), 12–13. (Gen)

3111. ——. "New York Jazz 1930–1950," *in* Barry Ulanov and George Simon (Eds). *Jazz 1950*. New York: Metronome, 1950. pp. 48–55. (Hist)

3112. ——. "... No Business Like ..." *Metronome*, LXVI (Oct., 1950), 34. (Pers)

3113. ——. "Not Just A Singer's Singer—But Everybody's", *Metronome*, LXIV (Apr., 1948), 19, 30. (Pers)

3114. ——. "Panassie Book Draws Reverse Rave," *Metronome*, LIX (Feb., 1943), 14, 21. (Rev)

3115. ——. "Andre Previn," *Metronome*, LXII (Apr., 1946), 20–1. (Pers)

3116. ——. "Righto!" *Metronome*, LXVI (Oct., 1950), 16–17, 29. (Geog)

3117. ——. "Jan Savitt," *Metronome*, LXIV (Nov., 1948), 17. (Pers)

3118. ——. "Shining Trumpets," *Metronome*, LXIII (Jan., 1947), 52–3. (Rev)

3119. ——. "Smart Alec," *Metronome*, LXIII (May, 1947), 16–17, 41–2. (Pers)

3120. ——. "The Sound; Stan Getz, That Is, and That's Cool Jazz," *Metronome*, LXVI (June, 1950), 13–14. (Pers)

3121. ——. "The Square Bear," *Metronome*, LXIV (Apr., 1948), 15, 36. (Geog)

3122. ——. "Thanks, Mr. Redman, For Modern Style," *Metronome*, LVII (June, 1941), 20–1, 25–6. (Pers)

3123. ——. "Those Good Old Days," *Metronome*, LXIV (June, 1948), 42. (Hist)

3124. ——. "3's No Crowd: The Trios Have Taken Over In a Big Way," *Metronome*, LIX (Nov., 1943), 14–15. (Ork)

3125. ——. "A Trip to Toronto," *Metronome*, LXIV (Mar., 1948), 20, 26. (Geog, Pers)

3126. ——. "The Twain Meet," *Metronome*, LXIV (July, 1948), 15. (Ork)

3127. ——. "U.S. Dominates Canadian Jazz," *Metronome*, LVII (Sept., 1941), 16–17, 35. (Geog)

3128. ——. "When Ralph Burns the Herman Band Is Fired By Brilliant Modern Manuscript," *Metronome*, LXI (Dec., 1945), 26, 48. (Pers)

3129. ——. "Where There's a Will ... There's a Classical Way," *Metronome*, LXIV (July, 1948), 11, 18–19. (Pers)

3130. ——. "Woody's New Band," *Metronome*, LXIV (June, 1948), 15, 27. (Crit, Ork)

3131. ——, and Dave Banks. "Jerks or Jocks?" *Metronome*, LXIV (Mar., 1948), 16–17, 30. (Pers)

3132. ——, and Stan Kenton. "Stan Kenton Joins the New Jazz Society," *Metronome*, LXVI (May, 1950), 25, 49. (Gen)

3133. ——, and George Simon (Eds). *Jazz 1950*. New York: Metronome, 1950. 104 pp.

3134. Valdez, Ildefonso P. "A Note on Blues," *in* Nancy Cunard (Ed). *Negro*. London: Wishart, 1934. p. 377. (Bl)

3135. Valentine, Gamewell. "Jazz and Syncopated Music," (lr) *Musical Courier*, LXXXVIII (Feb. 21, 1924), 51. (A & A)

3136. Vallas, Leon. "Lettre d'Amerique. IV–L'Apotheose du Jazz," *L'Edition Musicale Vivante*, III (Oct., 1930), 12–15. (Crit)

3137. Vallee, Rudy. *Vagabond Dreams Come True*. New York: E. P. Dutton, 1930. 262 pp.

3138. Vassenhove, L. van. "'Jonny' Ou Le Triomphe du Jazz," *Courrier Musical*, XXX (Mar. 1, 1928), 142–43. (J & O)

3139. Vechten, Carl van. "The Black Blues," *Vanity Fair*, XXIV (Aug., 1925), 57, 86, 92. (A & A, Bl, Pers)

3140. ——. "Memories of Bessie Smith," *Jazz Record*, 58 (Sept., 1947), 6–7, 29. (Pers)

3141. ——. *Nigger Heaven*. New York: Alfred A. Knopf, 1926. 286 pp. (Fict)

3142. Venables, R. G. V. "Britain's Webb, London Hot Club Fold Together," *Down Beat*, XV (Feb. 25, 1948), 15. (Geog)

3143. —— ——. "Discography—Frank Teschmaker," *Jazz Forum*, 1 (n. d.), 27–8. (Disc)

3144. —— ——. "A Discography of the Cotton Pickers, Tennessee Tooters and Allied Groups," *Jazz Forum*, 4 (Apr., 1947), 30–1. (Disc)

3145. —— ——. "Discography of the Mound City Blue Blowers," *Jazz Forum*, 3 (Jan., 1947), 20–1. (Disc)

3146. —— ——. "Full Discography of Ben Pollack and Band," *Down Beat*, XIII (Jan. 14, 1946), 19. (Disc)

3147. —— ——. "Ed Lang on Race Records," *Jazz* (New York), I (Dec., 1943), 6. (Disc)

3148. —— ——. "The Story of Sterling Boze," *Reprints and Reflections*, 4 (June, 1945), 1. (Pers)

3149. —— ——, and Clifford Jones (Eds). *Bix*. London: Discographical Society, 1945. 24 pp. (Pers)

3150. —— ——. *Cream of the White Clarinetists*. London: Dicographical Society, n. d. 16 pp. (Pers)

3151. —— ——. *Eye Witness Jazz*. London: Discographical Society, 1946. 24 pp. (Pers)

3152. —— ——, and C. W. Langston White. *A Complete Discography of Red Nichols and His Five Pennies*. Melbourne: Australian Jazz Quarterly, 1946. 15 pp. (Disc)

3153. —— ——. *Reminting the Pennies*. Tilford, Surrey: 1942. 8 pp.

3154. Ventura, Ray. "Non Le Jazz Ne Meurt Pas! Il Evolue..." *L'Edition Musicale Vivante*, IV (Sept., 1931), 7–9. (Hist)

3155. Verbeucken, Wim. "Jazzlife in Holland," *Swing Music*, 14 (Autumn, 1936), 21–2. (Geog)

3156. Verees, J. Paul. "Pessimistic View of Public's Taste," (lr) New York *Times*, Sept. 19, 1926, X, 14 : 6. (A & A)

3157. Vica, Carl. *Du Classicisme au Jazz*. Paris: Marcel Vigne, 1933.

3158. Vitalius, E. H. "Kind Words For Jazz," (lr) New York *Times*, Oct. 3, 1926, VIII 14 : 1. (Gen)

3159. Vizetelly, Frank H. "On the Trail of Jazz," New York *Times*, Oct. 18, 1934, 22 : 6. (Lang)

See: 589; 2604; 2953.

3160. Vuillermoz, Émile. "Rag-Time et Jazz-Band," *in* Emile Vuillermoz. *Musiques d'Aujourd'hui*. Paris: G. Cres, 1923. pp. 207–15. (A & A)

3161. —— ——. "Tempo di 'Jazz'," *Rassegna Musicale*, I (May, 1928), 304–08. (Gen)

3162. W. B. "America's Grab at the Jazz Business," *Musicians Journal*, 17 (July, 1925), 10–11. (Gen)

3163. W. H. A. "Rag-Time," *Metronome*, XV (May, 1899), 4. (Rag)

3164. W. M. "Tracing the Jazz Age," (lr) New York *Times*, Oct. 24, 1929, 28 : 7. (A & A)

3165. Wager, Walter. "London Jive," *Record Changer*, IX (Mar., 1950), 4, 19. (Geog)

3166. Walker, Alfred. "Jazz!" (lr) New York *Times*, Dec. 17, 1922, VII, 4 : 3. (J & C)

3167. Walkley, A. B. "Jazz," *in* A. B. Walkley. *Still More Prejudice*. London: William Heinemann, 1925. pp. 163–66, 148–52. (A & A)

3168. Ward, W. F. "Music in the Gold Coast," *Gold Coast Review*, III (July-Dec. 1927), 199–223. (A & A)

3169. Wareing, John H. "Some Reminiscences of Teddy Weatherford," *Jazz Forum*, 4 (Apr., 1947), 10–11. (Pers)

3170. Waring, Fred. (Ed: Rose Heylbut). "The Requirements of Rhythm Playing," *Etude*, LVIII (Sept., 1940), 583, 634. (A & A)

3171. Warner, J. E. "Blues for Bertha," *Record Changer*, IX (June, 1950), 5. (Pers)

3172. Waterman, Richard A. "'Hot' Rhythm in Negro Music," *Journal of the American Musicological Society*, I (Spring, 1948), 24–37. (A & A)

3173. Weaver, H. E. "Syncopation: A Study of Musical Rhythms," *Journal of General Psychology*, XX (Apr., 1939), 409–29. (A & A)

3174. Weaver, Jim. "Jazz and Ellingtonia," *Jazz* (New York), I (Dec., 1943), 13, 17. (A & A, Pers)

3175. Webb, H. Brook. "The Slang of Jazz," *American Speech*, XII (Oct., 1937), 179–84. (Lang)

3176. Webb, Les. "The McPartland Chronicle," *Jazz Journal*, II (May, 1949), 10–11. (Pers)

3177. Weber, Marek. "Salon—und Jazzmusik," *Anbruch*, XI (Mar., 1929), 136–37. (A & A)

3178. Webster, James D. "The Banjo Gave Us Jazz—Believe It or Not!" *Metronome*, LVI (Aug., 1940), 40. (Inst)

3179. Weil, Irving. "Jazz Gets a National Twist," *Musical America*, XLVIII (Aug. 25, 1928), 9, 21. (Geog)

3180. Weill, Kurt. "Notiz zum Jazz," *Anbruch*, XI (Mar., 1929), 138. (A & A)

3181. Weinstock, Bob. "Dizzy Gillespie, A Complete Discography," *Record Changer*, VIII (July, 1949), 8, 18. (Disc)

3182. Weirick, Paul. *Dance Arranging.* New York: M. Witmark, 1934. 142 pp.

3183. Weiss, Bernard. "Class In Dance Orchestration," *High Points*, XXX (Dec., 1948), 56–8. (Ed)

3184. Weissmann, Adolf. "The First German Jazz Opera," *Christian Science Monitor*, Mar. 19, 1927, 10. (Crit, J & O)

3185. ———. "The Standardization of Jazz," *Christian Science Monitor*, Oct. 22, 1927, 8. (A & A, Rev)

3186. Weller, Alanson. "Here and There in New York," *Jacobs' Orchestra Monthly*, XX (Sept., 1929), 53. (Pers)

3187. Welty, Eudora. "Powerhouse," *in* Eudora Welty. *A Curtain of Green.* Garden City: Doubleday, Doran, 1941. pp. 253–69. (Fict)

3188. Werrenrath, Reinald. "Jazz," *Musical Courier*, LXXXVI (Jan. 18, 1923), 18. (Gen)

3189. Wessem, Constant van. *Het Musiceeren en Concerteeren in den Loop der Tijden.* Amsterdam: De Spieghel, 1929. 159 pp.

3190. Wettling, George. "Lincoln Gardens," *Needle*, I (June, 1944), 13. (Hist)

3191. Wexler, Jerry. "Rhythm and Blues in 1950," *Saturday Review of Literature*, XXXIII (June 24, 1950), 49. (Bl, Disc)

3192. Wheelock, Raymond. "Did Swing Come From the Indians?" *Educational Music Magazine*, XXIII (Nov., 1943), 20–1, 50. (A & A, Sw)

3193. Whiston, Henry F. "'Watch Peterson,' Say Canadians," *Down Beat*, XVII (Mar. 10, 1950), 3. (Pers)

3194. Whitaker, Rogers E. M. "Spokesman With A Temperature," *New Yorker*, XXI (Apr. 28, 1945), 28–32, 35–7; (May 5, 1945), 28–32, 34–41. (Ork, Pers)

3195. White, Bob. "Are Modern Jazzmen Improving on Bix, Tesch?" *Down Beat*, VII (Sept. 1, 1940), 9. (A & A)

3196. ———. "Are the White Chicagoans of the '20's Overrated? No," *Music and Rhythm*, II (Oct., 1941), 45, 56. (Chi) *See*: 2249.

3197. ———. "Chicago Style?—It's A Phony Myth!" *Music and Rhythm*, I (Mar., 1941), 35–40. (Chi)

3198. ———. "Critics' Opinions Come 'A Dime A Bushel!'" *Music and Rhythm*, I (Apr., 1941), 54–7. (Crit)

3199. ———. "Dodds' Spirit Lives In Today's Jazz," *Down Beat*, VII (Sept. 1, 1940), 8. (Pers)

3200. ———. "Is the White Cornet Style Dead???" *Music and Rhythm*, II (Apr., 1942), 19–20. (A & A)

3201. Withe, Bob. "Gene Krupa Studied to be a Priest!" *Music and Rhythm*, II (May, 1942), 17, 47. (Pers)
3202. ——, "The Story of Jack Teagarden," *Music and Rhythm*, II (Mar., 1942), 11–12, 46. (Pers)
3203. ——. "The Truth About Trombonists," *Music and Rhythm*, II (May, 1942), 16, 36; (June, 1942), 24, 38. (Pers)
3204. ——. " Where Is Small-Band Jazz Going ?" *Music and Rhythm*, II (Dec., 1941), 18. (A & A)
   See: 2266
3205. White, C. W. Langston and R. G. V. Venables. "Spike Hughes and His Orchestra," *Jazz Journal*, I (Oct., 1948), 4. (Disc)
3206. White, William A. "A Sage Looks at Swing," *Time*, XXXV (May 20, 1940), 41. (A & A)
3207. Whiteman, Paul. "All-America Swing Band," *Collier's*, CII (Sept. 10, 1938), 9–12, 63–4. (Pers)
3208. ——. "How Jazz May Influence Modern Orchestras," *in* James Francis Cooke. *Great Men and Famous Musicians on the Art of Music*. Philadelphia: Theo. Presser, 1925. pp. 440–46. (Inst, Pers)
3209. ——. "In Defense of Jazz and Its Makers," New York *Times*, Mar. 13, 1927, IV, 4 : 1, 22. (A & A)
   See: 15; 17; 165; 168; 233; 558; 559; 560; 2337.
3210. ——. (Ed: Myles Fellowes). "Keep Jazz Within Its Limits," *Etude*, LXII (Aug., 1944), 437, 482. (Gen)
3211. ——. (Ed: James Francis Cooke). "New Concepts in Present Day Music," *Etude*, LVII (Apr., 1939), 227, 282. (A & A, Pers)
3212. ——. "Teach Jazz In the Schools," *Metronome*, XLV (Nov., 1929), 25, 39. (Ed)
3213. ——. "This Thing Called Jazz," *Rotarian*, LIV (June, 1939), 34–6. (Gen)
3214. ——. "What Is Jazz Doing to American Music ?" *Etude*, XLII (Aug., 1924), 523–24. (Infl, Inst)
3215. ——, and Leslie Lieber. *How To Be a Bandleader*. New York: R. M. McBride, c. 1941. 144 pp.
3216. ——. "So You Want to Lead a Swing Band," *Scholastic*, XXXIX (Oct. 13, 1941), 17–18, 24. Extract from: *How To Be a Bandleader*. (Gen)
3217. ——, and Mary Margaret McBride. " Jazz," *Saturday Evening Post*, CXCVIII (Feb. 27, 1926), 3–5, 90, 92; (Mar. 6, 1926), 32–3, 180, 185–86, 188, 191; (Mar. 13, 1926), 28–9, 136–37, 141–42, 147. Reprinted: *Jazz*. New York: J. H. Sears, 1926. 298 pp.
3218. ——, and David A. Stein. *Records For the Millions*. New York: Hermitage, 1948. 331 pp. (Disc)
3219. Whitton, Doug. "Down Under Blues," *Jazz Journal*, II (Feb., 1949), 6, 12. (Disc, Ork)
3220. Wiborg, Mary Hoyt. "The Three Emperors of Broadway," *Arts and Decoration*, XXIII (May, 1925), 48, 66, 72. (Pers)
3221. Wilder, Alec. "The State of Jazz," *House and Garden*, XCVIII (July, 1950), 49–50. (Bop)
3222. Wilkins, Eithne. " Jazz, Surrealism, and the Doctor," *Jazz Forum*, 1 (n. d.), 10. (A & A)
3223. Willems, Edgar. *Le Jazz et l'Oreille Musicale*. Geneva: Pro Musica, 1945. 46 pp.
3224. Williams, Cootie. "Why I Quit Duke Ellington After 11 Years," *Music and Rhythm*, I (Dec., 1940), 9, 97. (Pers)
3225. Williams, Eugene. "A History of Jazz Information," *Jazz Information*, II (Nov., 1941), 93–101. (Gen)
3226. ——. "New Orleans Today," *in* George S. Rosenthal (Ed). *Jazzways*. Cincinnati, 1946. pp. 59–87. (Geog, Pic)

3227. Williams, Eugene. "Lu Watters' Yerba Buena Band," *Jazz Information*, II (Nov., 1941), 37–9. (Ork)

3228. ——, and Marili Stuart. "Papa Mutt Carey," *Jazz* (New York), I, no. 7 (n. d.), 5–7. (Pers)

3229. Williams, Ned E. "Woody, Gastel Split Up; Still on Friendly Terms," *Down Beat*, XVII (June 16, 1950), 1. (Gen)

3230. Williams, Ralph Rex. *How to Build a Band and Make It Pay*. Chicago: Down Beat, 1940. 188 pp.

3231. Williams, Richard. "Basic Swing-lish," *House Beautiful*, LXXXVI (Feb., 1944), 27, 94–5. (Lang)

3232. Williams, Stewart. *Jazz in Chicago*. Cardiff, Wales, 1946. 24 pp.

3233. —— (Ed). *Jazz Information*. Cardiff, Wales, 1945. 24 pp.

3234. ——. *Junking in the Land of Jazz*. Cardiff, Wales: Tom Cundall, 1946. 16 pp.

3235. ——, and Brian Rust. *Jazz in New Orleans*. Cardiff, Wales, 1946. 28 pp.

3236. Williamson, Ken. *Jazz Quiz*. Durham City: Panda Publications, 1945. 24 pp.

3237. Willis, George. *Little Boy Blues*. New York: E. P. Dutton, 1947. 223 pp. (Fict)

3238. ——. *Tangleweed*. New York: Doubleday, Doran, 1943. 182 pp. (Fict)

3239. ——. *The Wild Faun*. New York: Greenberg, 1945. 179 pp. (Fict)

3240. Willmott, Peter. "Jazz and Society," *Jazz Forum*, 3 (Jan., 1947), 16. (A & A)

3241. Wilson, Earl. "The Brothers Dorsey Get Along—With Their Friends, But Not Each Other," New York *Post*, Jan. 19, 1942, 3 : 2–4. (Pers)

3242. ——. "'Just Kidded Around', That's How Lena Horne Got Film Job," New York *Post*, Dec. 1, 1942, 42 : 2–3. (Pers)

3243. ——. "Artie Shaw, Intellectual of Swing, Sees Some Ghosts," New York *Post*, Aug. 2, 1941, 3 : 1–7. (Pers)

3244. Wilson, Edmund. "The Jazz Problem," *New Republic*, XLV (Jan. 13, 1926), 217–19. (Crit, J & C, J & O)

3245. ——. "Shanty-Boy Ballads and Blues," *New Republic*, XLVII (July 14, 1926), 227–29. (Rev)

3246. Wilson, John S. "Anthony Shifts to Face New Situation," *Down Beat*, XVII (May 19, 1950), 8. (Crit, J & D, Ork)

3247. ——. "Armstrong Explains Stand Against Bop," *Down Beat*, XVI (Dec. 30, 1949), 3. (Bop, Pers)

3248. ——. "Birdland Applies Imagination to Jazz," *Down Beat*, XVII (Jan. 27, 1950), 3. (Crit)

3249. ——. "Bop at End of Road, Says Dizzy," *Down Beat*, XVII (Sept. 8, 1950), 1. (Bop, Pers)

3250. ——. "Brew Brews Bop on Pres Kick," *Down Beat*, XVI (July 1, 1949), 7. (Pers)

3251. ——. "Can Good, Pleasant Band Like Gene Williams' Make A Living in These Times?" *Down Beat*, XVII (Aug. 11, 1950), 2. (Crit, Ork)

3252. ——. "Cesana Forms Jazz Symphony Ork," *Down Beat*, XVII (Aug. 25, 1950), 7. (Ork)

3253. ——. "Charges Against Jazzmen 'Bear Unpleasant Truths'," *Down Beat*, XVII (Jan. 27, 1950), 1, 2. (Gen)

3254. ——. "Collectors' Item Dept.," *Down Beat*, XVII (Jan. 13, 1950), 3. (Gen)

3255. ——. "Complete Break With Past: Stan," *Down Beat*, XVII (Jan. 27, 1950), 1, 3. (A & A, Pers)

3256. ——. "Cornell Fared Well With 'It Isn't Fair'," *Down Beat*, XVII (Sept. 22, 1950), 2. (Pers)

3257. ——. "Jimmy Dorsey 'On Way Back'," *Down Beat*, XVII (Mar. 24, 1950), 3, 7. (Crit, Ork)

3258. ——. "Eileen Didn't Know What Was Comin'," *Down Beat*, XVII (June 16, 1950), 2. (Pers)

3259. Wilson, John S. "Flanagan Ork 'Gives Every Indication' of Being a Hit," *Down Beat*, XVII (May 5, 1950), 1, 19. (Ork)

3260. — —. "Freeman's Talents Blossom on TV," *Down Beat*, XVII (Aug. 11, 1950), 4. (Pers)

3261. — —. "Heywood Back, 'Won't Change Style'," *Down Beat*, XVII (Mar. 10, 1950), 8. (Pers)

3262. — —. "Peanuts Hucko Big Cog in New Joe Bushkin Unit," *Down Beat*, XVII (Dec. 1, 1950), 1, 19. (Ork, Pers)

3263. — —. "Interest in Flanagan Booming," *Down Beat*, XVI (Dec. 2, 1949), 6. (Ork)

3264. — —. "Israel Is 'Promised Land' for Jazzmen," *Down Beat*, XVII (Nov. 3, 1950), 7. (Geog)

3265. — —. "'JATP' To Make European Jaunt," *Down Beat*, XVII (June 2, 1950), 1. (Ork)

3266. — —. "Buddy Johnson Shows How To Keep a Band Working," *Down Beat*, XVII (Dec. 29, 1950), 4. (Ork)

3267. — —. "Memphis 5 Gives Dixie a Needed Shot in the Arm," *Down Beat*, XVI (July 1, 1949), 18. (Crit, Ork)

3268. — —. "Art Mooney Back to Playing Music," *Down Beat*, XVII (June 16, 1950), 12. (Crit, Ork)

3269. — —. "New Outlook on Life: Torme," *Down Beat*, XVII (Apr. 7, 1950), 1. (Pers)

3270. — —. "NYC Radio Forum Calls Mix Insincere, Irrelevant." *Down Beat*, XVI (July 15, 1949), 1, 19. (Crit)
See: 929; 2061.

3271. — —. "Our Success Due to TV, Says Stone 5," *Down Beat*, XVII (June 16, 1950), 4. (Ork, Rad)

3272. — —. "Pastor Crew 'A Competent But Undistinguished Ork'," *Down Beat*, XVII (Apr. 21, 1950), 3. (Crit, Ork)

3273. — —. "Revival of Dance Bands Won't Affect Us, Claims Combo-Minded Shearing," *Down Beat*, XVII (May 5, 1950), 3. (J & D, Pers)

3274. — —. "Says Roy Stevens Ork Is 'Off In Right Direction'," *Down Beat*, XVII (Mar. 10, 1950), 4. (Crit, Ork)
See: 2015; 2019; 2021; 2024; 2025; 2026; 2027; 2028; 3042.

3275. — —. "Scott Explains the 'Secrecy'," *Down Beat*, XVII (Apr. 7, 1950), 15. (Pers)

3276. — —. "Serge, Pres, Erroll Head Birdland Bill," *Down Beat*, XVII (Feb. 24, 1950), 3. (Crit)

3277. — —. "'Square' Produces Condon TV Shot," *Down Beat*, XVI (July 29, 1949), 1, 16. (Rad)

3278. — —. "The Street Just a Dead Alley Again," *Down Beat*, XVII (Feb. 10, 1950), 1. (Gen)

3279. — —. "Sullivan Piano Shines At N. Y. Dixieland Bash," *Down Beat*, XVII Apr. 21, 1950), 18. (Crit, Pers)

3280. — —. "TD's One of the Finest Dance Bands in Country," *Down Beat*, XVII (Sept. 8, 1950), 3. (Crit, Ork)

3281. — —. "Ventura Makes Bid As Dance Ork at Arcadia," *Down Beat*, XVII (Sept. 8, 1950), 1. (Ork)

3282. — —. "Vocalist Lists Horrors of Singing With Band," *Down Beat*, XVII (Apr. 7, 1950), 2. (Pers)

3283. — —. "Weston: What Became of Music?" *Down Beat*, XVI (Dec. 30, 1949), 7. (A & A)

3284. — —. "Why Barnet Had to Break Up," *Down Beat*, XVI (Dec. 2, 1949), 1. (Pers)

3285. Wimble, Ronald. "Swing, Sight and Sound," *Swing Music*, 14 (Autumn, 1936), 25, 89. (A & A)

3286. Winance, Yvan. "Le Hot Club au Congo Belge!!!" (lr) *Hot Club Magazine*, 18 (June 15, 1947), 18. (Geog)

3287. Winn, Edward R. "Ragtime Piano Playing," *Cadenza*, XXI (Mar., 1915), 6–7; (Apr., 1915), 4–6; (May, 1915), 2–4; (June, 1915), 3–4; XXII (July, 1915), 2–4; (Aug., 1915), 3–5; (Sept., 1915), 3–4; (Oct., 1915), 3–4; (Nov., 1915), 3–4; (Dec., 1915), 2–5; (Jan., 1916), 2–3; (Feb., 1916), 2–3; (Mar., 1916), 3–4; (Apr. 1916), 3; (May, 1916), 3; (June, 1916), 3; XXIII (July, 1916), 3–4; (Aug., 1916), 3; (Sept., 1916), 3–4; (Oct., 1916), 3–4. (Ed, Rag)

3288. Wister, Isabel. "Yes, I Teach 'Em Jazz," *Etude*, XLVI (Aug., 1928), 588. (Gen)

3289. Witmark, Isidore. *The Story of the House of Witmark; From Ragtime to Swingtime*. New York: Furman, 1939. 480 pp.

3290. Wolff, D. Leon. "Are Critics Jazz' Worst Enemy?" *Down Beat*, XIV (Apr. 9, 1947), 15–16. (Crit)

3291. ——. "'Big Bands — Phooey!'" *Down Beat*, IX (Oct. 15, 1942), 21. (A & A)

3292. ——. "Bix Half-Baked, Johnny Dodds Corny, Tesch Out of Tune," *Down Beat*, VIII (June 1, 1941), 8, 20. (A & A)
See: 1753.

3293. ——. "The Blues Are Dead!" *Music and Rythm*, II (Jan., 1942), 8, 50. (A & A, Bl)

3294. ——. "Bop Nowhere, Armstrong Just A Myth," *Down Beat*, XVI (June 17, 1949), 1, 19. (Crit)
See: 1944; 1947; 2070; 3295.

3295. ——. "Mix Hits Hysterical High," *Down Beat*, XVI (July 29, 1949), 12. (Crit)
See: 1944; 1947; 2070; 3294.

3296. ——. "Muggsy and Men Blow A Questionable Storm," *Down Beat*, XV (Feb. 11, 1948), 6. (A & A, Crit, Pers)

3297. ——. "The 10 Most Underrated Jazzmen Picked By Critic," *Down Beat*, X (Feb. 1, 1943), 17. (Pers)

3298. Wolff, Perry. "How Can We Justify Jazz To Those Who Don't Like It?" *Down Beat*, VIII (Aug. 15, 1941), 20. (A & A)

3299. Wood, Jasper. "The Blues in His Heart," *Jazz Record*, 22 (July, 1944), 9, 11. (Pers)

3300. ——. "Great Dixie Band is Discovered," *Down Beat*, XIV (Nov. 5, 1947), 6. (Ork)

3301. Wooding, Samuel. "Eight Years Abroad With A Jazz Band," *Etude*, LVII (Apr., 1939), 233–34, 282. (Hist, Ork)

3302. Woodruff, Duane. "Barney Bigard Has Been Among the Topnotchers For 14 Years," *Music and Rythm*, II (June, 1941), 52–5. (Disc, Pers)

3303. ——. "Coleman Hawkins Is Declining!" *Music and Rhythm*, I (Dec., 1940), 27–30. (Disc, Pers)

3304. Woodson, C. G. "Book Reviews," *Journal of Negro History*, XXXII (Apr., 1947), 249–50. (Rev)

3305. Woodward, Elizabeth (Ed). "Shaggin' On Down!" *Ladies' Home Journal*, LV (Feb., 1938), 6. (J & D, Pic)

3306. Woolf, S. J. "Toscanini's Ideas on Music Old and New," New York *Times*, Apr. 15, 1928, V, 3, 23. (A & A)

3307. Woollcott, Alexander. "The Story of Irving Berlin," *Saturday Evening Post*, CXCVII (Jan. 24, 1925), 6–7, 113–14; (Jan. 31, 1925), 16–17, 134, 137–38; (Feb. 7, 1925), 32, 34, 174, 177–78; (Feb. 14, 1925), 26–7, 50, 52, 55; (Feb. 21, 1925), 34, 36, 96, 99, 101. Reprinted: *The Story of Irving Berlin*. New York: Putnam, 1925. 237 pp. (Pers)

3308. Y. Y. "Plus Que Jazz," *New Statesman*, XXIII (Oct. 4, 1924), 729–31. (A & A, J & C)

3309. Yaw, Ralph. "What Is Swing?" *Metronome*, LII (May, 1936), 22, 35. (A & A, Sw)

3310. Ybarra, T. R. "'Jazz 'Er Up!' Boradway's Conquest of Europe," New York *Times*, Dec. 18, 1921, III, 3, 17. (Geog, Infl)

3311. ——. "Treason on the Blue Danube," *Outlook*, CLII (May 1, 1929), 6. (Disc, J & C)

3312. Yoder, Robert M. "High-Note Harry," *Saturday Evening Post*, CCXVI (July 24, 1943), 24–5, 40, 42. (Ork, Pers)

3313. Yohalem, Arthur E. "Peck Kelley Returns to First Club," *Metronome*, LVIII (Feb., 1942), 10. (Crit, Pers)

3314. Yost, Gaylord. "Does 'Jazz' Typify the American Spirit?" *Musical Courier*, LXXXV (Aug. 24, 1922), 15. (A & A, Gen)

3315. Young, Stark. "Shoat", *New Republic*, LIX (June 26, 1929), 153–54. (Hist)

3316. Zacheis, Les. "'Bixie'," *Jazz* (New York), I, no. 9 (n. d.), 6–8. (Pers)

3317. Zahl, Wesley H. "Jazz: A Blind Alley," *Jacobs' Orchestra Monthly*, XXII (Nov., 1931), 4–5, 40. (A & A)

3318. Zimmerman, Les. "Blowtop Joe," *Metronome*, LIX (Sept., 1943), 15, 18. (Pers)

3319. ——. "The Mad Mab," *Metronome*, LIX (Nov., 1943), 16–17. (Pers)

3320. Zolotow, Maurice. "The Duke of Hot," *Saturday Evening Post*, CCXVI (Aug. 7, 1943), 24–5, 57, 59. (Ork, Pers)

3321. ——. "Harlem's Great White Father," *Saturday Evening Post*, CCXIV (Sept. 27, 1941), 37, 40, 64, 66, 68. (Pers)

3322. Zweig, Arnold. "The First Jazz," *Coronet*, II (Sept., 1937), 153–54. (Gen)

3323. Zwonicek, Ernest. "All Jazz Is Dead in Europe!" *Down Beat*, IX (June 15, 1942), 14. (Geog)

3324. ——, and C. Dumont. "Armstrong in Switzerland," *Melody Maker*, XXV (Nov. 5, 1949), 9. (Crit)

JAZZ MAGAZINES

JAZZ MAGAZINES

1. L'ACTUALITE (Revue du Jazz International et du Spectacle). Ed., Roland Durselen; Pub., 155 Bd Adolphe Max, Bruxelles; monthly; 1944–?
2. AD LIB. Ed., W. E. Reid; Pub., 11 Webster Ave., Toronto; monthly; ?– July, 1947.
   Devoted to jazz from May, 1946, to demise.
3. AMERICAN JAZZ REVIEW. Ed., J. Robert Mantler; Pub., 144–42 Northern Blvd., Flushing, L. I.; monthly; Nov., 1944–?
   Supercedes the mimeographed AMERICAN JAZZ MONTHLY.
4. AUSTRALIAN JAZZ QUARTERLY (A Magazine For the Connoisseur of Hot Jazz). Ed., William H. Miller; Pub., William H. Miller, Box 2440 V, G. P. O. Melbourne; quarterly; Autumn, 1946–date.
5. BALLROOM AND BAND. Ed., Eric A. C. Ballard; Pub., London; monthly; 1934–1936.
6. BAND LEADERS. Ed., Walter H. Holze; Pub., Band Leaders, Mount Morris, Illinois; quarterly (monthly from 1944); Apr., 1942–date.
7. BASIN STREET. Ed., Pat Speiss; Pub., New Orleans; monthly; Mar., 1945–?
8. THE BEAT. Ed., Mike Williams; Pub., Jazz Publications, 4 Notts Ave., Bondi Beach, N. S. W., Australia; monthly; Sept., 1949–date.
9. BLUE RHYTHM. Ed., John W. Rippin and Maurice Gerdeau; Pub., Melbourne; monthly; Sept., 1942–Oct., 1942.
10. BULLETIN DU HOT CLUB DE GENEVE. Ed., Pierre Bouru; Pub., Hot Club de Geneve, 7 Pl. Longemalle, Geneva; 8 issues per year; Jan., 1950–date.
11. CLEF. Ed., Albert S. Otto; Pub., Otto–Marble Pubs., 1458 Lincoln Blvd., Santa Monica, California; monthly; Mar., 1946–Oct., 1946.
12. CLUB DE RITMO. Ed., ?; Pub., Club de Ritmo, Granollers, Spain; monthly; 1946–date.
13. COMBO (Nachrichtendienst für Künstler in Tanz- und Unterhaltungs-Orchetern). Ed., H. Knorn; Pub., Combo Verlag, Munchen-Pasing; fortnightly; Apr., 1949–date.
    Not exclusively devoted to jazz.
14. DIS-COUNTER. Ed., Roy Morser and Lester D. Wharton; Pub., 312 Powell Ave., Evansville 9, Indiana; monthly; Jan., 1948–date.
15. DISCOGRAPHY (For the Jazz Student). Ed., Clifford Jones; Pub., 110 B, High Road, Willesden, N. W. 10, London; fortnightly; Oct., 1942–1947. Published fortnightly until Apr., 1944, irregularly thereafter. Merged with JAZZ MUSIC in 1947.
16. THE DISCOPHILE. Ed., Derek Coller; Pub., 64 Romford St., Barking, Essex, England; bi-monthly; Aug., 1948–date.
17. DOWN BEAT. Ed., Jack Tracy; Pub., Norman Weiser, 2001 Calumet Ave., Chicago 16; fortnightly; 1934–date.
18. ESTRAD. Ed., Nils Hellstrom; Pub., Soderman's Bogtryckeri AB, Stockholm; monthly; 1938–date.
19. HOT CLUB JOURNAL (Mitteilungsblatt des Clubs "Der Schlüssel"). Ed., Teddy H. Leyh and Dieter Zimmerle; Pub., Stuttgart; bi-monthly; Jan., 1949–Aug., 1949.

20. HOT CLUB MAGAZINE. Ed., Carlos de Radzitzky; Pub., Willy de Cort, 34 rue d'Arenberg, Bruxelles; monthly; Jan., 1946–Aug. 1, 1948. Incorporated into JAZZ HOT in 1948.
21. HOT JAZZ CLUB. Ed., Albino Peretti and Rodolfo Doval Fermi; Pub., Hot Jazz Club, Sastre, Santa Fe, Argentina; quarterly; 1944–date.
22. HOT NEWS. Ed., Eric A. C. Ballard; Pub., London; weekly; 1935–? Absorbed by JAZZ MUSIC.
23. HOT NOTES. Ed., Eric Keartland; Pub., Eric Keartland, 81 Quay, Waterford, Eire; bi-monthly; Mar., 1946–Spring, 1948.
24. HOT REVUE. Ed., Rene Langel; Pub., Editions de l'Echiquier, Lausanne, Switzerland; monthly; Dec., 1945-May, 1947.
    Incorporated into JAZZ HOT.
25. HRS SOCIETY RAG. Ed., Charles Edward Smith, Heywood Hale Broun; Pub., Hot Record Society, 303 5th Ave., New York, 827 Seventh Ave., New York; quarterly, monthly; July, 1938–1942.
    Three "preliminary" numbers issued July, 1938, Sept., 1938, Jan., 1939.
    Monthly publication from Aug., 1940–Mar., 1941.
26. JAZZ. Ed., Victor Skaarup and Martin Goldstein; Pub., E. Pedersen, Copenhagen; monthly; 1934–35.
27. JAZZ. Ed., Robert Thiele and Dann Priest; Pub., 601 W. 26th St., New York; Monthly; June, 1942–Jan., 1945.
28. JAZZ. Ed., Carlos de Radzitzky; Pub., A. L. Van de Wege, Planckenbergstraat, Deurne-Antwerp; monthly; 1945.
    Flemish edition; six numbers appeared only.
29. JAZZ. Ed., Carlos de Radzitzky; Pub., J. W. Genin, 106 Ave. de l'Universite, Bruxelles; bi-monthly; Mar., 1945–Nov., 1945.
30. JAZZ. Ed., Tage Ammendrup; Pub., Rekjavik, Iceland; monthly; Mar., 1947–Nov., 1947.
31. JAZZ. Ed., Emmanuel Ugge; Pub., Gramoklub, Praha; irreg. (approximately monthly); May, 1947–Dec., 1948.
32. JAZZ. Ed., Douglas Forslundh; Pub., Gothenburg, Sweden; monthly; Oct., 1948–date.
33. JAZZ. Ed., Olaf Hudtwalcker; Pub., Bockenheimer Landstraße 69, Frankfurt am Main; monthly; Dec., 1949–date.
34. JAZZ-CLUB NEWS. Ed., Horst Lippman; Pub., Frankfurt am Main; monthly; Aug., 1945–Feb., 1948.
35. JAZZ COMMENTARY. Ed., Donald Biggar; Pub., Dalbeattie, Scotland; ?; 1944–1945.
36. JAZZ FORUM. Ed., Albert J. McCarthy; Pub., Delphic Press, East Mill, Fordingbridge, Hants., England; quarterly; May, 1946–July, 1947.
37. 'JAZZ HOME'. Ed., Gunter H. Boas; Pub., "The Two-Beat Friends," Frankfurt am Main; monthly; Apr., 1949–?
38. JAZZ HOT. Ed., Charles Delaunay and Hugues Panassie; Pub., 14 rue Chaptal, Paris 9; monthly, bi-monthly, monthly; Mar., 1935–Aug., 1939, Oct., 1945–date.
39. JAZZ HOT CLUB BULLETIN. Ed., O. Takeda; Pub., Hot Club of Japan, Tokyo; ?; ?
40. JAZZ INFORMATION. Ed., Eugene Williams; Pub., Box 6, Station H, New York; fortnightly; Sept. 12, 1939–Nov., 1941.
41. JAZZINFORMATION. Ed., ?; Pub., Selandia Bogtrykkeri A/S, Copenhagen; monthly; 1945.
    Originally TRIBUNE.
42. JAZZ JOURNAL. Ed., Sinclair Traill and Tom Cundall; Pub., Jazz Journal Pubs., 28 Ladbroke Sq., London, W. 11; monthly; May, 1948–date.

43. JAZZ MAGAZINE. Ed., Carlos L. Tealdo Alizieri and A. Cesar di Baja; Pub., Buenos Aires; monthly; Sept., 1945–Oct., 1946.
44. JAZZ MAGAZINE. Ed., James Asman and Bill Kinnell; Pub., Jazz Appreciation Society, Chilwell, Notts., England; ?; ?
45. JAZZ MUSIC. Ed., Albert McCarthy and Max Jones; Pub., Jazz Sociological Society, 140 Neasden Lane, Neasden, N. W. 10, London; monthly, bi-monthly; Oct., 1942–Apr., 1944, July, 1946–? Incorporates HOT NEWS.
46. JAZZ NEWS. Ed., Eddie Barclay; Pub., Blue Star Revue, 59–61 rue La-Fayette, Paris; ?; ?
47. JAZZ NEWS. Ed., ?; Pub., Hot Club of Zurich, Zurich; irregular (about every two months); Dec., 1940–Mar., 1942.
48. JAZZ NEWS. Ed., Jacques Meuris; Pub., A. Detry, 100 rue de la Cathedrale, Liege; bi-monthly; May, 1945–Oct., 1945.
49. JAZZ NOTES. Ed., John W. Rippin; Pub., Box 1482 G. P. O., Adelaide, South Australia; monthly; Jan., 1941–date.
50. JAZZ NOTES AND BLUE RHYTHM. Ed., C. Ian Turner; Pub., Box 2374V G. P. O., Melbourne; monthly; Jan., 1940–?
51. JAZZ PANORAMA. Ed., Marion Madgett; Pub., 22 Humberview Rd., Toronto 9; monthly, irregular; Dec. 1, 1946–May, 1948.
52. JAZZ QUARTERLY. Ed., Jake Trussell and Judy Downs; Pub., 1640 E. 50th St., Chicago; quarterly; Summer, 1942–1945.
53. JAZZ RAPPORTER. Ed., Børge J. C. Møller; Pub., Frantz Christtreus Bogtrykkeri, Copenhagen; monthly; July-Aug., 1943–1946.
54. THE JAZZ RECORD. Ed., Art Hodes; Pub., 236 W. 10th St., New York 14; monthly; Feb. 15, 1943–Dec., 1947.
55. JAZZ RECORD. Ed., James Asman and Bill Kinnell; Pub., Newark Notts., England; monthly; May, 1943–Apr., 1944.
56. JAZZ REVIEW. Ed., Max Jones and Albert McCarthy; Pub., Jazz Music Books, 140 Neasden Lane, London, N. W. 10; monthly; Jan., 1948–?
57. JAZZ RIFFS. Ed., ?; Pub., Antwerp Jazz Club, 85 van de Wervestraat, Antwerp; monthly; July, 1946–?
58. THE JAZZ SESSION. Ed., John T. Schenck; Pub., 1041 N. Rush St., Chicago 11; monthly, bi-monthly; Sept., 1944–Feb., 1946.
59. JAZZ TEMPO. Ed., John Rowe and Stan Wright; Pub., 39 Berkshire Gardens, N. 13 London; fortnightly, every three weeks, monthly; Mar., 1943–Apr., 1944.
60. JAZZ TEMPO. Ed., Ross Russell; Pub., Hollywood, California; monthly; Jan., 1946–?
61. JAZZ TIMES BULLETIN. Ed., John Gee; Pub., Society for Jazz Appreciation in the Younger Generation, Adeyfield Rd., Hemel Hempstead, Herts., England; ?; ?
62. JAZZ WAX. Ed., Louis D. Brunton; Pub., Birmingham, England; monthly; Aug., 1948–Oct., 1948.
63. JAZZETTE. Ed., Merrill Maynard; Pub., Beacon Jazz League, Boston; ?; ?
64. THE JAZZFINDER. Ed., Orin Blackstone; Pub., 439 Baronne St., New Orleans; monthly; Jan., 1948–Dec., 1948. Incorporated by PLAYBACK.
65. JAZZMEN NEWS. Ed., Vic Lewis; Pub., London; monthly; 1945.
66. JAZZOGRAPHY. Ed., ?; Pub., Society for Jazz Appreciation in the Younger Generation, 47 King St., Tring, Herts., England; ?; ?
67. JAZZOLOGY. Ed., Charles Harvey; Pub., Porthall Press, 208 High St., Harlesden, London, N. W. 10; monthly; 1944–Feb., 1947.
68. JUKEBOX. Ed., E. J. Wansbone; Pub., Wright & Jacques, 52 Albert St., Auckland; monthly; Aug., 1946–Apr., 1947.

69. MELODIE (Illustrierte Zeitschrift für Musik-, Film und Theater-Freunde). Ed., Gerhard Froboess; Pub., Musikverlag Melodie Froboess & Budde, Berlin N. 20; monthly; June, 1946-June, 1949.
    Not exclusively devoted to jazz.
70. MELODY MAKER. Ed., Ray Sonin; Pub., Melody Maker, 93 Long Acre, London, W. C. 2; monthly, weekly; 1926–date.
71. METRONOME (Modern Music and Its Makers). Ed., George Simon and Barry Ulanov; Pub., Metronome, 26 W. 58th St., New York 19; monthly; Jan., 1885–date.
    Not originally devoted to jazz.
72. 'MITTEILUNGEN' FÜR JAZZ-INTERESSENTEN. Ed., Dietrich Schulz-Kohn, Gerd P. Pick, Hans Bluthner; Pub., Berlin; three issues in photostat; 1943–Nov., 1943.
    Secretly issued under the Nazi regime.
73. MUSIC (Le Magazine du Jazz). Ed., F. R. Faecq; Pub., 13 rue de la Madeleine, Bruxelles; monthly; 1924–Dec., 1939.
74. MUSIC AND RHYTHM. Ed., Carl Cons and John Hammond; Pub., Music and Rhythm Pubs., 203 Wabash Ave., Chicago; monthly; Nov., 1940–1945.
75. MUSIC MAKER. Ed., Jim Bradley; Pub., Nicholson's, 416 George St., Sydney; monthly; ?
    Not exclusively devoted to jazz.
76. MUSICA JAZZ. Ed., Giancarlo Testoni; Pub., Galleria del Corso 4, Milan; monthly; 1945–date.
77. MUSIK-ECHO (Zeitschrift für Melodie und Rhythmus). Ed., Adalbert Schalin; Pub., Alberti G. m. b. H. Berlin W. 50; bi-monthly; June, 1930–Mar., 1934.
78. MUSIK PARADE. Ed., ?; Pub., Imudico, Copenhagen; monthly; July, 1949–date.
79. THE NEEDLE. Ed., Robert Reynolds. Pub., 35–15 75th St., Jackson Heights, New York; monthly; June, 1944–Summer, 1945.
80. NEW JAZZ TEMPO. Ed., Don Chester and Lee Wilder; Pub., Tempo Music Shop, 5946 Hollywood Blvd., Hollywood 28, California; ?; ?
81. OH PLAY THAT THING. Ed., Howard Burton and Jack Souther; Pub., San Francisco Record Society, 645 Divisadero St., San Francisco; irregular; July, 1948–?
82. ORKESTER JOURNALEN (Tidsskrift for Moderne Dansemusik). Ed., Harry Nicolausson; Pub., Lindberg's Tryckeriaktiebolag, Stockholm; monthly; 1934–date.
83. PHILHARMONIC. Ed., Johnny James; Pub., Dutch Hot Club, Herenweg 77D, Heemstede, Holland; monthly; Jan., 1950–date.
84. PICKUP (The Record Collector's Guide). Ed., Sinclair Traill and T. B. Denby; Pub., Pickup, 171 Quinton Road West, Harborne, Birmingham 32; monthly; Jan., 1946–Sept., 1947.
85. PLATTER CHATTER. Ed., W. C. Boswell; Pub., 905 Second Ave., Seattle 4; monthly; Sept., 1945–?
86. PLAYBACK. Ed., Orin Blackstone; Pub., 439 Baronne St., New Orleans 12; monthly; Jan., 1949–date.
    Incorporates THE JAZZFINDER.
87. PREHLED ROZHLASU. Ed., Emanuel Ugge (jazz section); Pub., Vilem Prager, Praha; monthly; Mar., 1932–Jan. 14, 1939.
    Not exclusively devoted to jazz.
88. RECORD ADVERTISER. Ed., Richard Turner; Pub., Northolt, Middx., England; monthly, bi-monthly; Jan., 1948–date.
89. THE RECORD CHANGER. Ed., William Grauer, Jr.; Pub., Changer Pubs., 125 LaSalle St., New York 27; monthly; Feb., 1943–date.

90. THE RECORD EXCHANGE. Ed., Harold Mills and Harold Tobin; Pub., 1681 Queen St., East, Toronto 8; monthly; Mar., 1948–date.
91. RECORDIANA. Ed., Jason G. Clark; Pub., P. O. Box 162, Norwich, Connecticut; monthly, irregular; May, 1944–Oct., 1944.
92. REPRINTS AND REFLECTIONS. Ed., William H. Miller; Pub., Box 2440V, GPO, Melbourne; ?; 1945–?
93. LA REVUE DU JAZZ. Ed., Hugues Panassie; Pub., Paris; monthly; Dec., 1948–date.
94. RHYTHM. Ed., Julien Vedey and Dan Ingman; Pub., London; monthly; 1926–1939.
95. RITMO Y MELODIA. Ed., Francisco S. Ortega and Alfonso Banda; Pub., Barcelona; monthly; 1943–date.
96. RYTHMER. Ed., Victor Skaarup; Pub., Vilh. Hansen's Musikforlag, Copenhagen; monthly; 1936–1942.
97. RYTMI. Ed., Paavo Einio and Johan Vikstedt; Pub., Fredrikenkatu 68. A. 2, Helsinki; monthly; Apr., 1934–1938, 1949–date.
98. SEAC JAZZ NEWS. Ed., Derek Coller; Pub., Colombo, Ceylon; irregular; Nov., 1946–July, 1947.
99. SOLID SET. Ed., Jack Myers and Peggy Griggs; Herb Beckford; Pub., St. Joseph, Missouri; monthly; 1943–Aug., 1945.
100. SONG HITS. Ed., Lyle K. Engel; Pub., Song Lyrics, Inc., Dunellen, New Jersey; monthly; May, 1937–date.
101. SWING. Ed., Harry Lim; Pub., Batavia, Java; monthly; 1937–38.
102. SWING (The Guide to Modern Music). Ed., Richard M. George; Pub., Swing Pubs., 55 W 42nd St., New York; monthly; Apr., 1938–1940.
103. SWING. Ed., Keith Brown; Pub., N. Player, 35 Ropato St., Lower Hutt., Auckland; monthly; Oct., 1941–Aug., 1942.
104. SWING MUSIC. Ed., Leonard Hibbs; Pub., 1a Middle Temple Lane, London; monthly, quarterly; Mar., 1935–Autumn, 1936.
105. SWING SESSION. Ed., Cav Nichol; Pub., Cav Nichol, 37 Rodrigo Rd., Kilbirnie, Wellington, New Zealand; monthly; Jan., 1947–Oct., 1948.
106. DIE SYNKOPE. Ed., Walter Kwiecinski; Pub., Hot Club of Hannover, Hannover; monthly; Mar., 1948–Jan., 1949.
107. TEMPO (The Modern Musical Magazine). Ed., Charles Emge; Pub., Los Angeles; monthly; June 15, 1933–May 15, 1940.
108. TEMPO (The Australian Musical News Magazine). Ed., Frank Johnson; Pub., 350 George St., Sydney; monthly; 1936–date. Not exclusively devoted to jazz.
109. TUNESMITH (The Magazine for Songwriters). Ed., Irving Bell; Pub., Tunesmith, 23 S. Spring St., Concord, New Hampshire; monthly; 1937 (?)–date.
110. UNIVERSAL JAZZ. Ed., Ron Russell; Pub., Reading, Berks., England; monthly; May, 1946–? (late 1946).
111. VIER VIERTEL (Zeitschrift für Musik und Tanz). Ed., Kurt Balzer; Pub., Capriccio-Musikverlag G. m. b. H., Berlin N 20; fortnightly, monthly (since Oct., 1949); Nov. 1, 1947–date. Not exclusively devoted to jazz.
112. THE WHEEL (A Record Collector's Rag). Ed., Ed Nickel; Pub., W. W. Mull, West Avenue, Kannapolis, North Carolina; monthly; May, 1948–Sept., 1948.
113. YAM. Ed., Jaakko Vuormaa; Pub., Helsinki; monthly; Jan. 15, 1942–May 15, 1944.

INDICES

SUBJECT INDEX

A & A Analysis and Appreciation 3, 10, 12, 13, 15, 17, 25, 40, 42, 43, 45, 81, 83, 85, 93, 102, 107, 151, 163, 164, 165, 167, 168, 170, 173, 211, 216, 224, 233, 250, 254, 294, 329, 331, 332, 346, 347, 351, 352, 360, 362, 363, 370, 377, 388, 389, 400, 403, 404, 406, 407, 409, 421, 422, 424, 434, 444, 473, 483, 513, 534, 548, 558, 559, 560, 565, 593, 598, 608, 611, 615, 638, 650, 654, 656, 668, 705, 710, 711, 712, 715, 723, 732, 738, 754, 757, 758, 760, 774, 785, 787, 792, 799, 800, 801, 803, 807, 817, 820, 825, 840, 841, 842, 843, 845, 851, 852, 873, 883, 911, 913, 914, 915, 918, 923, 924, 925, 930, 932, 933, 934, 936, 937, 944, 947, 948, 954, 960, 962, 969, 970, 998, 1031, 1035, 1037, 1039, 1041, 1042, 1045, 1047, 1049, 1051, 1053, 1058, 1062, 1072, 1076, 1083, 1085, 1087, 1093, 1094, 1097, 1103, 1128, 1131, 1132, 1133, 1135, 1137, 1140, 1141, 1144, 1153, 1155, 1162, 1175, 1177, 1178, 1182, 1185, 1197, 1204, 1206, 1209, 1211, 1224, 1227, 1239, 1245, 1270, 1272, 1273, 1274, 1275, 1276, 1277, 1286, 1292, 1301, 1307, 1325, 1327, 1349, 1350, 1351, 1363, 1365, 1367, 1368, 1371, 1372, 1374, 1375, 1388, 1402, 1419, 1427, 1428, 1432, 1433, 1445, 1447, 1450, 1456, 1460, 1463, 1477, 1478, 1480, 1493, 1500, 1510, 1517, 1518, 1519, 1521, 1523, 1524, 1525, 1526, 1527, 1532, 1544, 1547, 1552, 1560, 1568, 1569, 1572, 1574, 1575, 1581, 1592, 1594, 1601, 1609, 1611, 1612, 1613, 1614, 1616, 1617, 1636, 1648, 1650, 1654, 1655, 1656, 1657, 1659, 1672, 1676, 1679, 1684, 1689, 1707, 1708, 1709, 1711, 1712, 1718, 1725, 1731, 1732, 1733, 1734, 1735, 1737, 1740, 1741, 1742, 1747, 1753, 1759, 1763, 1797, 1830, 1838, 1842, 1853, 1855, 1856, 1858, 1862, 1863, 1864, 1866, 1874, 1878, 1882, 1883, 1899, 1902, 1903, 1908, 1916, 1917, 1924, 1925, 1933, 1936, 1948, 1952, 1973, 1975, 1982, 1987, 1990, 1996, 1998, 1999, 2010, 2016, 2036, 2044, 2045, 2055, 2058, 2059, 2067, 2073, 2074, 2078, 2084, 2086, 2087, 2090, 2091, 2096, 2102, 2111, 2115, 2120, 2133, 2142, 2157, 2158, 2159, 2176, 2179, 2186, 2201, 2203, 2207, 2208, 2209, 2213, 2214, 2225, 2230, 2231, 2232, 2235, 2246, 2253, 2258, 2259, 2266, 2267, 2290, 2308, 2319, 2320, 2322, 2323, 2335, 2336, 2337, 2346, 2347, 2349, 2350, 2353, 2361, 2363, 2381, 2382, 2384, 2387, 2393, 2394, 2397, 2401, 2422, 2434, 2435, 2437, 2452, 2453, 2459, 2460, 2462, 2463, 2518, 2519, 2529, 2533, 2537, 2542, 2546, 2553, 2557, 2562, 2564, 2599, 2605, 2606, 2609, 2618, 2619, 2620, 2627, 2628, 2634, 2637, 2647, 2654, 2656, 2662, 2667, 2668, 2671, 2672, 2674, 2675, 2676, 2689, 2696, 2699, 2701, 2702, 2706, 2707, 2708, 2712, 2714, 2716, 2717, 2718, 2727, 2730, 2731, 2732, 2735, 2736, 2737, 2739, 2741, 2742, 2743, 2746, 2750, 2755, 2756, 2760, 2761, 2764, 2765, 2767, 2768, 2770, 2771, 2772, 2778, 2787, 2789, 2792, 2814, 2852, 2854, 2856, 2857, 2860, 2861, 2862, 2863, 2868, 2869, 2884, 2885, 2886, 2893, 2895, 2897, 2898, 2906, 2916, 2917, 2918, 2919, 2920, 2924, 2926, 2928, 2931, 2933, 2934, 2942, 2952, 2954, 2955, 2959, 2960, 2963, 2964, 2968, 2969, 2992, 2993, 2997, 3002, 3003, 3004, 3007, 3010, 3011, 3012, 3013, 3019, 3027, 3038, 3056, 3058, 3062, 3066, 3068, 3069, 3070, 3079, 3090, 3102, 3135, 3139, 3156, 3160, 3164, 3167, 3168, 3170, 3172, 3173, 3174, 3177, 3180, 3185, 3192, 3195, 3200, 3204, 3206, 3209, 3211, 3222, 3240, 3255, 3283, 3285, 3291, 3292, 3293, 3296, 3298, 3306, 3308, 3309, 3314, 3317

Bibl Bibliographies of Jazz 134, 714, 1492, 1682, 2223, 2365, 2372

Bl Blues 76, 85, 115, 584, 616, 690, 827, 933, 971, 1081, 1082, 1111, 1447, 1506, 1581, 1674, 1676, 1752, 1907, 1934, 1961, 1969, 2003, 2088, 2227, 2242, 2247, 2301, 2346, 2352, 2354, 2373, 2379, 2380, 2386, 2398, 2399, 2421, 2450, 2528, 2610, 2612, 2708, 2710, 2711, 2886, 2910, 2914, 2949, 3077, 3134, 3139, 3191, 3293

Bop Bop 39, 40, 62, 63, 81, 87, 88, 122, 235, 312, 611, 650, 903, 918, 975, 1053, 1067, 1089, 1211, 1374, 1377, 1385, 1397, 1399, 1447, 1582, 1597, 1605, 1634, 1666, 1697, 1730, 1737, 1824, 1926, 1948, 1952, 2011, 2016, 2055, 2165, 2235, 2467, 2468, 2571, 2590, 2603, 2671, 2672, 2674, 2675, 2707, 2732, 2793, 2794, 2795, 2931, 2952, 2956, 2983, 3058, 3221, 3247, 3249, 3294

INDEX TO PERIODICALS
ENTRIES CITED

M

Melodie (Berlin) 42, 325, 641, 815, 1714, 1718
Melody (Boston) 163, 411, 1658, 2087, 2111,
2157, 2312, 2557, 2567, 2720, 2905
Melody Maker (London) 29, 830, 1390, 1897,
1926, 3044, 3324
Melos (Berlin) 925, 1097, 1227, 1844, 1856,
2737, 2741, 2742, 2761, 2762
Menestrel (Paris) 1160, 1841
Metronome (New York) 9, 16, 19, 33, 41, 49,
50, 51, 52, 65, 66, 67, 86, 99, 111, 116, 133,
153, 155, 159, 162, 164, 195, 202, 203, 208,
217, 238, 263, 268, 273, 288, 306, 321, 323,
324, 351, 367, 429, 490, 514, 515, 516, 517,
518, 522, 526, 538, 541, 542, 568, 575, 580,
586, 591, 605, 616, 627, 630, 631, 646, 675,
677, 679, 680, 683, 685, 687, 696, 708, 740,
756, 758, 775, 787, 827, 847, 848, 893, 894,
895, 896, 897, 898, 899, 900, 901, 913, 919,
951, 953, 958, 968, 1044, 1136, 1141, 1144,
1168, 1176, 1183, 1217, 1280, 1321, 1326,
1377, 1378, 1380, 1381, 1382, 1383, 1386,
1387, 1389, 1396, 1397, 1401, 1403, 1405,
1407, 1408, 1409, 1497, 1504, 1521, 1531,
1580, 1613, 1636, 1638, 1643, 1660, 1736,
1749, 1771, 1772, 1773, 1774, 1775, 1776,
1777, 1778, 1779, 1780, 1781, 1782, 1783,
1784, 1785, 1846, 1847, 1886, 1983, 1991,
1996, 2001, 2005, 2006, 2007, 2014, 2017,
2023, 2029, 2082, 2132, 2134, 2171, 2179,
2230, 2438, 2546, 2602, 2611, 2638, 2639,
2651, 2668, 2681, 2689, 2731, 2774, 2792,
2793, 2794, 2795, 2796, 2797, 2798, 2799,
2800, 2802, 2803, 2804, 2806, 2807, 2809,
2810, 2811, 2812, 2813, 2814, 2815, 2816,
2817, 2818, 2819, 2820, 2821, 2822, 2823,
2824, 2825, 2826, 2827, 2828, 2829, 2830,
2831, 2832, 2833, 2834, 2835, 2836, 2837,
2839, 2840, 2843, 2847, 2927, 2962, 3026,
3058, 3074, 3075, 3076, 3078, 3079, 3080,
3081, 3082, 3083, 3085, 3086, 3087, 3089,
3090, 3091, 3092, 3093, 3094, 3095, 3096,
3098, 3099, 3100, 3101, 3103, 3105, 3106,
3107, 3108, 3109, 3110, 3112, 3113, 3114,
3115, 3116, 3117, 3118, 3119, 3120, 3121,
3122, 3123, 3124, 3125, 3126, 3127, 3128,
3129, 3130, 3131, 3132, 3163, 3178, 3212,
3309, 3313, 3318, 3319
Modern Music (New York) 1063, 1064, 1130,
1178, 1750, 2073, 2176, 2177, 2178, 2399,
2532, 2559, 2618, 2766, 2967, 3012, 3013
Monde Musical (Paris) 970, 2773
Monthly Musical Record (London) 322, 957,
2086
Moradas (Lima) 2432
Music (Brussels) 978, 995, 998, 1000, 1012
Music and Letters (London) 883
Music and Musicians (Seattle) 433
Music and Rhythm (Chicago) 56, 77, 190,
271, 337, 714, 738, 777, 819, 825, 930, 1169,

1171, 1189, 1258, 1261, 1268, 1279, 1281,
1341, 1455, 1467, 1471, 1476, 1477, 1669,
1671, 1672, 1677, 1960, 1971, 1979, 1992,
2249, 2250, 2251, 2254, 2257, 2258, 2259,
2266, 2267, 2340, 2411, 2412, 2413, 2464,
2487, 2489, 2493, 2503, 2512, 2697, 2756,
2757, 2778, 2785, 2902, 2915, 2917, 2957,
2974, 2990, 3196, 3197, 3198, 3200, 3201,
3202, 3203, 3204, 3224, 3293, 3302, 3303,
Music Educator's Journal (Ann Arbor) 1109,
1152, 1711, 1712, 2403
Music Educators' National Yearbook (Chicago) 840, 1109
Music Lover's Magazine (Portland, Oregon)
45, 1356
Music News (Chicago) 458, 593, 1854, 2459,
2661
Music Teacher (London) 1195, 1196, 1357
Music Teachers' Review (Brooklyn) 1047
Music Trade Review (New York) 420, 746
Music Trades (New York) 435
Musica d'Oggi (Milan) 36
Musical Advance (New York) 2712
Musical America (New York) 198, 232, 278,
329, 339, 362, 432, 558, 770, 1197, 1371,
1857, 1924, 1940, 2187, 2248, 2285, 2318,
2328, 2626, 2627, 2685, 2765, 2848, 2959,
3004, 3006, 3008, 3017, 3179
Musical Canada (Toronto) 172, 1520
Musical Courier (Philadelphia) 43, 212, 213,
318, 331, 354, 378, 396, 401, 404, 417, 418,
425, 436, 437, 454, 455, 482, 492, 505, 595,
620, 637, 800, 914, 954, 1085, 1105, 1108,
1131, 1132, 1151, 1363, 2079, 2080, 2081,
2398, 2400, 2408, 2462, 2463, 2619, 2688,
2696, 3135, 3188, 3314
Musical Digest (New York) 406, 789, 1128,
1204, 2074
Musical Leader (Chicago) 289, 363, 384, 397,
407, 409, 410, 709, 936, 937, 938, 939, 1269
Musical Monitor (Chicago) 137
Musical News and Herald (London) 1206,
1647, 1733, 2900
Musical Observer (New York) 188, 252, 427,
2108, 2366, 2686, 2916
Musical Opinion (London) 20, 316, 372, 884,
911, 1042, 1734, 2186
Musical Progress (Washington, D.C.) 2753
Musical Quarterly (New York) 1285, 1352,
1679, 2010, 2206, 2352, 2635, 2700, 2963
Musical Record (Boston) 1872
Musical Standard (London) 419, 598, 1372,
2460, 2969
Musical Times (London) 12, 1369, 1609, 2699,
2738
Musicalia (Havanna) 1881
Musician (Philadelphia) 105, 166, 180, 623,
799, 817, 831, 962, 1019, 1402, 1499, 1589,
1868, 1961, 2039, 2040, 2041, 2184, 2534,
2543
Musician's Journal (Manchester) 3162